Negotiating Adolescence in Rural Bangladesh

Negotiating Adolescence in Rural Bangladesh

A Journey through School, Love and Marriage

NICOLETTA DEL FRANCO

zubaan

Published in 2012 by
ZUBAAN
An imprint of Kali for Women
128B Shahpur Jat, 1st floor
New Delhi 110 049
Email: contact@zubaanbooks.com
Website: www.zubaanbooks.com

10 9 8 7 6 5 4 3 2 1

ISBN: 978 93 81017 17 3

Zubaan is an independent feminist publishing house based in New Delhi, India, with a strong academic and general list. It was set up as an imprint of the well-known feminist house Kali for Women and carries forward Kali's tradition of publishing world-quality books to high editorial and production standards. *Zubaan* means tongue, voice, language, speech in Hindustani. Zubaan is a non-profit publisher, working in the areas of the humanities and social sciences, as well as in fiction, general non-fiction, and books for young adults that celebrate difference, diversity and equality, especially for and about the children of India and South Asia, under its imprint Young Zubaan.

Typeset by Jojy Philip, New Delhi 110 015
Printed at Raj Press, R-3 Inderpuri, New Delhi 110 012

To
Franca Contini (1960–82) and Nasreen Huq (1959–2006)
for their strong love and passion for life.

Contents

Acknowledgements

This book represents a further important step in an intellectual and emotional journey that started in 1980, when I ventured for the first time, for a short period, into rural Bangladesh for the fieldwork of my degree dissertation. From that time I have always wished to have the opportunity to go back to Bangladesh for long-term research and work.

I owe the initial encouragement for undertaking this work to my mentor DPhil supervisor Professor Ann Whitehead who gave me confidence from the beginning, encouraged me to turn my thesis into a book and sustained me through all my ups and downs with invaluable intellectual, emotional and practical support. I am lucky that she has become a friend beside being an endless source of intellectual challenge. Joe Devine also has an important role in encouraging and supporting this endeavour and I want to thank him for his patience, advice and friendship throughout the last 14 years.

I am indebted to many people from Bangladesh. I would like to mention first of all the students, teachers and principals of the two colleges where I did my fieldwork and the people of Tarapur and Chadnagar. Thanks to them I remember my fieldwork as a very enjoyable period and consider that area of Bangladesh as my third home. Together with some of the young people from the colleges and the two villages – Palash, Shuma, Jhorna, Masud, Liton, Mamun, Gabriel, Resma, Parul, Ambia, Anis, Farook, Sonia, Tonu, Tahomina and my 'little brothers' in Dhaka – I want to mention and thank the Xaverian Fathers in Dhaka, Khulna and Chadnagar and in particular

Father Pier Lupi who first welcomed me in Bangladesh in 1980 and introduced me, together with Father Luigi Paggi, to people and places that have become an important part of my life.

When I started my fieldwork I was lucky to meet Laura Giani who offered me a place to stay in Dhaka and, more importantly, has been an invaluable friend ever-since: thank you!

There are many friends I have to thank for their support and for sharing ideas and discussions during my DPhil – Laura Maritano, Shahin, Lorella, Angela, Kanwal, Titti, Giampaolo, Clare, Niki, Marzia, Saverio, Igor and Tapan.

More recently, while this book was being revised and edited I was once again in Bangladesh working for an NGO. Thanks to Patrizia, Manuela and all the others I worked with, I not only had a great time, but also the opportunity to reconcile research and development work and find new motivation and ideas for both.

I owe financial support for the fieldwork on which this book is based to the Simon Population Trust that provided a grant and to Silvia Carzaniga and her friends who raised funds for my research in very creative ways.

A special thank goes to Cesare Rusconi, my school teacher of philosophy who was the first to take care of my 'intellectual life'.

Finally I am indebted and grateful to my mother Gabriella who has always accepted my choices and bravely coped with my long absences.

Many thanks to Francesco Cabras for the cover photograph and for being sensitive enough to really *see* the people while taking pictures of them.

ONE

Adolescence, Self and Social Relations

A BEGINNING

In August 1998, during a visit to Bangladesh, I was introduced by a Bangladeshi friend to some young women who had been attacked and severely disfigured with sulphuric acid. I also met the representative of an Italian non-government organisation (NGO) and some members of Naripokkho, a Bangladeshi feminist advocacy organisation who were discussing ways to help acid survivors and counteract the phenomenon. In July 1999, I returned to Bangladesh to carry out research into acid violence (Del Franco 1999) and I had longer conversations with survivors in the Naripokkho office and in the Dhaka Medical College hospital where some girls were being treated for acid burns. Maheen[1] was 15 years old when she was attacked. Given here is her account of the experience:

It happened to me in August 1996. I was a student, 15 years old. My family is from Bogra but now I live in Dhaka with my mother and the family of my uncle. My father left us. Sometimes I stay here in Nasreen's[2] house and it is like having two families. The real target of the attack was my cousin whom I am living with. The reason of the attack was prem (love). Sometimes boys think they love girls but we might not like them. You don't marry somebody that you don't love. First you will see who he is, you will talk with him and then if you like him you might decide to marry him. We hadn't see him (the one who attacked me) before the incident. We had been invited to celebrate a birthday and that was the first time we saw that boy. He was 22. He spoke of marriage in front of my cousin's mother.

Time to time, the boy used to come to our house. The night of the attack, he probably wanted to kidnap us. We were asleep, but when I realised what was happening I stood in front of him to protect my cousin and I was hit by the acid he threw. I tried instinctively to stop him and I ran after him but when I saw that he had a pistol in his hand I gave up. I saw eleven persons outside waiting for him. My uncle intervened and was beaten by them with a stick. Acid also hit my mother. The same night we all went to the hospital.

I think that Dano attacked us because he thought that if he couldn't marry my cousin, nobody else would. Boys are very bad, like animals. He didn't behave like that only with us. He did the same with other girls. He was inolved in politics and didn't have any job. He worked for others who paid him for robbing and other things, like threatening people for money.

I was in the hospital for eight months and I underwent eight operations. Then I met people from Naripokkho. Naripokkho gives genuine help, mon theke (from the heart). They started encouraging us to go out and asked why we were staying all the time at home. We were afraid at the beginning, of going out: what would people say? People might be afraid of us.

My mother now works in a garment factory. She started there one year ago. Everybody is treating her well, probably because everybody knows our story. Time to time they see me on television. They treat me nicely when I go to see my mother. I get some money from Naripokkho for the work I do and together we can afford living in Dhaka.

My uncle's family lives with us. Before the incident my cousins were studying, but now, after paying all the money for my treatment, they have to work. With you all your family goes down. Your family goes down, you lose your face and you won't have it back, never. Sometime I would like to do the same to the boy who attacked me. Boys do that to girls so that they can't get married anymore. If I really love somebody, how could I throw acid on him? They consider girls to be toys, like dolls. They want something without marrying. If the girl does not agree they throw acid.

The stories of Maheen and the other young survivors I met in 1999 and later on in 2002 are very typical of one particular pattern of acid violence where the immediate reason given for the attack is the rejection of a marriage or 'love' proposal. According to Ain o Shalish Kendra (ASK) statistical reports, in 2002, 250 women were attacked with acid and about 20 per cent of the cases concerned the refusal of love, marriage proposals or sexual relationships. These incidents steadily increased through the 1990s and then slowly decreased from

2003 to 2009. They have key elements in common. The girls are usually teenagers and personal accounts indicate that in many cases they have been approached by their suitors on the way from or to school. Most of the attacks take place at night, at the girls' houses and are often preceded by various threats. The aim of the rejected suitors appears to be to ruin the girls' potential for future marriage by dishonouring them and their families. The press tends to represent these incidents mainly in terms of individual deviance and the state responds by addressing them as 'law and order' issues. Clearly, the attacks are criminal acts. Some of the survivors (or their parents) have described their attackers as *mastaans* or musclemen earning a living from illegal activities, sometimes on the payroll of powerful people, or as drug or alcohol addicted unemployed youth. There is also a strong gender dimension to these attacks; acid is not a weapon like others. Acid scars are permanent and have a powerful social and symbolic connotation. Disfigurement is something that lasts forever; it hinders the public life of the victims and their chance at marriage, and ultimately forces them back home. Women's refusal of a love proposition is an insult to men's sense of prestige and they take revenge by forcing their victims to a life of seclusion and hiding. Besides young unmarried adolescents who refuse 'love' propositions, cases of acid violence are also found among married women who are attacked by their husbands or in-laws if they or their families fail to satisfy dowry requests, or are involved in property or other disputes. These incidents and the many other forms of gender violence need to be understood according to feminist researchers, in the broader context of the socio-economic, political and cultural transitions in Bangladesh. These changes include an increased visibility of women into previously male dominated public spaces as NGO activists, garment factory workers or students, and the challenges to the gender division of labour and gender relations in general that these changes imply (Del Franco 1999; Akhter and Nahar 2003; Kabeer 2000; Chowdhury 2005).

However, this is not a strong enough explanation to fully understand the context in which these kinds of events occur. During a long conversation with Nasreen, she suggested that in order to understand the cases where unmarried adolescents are involved, we must first consider the young age of the persons involved: 'These are crimes committed by young people against young people'. She further suggests we consider the way they are educated and how that does not allow the development of a friendship between males and females: 'Where they can mix freely, they understand a little bit more about each other, but in our society they are totally separated and this is very unhealthy'. But there is a contradiction between an education that stresses the separation of the sexes and prohibits any kind of cross-gender relationships before marriage, and a reality that allows contact between male and female adolescents who are not equipped with the instruments to recognise and deal with their emotions and sexual desires:

Boys and girls can find themselves in situations in which it is very natural to be attracted to each other and in some cases it may happen that this attraction is expressed simply through eye contact. This may be enough for a boy to think that the girl has expressed some kind of consent and from that to believe that she already belongs to him. In a society where boys and girls meet each other more freely, the tension can be defused; but not here. Where they can mix freely, they can understand a little bit more about each other, but in our society they are totally separated and this is very unhealthy'.

To me, the peculiarity and interest of these attacks lies mainly in the fact that they are related to the domain of emotional and sexual relationships between girls and boys. They concern gender relations and involve a discussion of the cultural norms and practices that regulate the relationship between boys and girls, but they also concern the way these practices and the modalities of the transition to adulthood are changing.

Nasreen's comments on the separation between boys and girls undoubtedly capture important aspects of what it means to be a teenager in Bangladesh. Earlier ethnographies (Aziz and Maloney 1985; Kotalova 1993) also suggest that in the social context of rural Bangladesh, puberty used to correspond to the immediate acquisition of adulthood for many girls in so far as early marriage was a predominant reality. From puberty onwards, girls were taught an attitude of modesty and shame that had to be expressed by the way they behaved and dressed, and purdah was enforced so that their physical world was restricted to the house and its surroundings, and contact with boys limited. Boys enjoyed more mobility but they could not engage in any form of close interaction with girls, unless in groups and under the control of adults. While for girls adulthood was mostly linked to puberty and marriage, for boys becoming an adult was connected with being married and economically capable to support their own family. Nasreen's comment raises a core issue that can be expressed thus:'What kind of ideas do young people possess to recognise and deal with their emotions, sentiments and sexual desires, particularly in a context that allows *de facto* new opportunities for encounter and for developing forms of relationships?' How are these everyday opportunities and young people's emotions reconciled with hegemonic values about affection, attachment and premarital cross-gender relationships?

My encounter with girl survivors of acid burns, some of their parents and some members of Naripokkho, as well as my previous[3] acquaintance and discussions with young male college[4] students in Dhaka helped bring out some of the themes I develop in this book. The acid survivors were all students and most of them intended to continue their education after grade 10 and matriculation. Education opens spaces in which boys and girls have multiple occasions of contact. These spaces are created when young people move to school but also, as Maheen said, on occasions like birthday parties and other social events. This is true both for urban and rural areas. Young people talk of 'love' and reflect on cross-gender relationships. One of the boys I used to live with in Dhaka during 1994–96 used to proudly show me the love letters he had received from a girl with the imprint of her lips forming a kiss shape.

The impetus for the field research I conducted between 2001 and 2003, on which this book is based, lies in an interpretation that acid attacks can be understood in the context of changes in the adolescent experience. In rural Bangladesh, as elsewhere, processes of socio-economic change and new educational opportunities contribute to more differentiated life trajectories and create new spaces for the emergence of adolescence as a stage of life.

National statistics show a trend favouring an increase in marriageable age for both men and women (NIPORT 2009). For girls, this goes hand in hand with a steady increase, since the early 1990s, in the number of them enrolled in secondary and higher secondary education (BANBEIS 2006). For boys, the transition to adulthood is more complicated and somewhat delayed in the contemporary reality of more diversified employment opportunities and, for some, increased land scarcity and rural poverty. Agriculture has ceased to be the only main occupational aspiration for many, and other employment choices such as public services or small business, or in some areas overseas migration, are more desirable. Education is seen as the means to acquire the skills and qualifications for highly valued white-collar jobs in the public or private sectors or for initiating a successful business. For some young men, economic independence and marriage are therefore postponed until the end of tertiary education.

This book documents and describes the everyday reality of this changing gendered transition; it interrogates the experience of being young and becoming adult in rural south-west Bangladesh. There are significant temporal, spatial and cultural dimensions. With the delay of marriage, the acquisition of adult status and responsibilities is also postponed. Access to higher education contributes to the creation of new social spaces for same and cross-gender interaction and opens up opportunities for employment that allow boys and girls to imagine and pursue different life trajectories. Young people are caught in the midst of the contradiction between the hegemonic values and patterns of behaviour that define their belonging to the moral community (*samaj*) and the new models of intimacy and romantic love that are spread through the media even in the more remote rural areas. I focus on three main areas that are central to their experience: (*a*) those of college and student life; (*b*) friendships and relationships with those of the same sex and across sexes; and (*c*) marriage and the issues involved in the choice of a marriage partner.

In Europe, and in reference to industrial societies, adolescence was and is conceptualised as being linked to a psychological process of self-definition resulting in the development of a coherent self concept, and adulthood to the acquisition of a social identity in terms of occupation, definition of one's place inside different social contexts and the capacity of entering intimate relations. The context is one in which contractual market relations and impersonal relations between citizens and the state, both of which construct the persons as individuals, dominate the contour of social relations. I argue in this book that processes of self-definition and the active acquisition of social identity, for adolescents, are also occurring in rural Tarapur but in a different way and with much less public recognition.

In rural Bangladesh the social context does not encourage youth, especially females, to develop initiative and autonomy in decision making and independence from familial networks. Every individual is attributed a defined position and entitlements inside a net of hierarchical relationships as a member of the samaj (society or moral community), of a group of *attiyo swajan* (one's own people), of a lineage or a caste, of a *bari* (extended family), and finally of a *songsar* or *parivar* (nuclear family). The capacity to be and to act independently from complex sets of social relations is quite limited, but I will argue that a profound process of social and economic change is opening up spaces for young people to share and live 'adolescence' as a personal and social experience. I will explore the modalities of these processes, and how they translate, for boys and girls, into different degrees of control over important life choices and into the possibility to choose the direction one's life is going to take.

To do this it is necessary to unpack social relations to look at how social identities are constructed at the symbolic and material levels. At the discursive level this means to look at how boundedness and interdependence or separation and autonomy are constructed in cultural representations and played out in language, and how this is reflected at the level of daily interaction and social practices. Theoretically, the books aims at re-asserting the importance of the analytical idea of adolescence for the study of young people because of its emphasis on the idea of critical age-related transitions. These can be understood by exploring two trajectories: one linked to socio-economic changes that open up opportunities for differentiated life chances, and another occurring as individuals pass through different developmental phases. I discuss these intersecting adolescent transitions in the social and personal world of Bangladeshi rural adolescents through the lens of gender and class.

Locating Adolescents

The material on which this book is based was collected from October 2001 to April 2002 and again from October 2002 to April 2003, in the sub-district of Tala in Satkhira district. The identification of a research area and of a place to stay was made easier by my previous acquaintance with the director of a local NGO, and by my past experience in the area. I had ventured for the first time in south-west Bangladesh, in Satkhira district and precisely in Chadnagar in 1980–81 for a study about a group of low caste Hindus, the Rishi. Then, after short visits in 1990, 1991 and 1992, I spent two years, from 1994 to 1996, in the south-western town of Jessore, working with a Bangladeshi NGO that was running an integrated development programme targeted at 'empowering' rural women. During that time, I learned to speak Bengali, thanks to the patience and friendship of two young NGO officers and the conversations with the programme's beneficiaries. Having made friends in Jessore and Dhaka I returned to Bangladesh regularly in subsequent years, and in the summer of 1999 I conducted research for my MA dissertation which focused on the problem of acid violence. In the summer of 2000, I worked again in Dhaka for an Italian NGO which was running a programme of medical assistance for acid survivors. I was not, therefore, a complete outsider in Tarapur, the village where I settled down in October 2001, where I occupied a small guest house that had been originally used by the NGO. I chose three main research sites: the village of Tarapur, two colleges (one mixed and one for girls only) in Tala, the urban centre after which the sub-district is named. During my fieldwork I used to frequently visit Chadnagar, where I stayed for a few months between 1980 and 1981. Some of the people and events mentioned in this book are from Chadnagar. By choosing a rural area for my fieldwork I was able to contextualise my understanding of the emergence of adolescence in the thick network of face-to-face social and economic relationships that embed the individual experience in rural Bangladesh; another reason for me to locate my study in a village in the south-west part of the country was to build on my previous knowledge of the area and deepen my understanding of it by looking at social dynamics from a different angle.

My knowledge of spoken Bengali allowed me to enjoy direct and immediate communication with both adults and young people. Tarapur villagers were used to foreigners, mostly donor representatives, visiting them. Halima, the woman who cooked at the guest house, and others used to recount these encounters as unpleasant experiences because of the lack of direct communication. They were surprised and relieved to discover that I could understand and speak with them. It is common for foreigners in Bangladesh to be told by local people: 'you can't understand us' in the sense of what they call *'amader* culture' (our culture, they use the English word for culture). Being able to speak the language helped to overcome this problem.

The little building where I lived had the same structure as the mud huts in which lives 99 per cent of Tarapur's population. The building's structure allowed little if any privacy. Thus the villagers, close neighbours, students from the two colleges and the nearby high school used to come to visit, sometimes just to 'see' me. During the first few months, Halima, the cook, stayed over during the day and she introduced me to different people in the village. Through her I managed to gain access to the households of west Tarapur. Halima felt in some way responsible for me and my security. She ended up having a sort of paternalistic attitude towards me and tried to act as a filter between me and my visitors. This became a hindrance because I didn't feel completely free to talk and meet whomsoever I wanted. I had the impression that the more I became well acquainted with a number of people and households or the more I became accepted by the villagers, the more I was subjected to some form of social control. I became more aware that my interactions with people were observed and evaluated. On the other hand, the fact that I used to talk openly to everyone without much concern for social hierarchies, and that I showed particular interest in talking with poor people, was appreciated. While at the beginning I was associated with the NGO and with the affluent family of the NGO director, later on I became known as *didi* (elder sister) to most of the people.

My status as an unmarried adult woman was the object of much curiosity. It triggered interesting discussions about marriage and about 'love marriages' as opposed to arranged ones. Another frequent topic for discussion was the cultural difference between 'us' and 'them'. All these discussions took place in very informal ways: either while sitting on the verandah of a house with all the neighbours around and the children screaming during visits to people's houses, or while in a van on the way home, or during NGO groups meetings where I was invited to audit, or while sitting in the school courtyard and watching a football match between the student teams, etc. All of this was quite time consuming but the conversations proved to be rich and insightful.

In the second period of my fieldwork, I intensified the visits to the colleges and to the high school. In the colleges my work was facilitated by the courtesy and availability of the two principals and the teachers who allowed me free access to the students. At the beginning I was addressed as 'madam' by both boys and girls during the English classes and as 'auntie' by the girls during the more informal conversations we had in their room at college. As a foreign 'madam' I was the object of respect and curiosity; as 'auntie' I slowly became for some girls a confidant. The conversations in the girls' room were often very intimate and warm. We talked about a range of issues including their relationships with their parents and their perception of society, their relationships with boys and their expectations and hopes for the future. They talked quite openly, especially when they could do so indirectly by referring for example to another classmate who was not present, and sometimes they would just make jokes or sing. Since I was perceived as someone that would not judge them, they felt that they could express themselves openly and frankly. Instead, what prevented them (especially the younger girls attending first year of college) from being completely free with me was their lack of trust in their classmates. In other words, they were afraid that they would be gossiped about after our meetings.

I often visited the girls' and boys' homes and met their parents and neighbours. This was an important activity since it built trust with them and allowed me to know more about their personal circumstances, even if the visits themselves did not produce any 'hard data'. First, it was impossible to have some privacy with the family because all the neighbours would come 'to see' me. Second, parents were as curious about me as I was about them. Half our conversations would be about me talking to them about my relatives, my life in Italy and my personal circumstances.

The male college students were also quite curious and willing to talk. In a way similar to the situation with the girls, the fact that I was not considered a member of the samaj, but was literate enough about their society, encouraged dialogue and nurtured relationships of trust. The boys' group was much larger and so I began with casual conversations with small groups of them in the courtyard. However, I struggled to remember all their names, never mind learn of their lives and history. I established better personal relations with the group I taught English to. I recorded two interviews after the English classes. Through Prodip, an intermediate student who was also a close neighbour, I built an especially good rapport with his male friends. Prodip was also responsible for carrying out my survey of the village. Together, we visited about 20 families and during long walks in the countryside he started asking me questions about issues that, he claimed, he could not talk about to anyone else. The issues he was most concerned about related to sexuality and cross-gender relations. These conversations opened to me his more intimate world and through him I was able to develop a good rapport with his best friends, all of whom attended Tagore college and lived in the nearby villages. I had many informal conversations with this group of boys and they also participated in interviews that I recorded.

In general, both boys and girls seemed much more constrained by the social pressure coming from their parents, elders and other villagers. At college, on the other hand, they were more self-confident. I also experienced the colleges as more familiar places where I was observed less and where I could have more direct communication with students and staff. The colleges were also realistically the best place for meeting the girls and spending time with them, as their mobility was more limited than the boys', and they couldn't freely come to my place or meet me in other public spaces.

Setting the Scene

In the remaining part of this chapter I discuss how adolescence
and youth-hood have been addressed in the anthropological and
psychological fields in relation to some core themes: the transition
to adulthood and process of definition of self-identity, youth-parental
relations, the role of the peer group, and the process of socialisation.
I explore the strengths and weaknesses of different psychodynamic
approaches to adolescence as a critical age-related transition. Turning
then to the anthropological field, I give an account of the debate in
the South Asian scholarship about the concepts of the self and the
individual that has brought some authors to argue that the socio-centric
nature of some cultures can be counterpoised to the individualism
of the West. I also discuss the more recent anthropological literature,
which, instead, theoretically and empirically points out the spaces for
and the instances of individual agency. I do this in order to delineate
a map of concepts that might constitute a framework to interpret
Bangladeshi adolescents' personal and social world and to formulate
the key questions that I intend to address. The main underlying
concern in exploring and counterpoising this literature is to raise
significant questions about how social links can be conceptualised and
to think about the relation between the self, individual identity and the
social. The issue of establishing the self through separation and that of
autonomy *versus* social connectedness are particularly significant ones
to consider in adolescence and in different socio-cultural contexts.

ADOLESCENCE CROSS-CULTURALLY: ANTHROPOLOGICAL UNDERSTANDINGS

Social anthropologists have long been wary of psychological theorising
about adolescence and this is evident in the various themes that occur
in the anthropological literature on adolescence. One such theme
is whether or not the acquisition of adulthood involves a series of
predictable transitions and whether the timetable for these transitions
rests on psycho-biological universals or is determined by socio-cultural
factors. Mead's ethnographic work on Samoa (1928) was specifically

undertaken to question the biological determinism that views adolescence as a period of storm, stress and turmoil, and to show the importance of culture and culturally determined socialisation processes in shaping children's and adolescents' behaviour in different cultural contexts. In another form of cross-cultural comparison, Schlegel and Barry (1991) and again Schlegel (1995) advocated a biosocial approach to the study of adolescence and focused on reproduction as the key to understanding its universal character. In their perspective adolescence is seen essentially as a period of preparation for marriage and for learning adult roles that may or may not be in step with the acquisition of the physical capacity to reproduce (ibid.). Their research however also showed the wide range of cultural variations in adolescent activities and behaviours in relation to such topical issues as sexuality, courtship, marriage, relations with parents and the peer group, and deviant and antisocial behaviour. This implies that cross-cultural differences appear to be more numerous than cross-cultural commonalities (Schlegel and Barry 1991).

In parallel with Schlegel and Barry's study, Whiting and Whiting's[5] 'Harvard Adolescence Project' focused on the impact on adolescent life and behaviour of the processes of socio-economic change described in terms of 'modernisation'. Schooling appears to play an important role in removing teenagers from their houses and in allowing young people of both sexes to meet without parents' supervision. It prepares them for occupations different from their parents' and inevitably increases girls' age at marriage. New forms of employment are made available within a monetized economy and higher levels of education are valued and required to access them.

Schlegel and Barry's assertion of the universality of adolescence as a social stage is based on quite a narrow conceptualisation of adolescence itself. By identifying as a fundamental characteristic of adolescence the capacity to reproduce, their 'biosocial' approach overemphasises the idea that what happens in adolescence is all about physiological maturity. The same authors, together with Whiting and Whiting and all the other participants in the Harvard Adolescence Project, talk of adolescence as a life stage within a socialisation framework in which adolescents are seen as passive recipients of adult values and social norms and in some senses 'on trial for the roles they will assume as spouses and affines'

(Schlegel 1995: 23). Moreover, and more importantly, the notion of the psychological used in most of these studies is not informed by the notion of psychodynamics and does not take into account the intra-psychic processes that are assumed by psychoanalysis to occur in adolescence. The attention, in a typical cross-cultural perspective, is rather on how culture defines certain psychological traits of the individuals. A smooth and non-problematic process of transition to adulthood is assumed to occur through socialisation and the adherence to some sort of predetermined social roles. Finally, change, in terms of modernisation, is seen exclusively as something that comes from the outside disrupting the traditional system of attributed roles and putting young people in a state of psychological stress that eventually results in antisocial behaviour. Conflict between generations in these studies is seen essentially as due to the tension between traditional models that parents want to inculcate in their children and the new attitudes, values and behaviours that children may want to adopt. Adolescents are seen as potentially deviant because as incomplete human beings they can be more influenced by the external environment and by the changes brought about by modernisation.

In contrast to North American cultural anthropology, British social anthropology has been less concerned with the psychological dimension of the processes that take place in adolescence, and up to the 1970s ethnographies dealt mainly with two themes: initiation ceremonies by which adulthood is acquired, and age set and age grades, particularly in East African pastoralist societies (Richards 1970). After the 1970s, more attention was given to adolescence and youth-hood as social stages interpreted in terms of the processes of socialisation. Socialisation constituted the focus of an annual Association of Social Anthropologists (ASA) meeting in 1967 that resulted in a volume published in 1970. The four chapters that deal with adolescents look at aspects of conflict between young people and elders in terms of competition for power in different domains (La Fontaine 1970; Mayer 1970; Spencer 1970; Wilder 1970). Some of the authors of the 1970 volume are also among the contributors to another ASA monograph published in 1990. The volume is organised around a theme of ascendant life course passage from adolescence to late adulthood;

four chapters deal in particular with adolescence conceptualised as a transient phase, and with different aspects of this transition. Both the 1970 and 1990 volumes can be located inside the particular tradition of British anthropology with its focus on categorical relations, social roles and social relations.

My research resonates better with recent anthropological studies on young people that draw extensively on approaches to youth culture initially developed outside anthropology. In the introduction to the volume *Youth Cultures: A Cross Cultural Perspective*, Helena Wulff advocates an approach that deals with 'youth culture in its own right' (Wulff 1995: 2). Instead of treating young people in adult terms either as resisters, victims or in the process of acquiring predetermined adult identities, she argues that we focus on them as cultural agents in a context where identities are shaped by elements of local culture as well as by globalisation and transnationalism. The focus on youth as cultural agents had developed since the 1970s and 1980s in Britain, particularly in the field of cultural studies, in a Marxist-Gramscian framework, with the Birmingham school. Here the focus was mainly on working class youth in industrial societies. In the 1995 volume quoted above and in other more recent studies reviewed by Bucholtz (2002), the contexts considered vary considerably from Europe to North America, to Africa and Asia, and the impetus of this research corpus lies more in a trans-cultural or multicultural paradigm rather than in a cross-cultural, comparative one. This approach is also apparent in the growing interest in contemporary middle-class urban and rural youth in South Asia, which includes studies that focus on the performance of masculinity, models of consumption and popular culture (De Neve 2004; Fuller and Narasimhan 2007; Nisbett 2004; Osella and Osella 2004), courtship and sexuality (Abraham 2002 [in Bombay]; Osella and Osella 1998, 2000, 2002 [in Kerala]), and marriage and the dynamics of conjugality (Ahearn 2001a; Donner 2008; Grover 2009).

This research on youth culture with its emphasis on young people as active agents within complex social contexts and on the construction of social identity through ongoing processes of negotiation within social relations, provides many useful insights for my own study. However, this perspective leaves in the background a dimension of youth-hood which is particularly relevant in my own approach, one that is apparent in the use of the term adolescents to refer to Bangladeshi teenagers. I prefer to talk of adolescents rather than youth because this places teenagers within a developmental stage entailing a complex and multifaceted process of transition, which involves physical, psychological and social dimensions. However, my perspective is not one where adolescents are seen as incomplete human beings, in the process of being 'socialised' into adult social roles as a 'socialisation' framework would see them. On the contrary, I intend to put young people at the centre of the scene and to give voice to their own perceptions and experiences about what it means to be young. At the same time, my perspective wants to take into account also that as 'adolescents' they live a particular phase of transition and maturation, and that to make sense of this it is important to consider psychodynamic perspectives. In psychodynamic perspectives, conflict between generations in adolescence is essentially read as a manifestation of the intra-psychic dynamics of separation and differentiation that characterise adolescence as a period of search for self-identity. These perspectives thus focus on identity not as defined in terms of occupational, marital or any other social position, but more profoundly as a sense of selfhood, a sense of 'I' that is also, but not only, made of one's social position. The notion of intra-psychic separation is thus at the heart of the processes required for the development of a sense of selfhood and at the heart of the capacity of agentful behaviour.

In order to gain insight into how intra-psychic dynamics have been interpreted in relation to adolescence as a developmental stage, I discuss in the next section important themes found in the psychological literature.

Adolescence as a Developmental Phase: Dominant Psychological Understandings

Strengths and Weaknesses of Erikson's Psychosocial Approach

In psychological understandings of adolescence one most influential work is undoubtedly that of Erikson (1968), representative of the school of Ego Psychology.[6] His theory of adolescence was developed subsequently by Marcia (1980) and his work has actually set the standards against which different scholars compare and assess their work on identity formation (Muuss 1996). Erikson was the first to enquire into the issue of identity formation in adolescence and his approach diverges from a strictly Freudian perspective by the importance given to the environment and to the study of the Ego in relation to the external reality and in its adapting to it.

According to Erikson, during adolescence the physiological changes of puberty trigger a process of psychological development that implies a major reorganisation of the self and opens the way for the development of a mature adult identity. Coleman and Hendry (1999: 52), in presenting Erikson's theorisation of the acquisition of self-identity, synthesise what can be called a process of 'individuation' saying: 'the individual struggles to determine the exact nature of his/her self, and to consolidate a series of choices into a coherent whole which makes up the essence of the person clearly separated from parents and other formative influences'. Erikson interprets adolescence as a period of search for one's own identity linked to a process of individuation. Adolescents try to understand who they are and who they want to become, their personal values and their direction in life. This conceptualisation of adolescence as a period of maturation and unfolding individuality is underpinned by the notion of Ego identity, that Erikson defines as 'the awareness of the fact that there is a self-sameness and continuity to the Ego's synthesizing methods'. Identity is a core concept in Erikson's analysis, but also a very contested and problematic one. First, the notion of an inner identity that constitutes the essence of a person is arguably very culturally specific. Anthropologists have long shown that 'the trascendental subject and the Western idea of the person are far from universal' (Moore 1994: 33). There is cross-cultural variability in the way the self and the person are defined and understood and also multiple models within cultures and societies (Moore 1994). In the psychoanalytic field, the approach of J. Lacan has definitely questioned the existence of a self-conscious and self-centred rational subject and has demonstrated that the self is split and fragmented, the identity multiple and contested. The self is seen not as an autonomous agent, as in the Ego psychologists' perspective, but as a fluid, mobile series of identifications, internalisations of images/perceptions invested with libido (Grosz 1990). My own use of the word identity has to be intended thus in a much looser sense than in Erikson's analysis and as a synonym of selfhood and self-awareness.

Even the universal character of adolescence as a period of psychosocial moratorium in which young people can delay major choices and experiment with different roles in a kind of inner soul searching is controversial and historically specific. However, Erikson himself acknowledges this. He recognises that the emergence of adolescence as 'an even more marked and conscious period' and the identity crisis that may characterise it are linked to the technological and economic changes that prolong the period between school life and the access to specialised employment (Erikson 1968: 128).

In this sense Erikson recognises, in part, the relative nature of adolescence as a stage in the life cycle that may vary in different societies in terms of 'duration, intensity and ritualization' (ibid.: 155). One of the strengths of his analysis is the importance attributed to history and society in the process of identity formation that takes place in a continuous interplay between the psychological and the social: 'we deal with a process located in the core of the individual and also in the core of its communal culture' and a 'process which establishes in fact the identity of those two identities' (ibid.: 22). A further critical element in Erikson's analysis is his clear distinction between identity formation during adolescence and the childhood processes of introjection and identification that give the individual a first minimal sense of 'I'.[7] The 'I' that is supposed to develop in adolescence is more complex because in its formation the real 'others' and the social play an increasingly important role and the individual plays an active role in discarding some identifications and selecting others, in other words, in crafting one's self.

On the controversial issue of the need for emotional disengagement from parents as a condition for the acquisition of adult autonomy, Erikson departs markedly from Freud and, instead of viewing others as objects of cathexis (investment) important to intra-psychic functioning, he sees the 'others'—the real ones—as providing the context for the

Ego development and functioning. Parental figures, according to Erikson, are important especially in adolescence for the formation of self-identity as bearers of values and for providing an ideological framework against which young people can rebel and forge their own values. We can thus say that in Erikson's approach the interpersonal dimension has a central role.

Other psychoanalytic theorists, in line with Freudian orthodoxy, analyse and describe the transition to adulthood by focusing on the intra-psychic dynamics of separation/individuation. According to Blos (1966, 1967), adolescence is characterised by the 'second individuation process', the first one being that described by Mahler (1963) and Mahler et al. (1975). According to Mahler, whose analysis is informed by other object relations theorists,[8] the infant goes through a process of progressive separation/individuation from the mother which ends during the third year of life when the toddler finally accepts the reality of separation from the mother and gives up the desire to return to a sort of self-object fusion (ibid.: 109). Incorporating the image of the mother allows the infant to separate from her and give foundations to his/her intra-psychic structure.

Both the first and second individuation imply emotional disengagement from the infantile love objects and from the internal representations of the parents and other carers and the establishment of a sense of self able to control the demands of the superego and to take increasing responsibility (Blos 1967).

Intergenerational Relations in Adolescence: From Intra-psychic to Interpersonal Dynamics

An important and controversial aspect of the psychoanalytic theorisation of adolescence concerns the conceptualisation of individuation in terms of autonomy and independence from the parents. From Anna Freud to Erikson, theorists of adolescence have stressed the establishment of emotional autonomy and independence from parents as a feature of adulthood. For some, the disengagement from parents occurs at the intra-psychic level, as a process of disinvestment from internalised parent images, and implies a painful sense of loss of the infantile love objects associated with the fear of becoming an adult, and as such alone. The internal turmoil may manifest itself in an ambivalent attitude towards attachment figures. Winnicott sees adolescents 'in the doldrums'; their ambivalent attitude, the coexistence of a sort of defiant independence and regressive dependence, is the way in which is manifested the internal conflict between being a child, and as such in need and dependent, and becoming an adult, and as such alone. On the other hand, it is precisely the closeness of the parents and the successful internalisation of their images in the preceding phases that can give the individual the strength to overcome the fear of growing up (Winnicott 1965). Erikson instead gives a central role to the real parents and to parent-child interpersonal relationships in the trajectory of adolescence. Informed by both Erikson and Blos, empirical, psychodynamic research has subsequently developed in the direction of finding ways to measure the process of individuation and the attention has focused mainly on the interpersonal dimension and on the actual interaction between adolescents, parents and other significant adults. Many recent studies try to demonstrate that there can be autonomy together with 'social responsibility' (Greenberger 1984), or 'interdependence' (Youniss and Smollar 1985) or again 'connectedness'[9]. Rather than based on severing affective links with the parents, a successful process of growth is seen by these authors as linked to the development of qualitatively different relations inside the family, implying increased symmetry of reciprocal influence. Thus an increased degree of self-assertion and decisional autonomy by adolescents is not incompatible with keeping the relationships going, but rather is actually favoured by it. In these approaches, self and identity are constituted in relation as much as a 'mature external relational world characterized by mutuality depends on a firmly established internal one' (Marcia 1993: 105). A separated, autonomous self is seen not as an end in itself but as the prerequisite for relating to others. 'I think 'separation can be better understood to describe a process in the serving of allowing more mature levels of relating to come into being' (ibid.: 110).

Even the opening up to a larger social world outside the family boundaries is supposed to serve the task of self-definition and formation of identity/selfhood typical of the work of adolescence. Establishing mature intimate relationships presupposes the constitution of a firmer self-identity and the capacity to relate with the 'Other' as separate and independent from one's self.

INDIVIDUAL OR COLLECTIVE SELF?: THE INDIAN DEBATE

The Paradigm of Collectivity and Its Criticism

The issue of the role of the social in relation to individual identity has been the focus of considerable debate in the anthropological field. As mentioned above, the literature shows examples of local theories of the person and the self where these are not necessarily conceived as bounded entities and embodiment is not the essence of identity.[10] With regard to the Indian subcontinent, a 'paradigm of collectivity' (Arnold and Blackburn 2004) dominated in the scholarship in the field of anthropology, history, politics and religious studies in the 1960s and 1970s. Indian society was represented as a socio-centric one, where there was no space for consideration of notions of selfhood and individual identity, and where individual personality and interests were totally subsumed into the caste, familial and group identities.

Dumont argued, for example, that hierarchy rather than equality is the principle that structures Indian caste society and the individual's desire, happiness and autonomy are irrelevant because the emphasis is placed on the collective whole.

To say that the world of caste is a world of relations is to say that the particular man and the particular caste have no substance: they exist empirically, but they have no reality in thought, no Being. ...At the risk of being crude...on the level of life in the world the individual is not. (Dumont 1970: 272)

Drawing evidence mainly from texts and rituals, to examine the indigenous logic of what constitutes a person, Marriott (1976) argued that in India persons are conceptualised as 'dividuals' rather than individuals, because the person's substance is divisible and transferable.[11] Marriott, again in 1990, emphasises that 'the investigator who seeks ways of asking in rural India about equivalents of Western 'individuals'…risks imposing an alien ontology and an alien epistemology on those who attempt to answer'.[12] Similarly, Shweder and Bourne, after discussing a great deal of cross-cultural literature, conclude by counterposing an 'egocentric' western self to the 'socio-centric' Indian self where interests are subordinated to the good of the collectivity and interdependence rather than autonomy is valued (1984: 190). The sharp dichotomy these views assume between a western self as characterised by independence, autonomy, differentiation and self-awareness and the non-western as 'unindividuated' (Marsella 1985: 209), interdependent and with fluid boundaries, have been criticised from a number of perspectives.[13]

According to Spiro (1993: 113), on 'conceptual/terminological and methodological grounds' it can be argued that in most of these studies the term 'self' remains undefined and sometimes confused with other concepts such as person, individual, personality and so on. We can draw a clear distinction between conceptions of the self expressed by sets of cultural symbols and representations and the actual experience that the actors have of their own self, expressed by the way they talk of their experience and by their actual behaviour (Spiro 1993; Moore 1994). In this vein, Wilce questioning the empirical foundations of Dumont's statement, asks: 'how true is (this view) to life on the ground, to the lives of all sorts of people in and out the caste system?' (Wilce 1998: 37). Moore explains this argument as follows: 'even if persons in some societies might be thought of as inseparable from other persons this does not mean that individuals do not exist, or that people's actions are not evaluated in terms of an individual life trajectory or career' (Moore 1994: 33). Mines (1988) provides an interesting example of how Indians depict themselves privately as active agents, pursuing private goals, counter to Dumont's and Marriott's views that individualism is devalued in India. On the basis of 23 case studies of Indian men and women of different socio-economic backgrounds, she observes that although most of the people in her sample had moved into adult roles (marriage and work) at about 17 to 22 years of age, in conformity with societal norms and values, they had manifested a more complete control over their lives in terms of autonomous decisions only when external circumstances, effective economic independence for example, had allowed them to challenge familial and societal values and follow those preferences and goals that at a younger age they hadn't been able to pursue. So she argues that persons perceive themselves as having interests and needs distinct from those of their social group and this translates into an actual possibility of choice 'to comply or not comply' (ibid.: 570). These arguments and counter arguments are understandable within the debates that counterpoised before the 1970s universalist and culturalist perspective on the relation between self and culture (Holland 1997).

Another critical point can be raised from the perspective of a critique of past representations of 'culture'. The universalism versus relativism debate is underpinned by an idea of culture as a holistic, coherent and integrated system of values, belief and representations. As Holland underlines, this does not account for different social positions, for differentiations based on wealth, religious community, caste and gender and for power relations.[14] Marriott's and Dumont's approaches can also be criticised, according to the same author, because their 'holistic' perspective does not take into account history and presents a timeless society and culture. Marriott and Dumont give a static picture of Indian society as much as they draw their evidence mainly from ancient texts and rituals.

As a further critique of this 'cultural difference' approach, I would argue that the idea of western individualism itself, as well as the idea of 'socio-centric', have to be deconstructed. It would be misguided to interpret the assumed 'western individualism' as an issue of culture and consider it only in the terrain of cultural representations. The historical emergence of the 'individual' is connected with capitalism and the market economy, where the abstract 'homo oeconomicus' is conceptualised as the rational and self-interested subject of economic choices inside a network of impersonal relations mediated by the market. Historically, in the West, there has been a transition from pre-institutions of embededdness to institutions that, at least formally, give the individual a pre-eminent role, together with an abstract power to choose and to forge one's own life. This view of the individual is anchored in contractual relations with the state and the market where the individual is relatively free from the social obligations and responsibilities that characterise precapitalist rural societies where relations of production based on patronage and clientelism prevail. Together with the development of market economies, there has been also the development of a normative conception of the individual pertaining to the socio-legal sphere, where every person is a bearer of natural rights and entitled to legal action to enforce them. Thus, being a person in the West is not just about some kind of 'Westerness', it is about generalised capitalism, generalised market economies and the socio-legal nature of citizenship within states based on these economies.

Another way of making sense of Dumont's and Marriott's interpretation would be to acknowledge that Indian society does not construct adult identity as an individuated one and that in a situation of social embeddedness there is not much recognition in the hegemonic discourse of a process of individual development in terms of 'individuation'. I would then add, following Moore, that even if persons are thought of as inseparable from others or bound into complex webs of relationships, 'this does not make the individuals concerned as incapable of agency and intention' (Moore 1994: 33). Thus the notion of individual self-interest is not the only basis for agency.

Socio-psychological Approaches in South Asia: Women's Identity

Some of these lines of thought have been developed in studies that examine the relation between the person and the social in South Asia through looking specifically at women's identity in socio-psychological studies that have focused on intra-family dynamics in a South Asian context. Roland (1988), while arguing that a strong enmeshment of the individual in the group is fostered inter alia by child rearing practices, acknowledges on the other hand that precisely the 'prolonged symbiotic nurturing maternal relationships' (ibid.: 240) favour the development of individuality. According to him: '...this is richly developed in certain ways in Indians' and 'Hindu culture not only recognizes the particular proclivities of a person but also accords a remarkable degree of freedom in feeling, thinking and maintaining a private self' (ibid.). In other words, social embeddedness is good for the psyche.

S. Kakar, an Indian socio-psychologist, also has a very nuanced view of the link between women's self-identity and their embeddedness in the family. For him, social embeddedness is very constraining. He describes women as passing their life 'entrapped' in a network of familial relations where their personal identity seems to be entirely subsumed in the roles they perform, first as daughters, then as wives and mothers. 'An Indian woman does not stand alone; her identity is wholly defined by her relationships to others' (Kakar 1978: 56). 'The dominant psycho-social realities of their life can be condensed into three stages: first she is a daughter to her parents; second she is a wife to her husband (and in laws); third she is a mother to her sons and daughters' (ibid.: 57). 'The feminine role in India crystallizes a woman's connections to others, her embeddedness in a multitude of familial relationship' (ibid.: 62). He describes the process of socialisation of adolescent girls as one that does not foster the development of self-esteem, saying that during early adolescence girls' self-esteem 'falters' and they tend to 'over conform to the prescription and expectations of those around' (ibid.). On the other hand, he acknowledges that this is not reflected in the psychology of Indian women in terms of propensity to 'feelings of worthlessness and inferiority or low self esteem and depressive moodiness' (ibid.:60). Kakar acknowledges that the context is actually one where women have a great deal of space and sphere of activity on their own 'within which to create and manifest those aspects of feminine identity that derive from intimacy and collaboration with other women' (ibid.). For Kakar, what counts in giving an initial foundation to girls' self-esteem is their infantile relation with their mothers, which he describes as being based on trust and acceptance: 'The capacity to be truly alone is greatest when the 'Other' originally equated with the accepting, giving 'good mother' has become a constant and indestructible presence in the individual's unconscious and is fused with it in the form of self-acceptance' (ibid.: 87).

Ewing (1991), in an attempt to answer the question of the applicability of psychoanalytic theories to the context of South Asia, builds on the idea that emotional maturity depends on the capacity to rely trustingly on others. She introduces a distinction between 'intra-psychic autonomy' (as conceptualised by Cohler and Geyer 1982) and 'interpersonal engagement' as the key to analyse the cases of two Pakistani women who experienced depression as they were trying to adjust to marriage. Intra-psychic autonomy defined as 'the ability to maintain enduring mental representations of sources of self esteem and comfort' is, according to Ewing (1991: 193), what permits Pakistani women to adapt and cope with the demands of the family environment and the strong interpersonal engagement that this entails. On the other hand, the lack of it, due to the unsatisfactory internalisation of maternal representations in early childhood, may lead to psychological disturbance.

When one keeps in mind a distinction between interpersonal and intra-psychic autonomy, there is considerable evidence to suggest that in many South Asian families, individual family members do in fact act in an autonomous fashion intra-psychically, though they operate within a highly 'engaged' interpersonal network of family relationships and expectations. Despite a high degree of interpersonal engagement, South Asians often display a considerable ability to maintain their own perspective and remain attuned to their own needs and the needs of others while accepting the demands for conformity within the family. (ibid.: 139)

Ewing quotes other studies that underline manifestations of self-esteem and agency in the behaviour of South Asian women although not exclusively in terms of psychoanalytic categories. More than just the awareness of one's boundaries, self-esteem allows women to perceive their needs and to 'act tactfully' (Roy 1975) in pursuing them, eventually to rebel against hierarchical superiors (Mines 1988) while remaining engaged in a complex network of obligations and reciprocal expectations. In brief 'intra-psychic autonomy' allows women a sphere and a possibility of action. The possibility of agentful behaviour is linked to an individual's self-esteem and is seen as the ability to negotiate social relations while at the same time remaining part of the network. Ewing concludes that even in the context of an extended family, where the place of the new bride is strictly defined by age and gender hierarchies, there must be some flexibility 'behind the scenes' to accommodate individual needs. If some space for negotiation is not granted, however strong a woman is in terms of self-esteem, some psychological disturbance may occur (Ewing 1991).

These examples show that if we look at self and identity 'in action' through the words, experiences and behaviour of the actors, we see that identity as perceived, played out in interaction and lived in choices is far more complex than simply being shaped by discourses about the importance of the collective. Wilce (1998), in his analysis of Bangladeshi 'troubles talk', points out how expressions of dependence and assertiveness are intertwined in the way people narrate their own experience of illness and how the self that is played out in the dialogues reveals a dialectic of self-assertiveness and dependence. 'Complaining' can at the same time be read as a self-assertive act and as a way of claiming help from patrons on the basis of a dependent client status. Wilce underlines also that 'troubles talk' is a gendered act and that: 'Self-hood, here, the strong self-indexing entailed in troubles telling, can be conceived of as an unequally distributed privilege rather than as a biological given' (ibid.: 40). Moreover, from Mines' analysis it appears, even if she doesn't particularly underline this aspect, that the nature of the economy and the opportunities it offers played an important role in motivating the 'autonomous' choices of some of her interviewees. The 'distinctive personal interests' (Mines 1988: 570) that they had shown were in many instances connected to employment choices that could only be realised when some sort of economic independence from the family had been acquired. In some cases this allowed them to disregard the loyalty due to parents and extended family.

The Space for Agency and Resistance: Anthropological Accounts

These interesting socio-psychological accounts parallel the developments in anthropological and social research in South Asia in the last 20 years, following the path opened by Scott (1985) and the school of 'subaltern studies'.[15] The focus has shifted from social structure and culture, described earlier, to the place of the individual actors in society and to the everyday experiences of people and their voices. This opens up the analysis of conflict and resistance (Haynes and Prakash 1992) and spaces for the manifestation of agency in societies that earlier studies depicted as harmonious and holistic. This is apparent in recent studies of gender relations in South Asia that have been focusing on the different strategies that women employ to actively shape their lives and struggle against social hierarchies. Western feminist thinking has been criticised for its assumption of universality based on a western-defined concept of sexual difference and patriarchy where: 'Third World women are produced by the Western imaginary as homogeneously poor, oppressed, with shared needs and interests that lead to the suppression of differences' (Mohanty 1988: 61). Against this stereotype of women as passive and oppressed victims, these studies emphasise women's resistance and alternative discourses. Women's subjectivity, their capacity to act in accordance with their perceived needs and to voice their concerns, in short, their agency, has been underlined in several accounts (Hynes and Prakash 1992; Jeffery and Jeffery 1994, 1996; Raheja and Gold 1994). This perspective, countering the image of Indian girls and adult women as powerless and demure, obedient and oppressed, emphasises how they negotiate and resist aspects of their situation in the everyday (Jeffery and Jeffery 1994). The same studies have raised relevant questions about how agency and resistance can be conceptualised in a context that remains one of strong social embeddedness where social punishments sanction those who step too far out of line (Jeffery and Jeffery 1996). Although these contributions have provided important insights, there is a danger of overusing the idea of resistance to describe women's actions.

I do not want to rehearse these issues too fully. Jeffery and Jeffery point out, drawing from Mani (1990) and Abu-Lughod (1990), that:

...the twin tendencies of romanticizing women's resistance and seeing it as coterminous with agency contain their own difficulties. It is important not to exaggerate the potential of women's everyday resistance to alter the terms under which they lived nor to render invisible the ways women were coopted by the protective and may be comforting certainties of the structures in which they were embedded'. (Jeffery and Jeffery 1996: 16)

The perspective of seeing agency only in actions that resist domination is misguided because according to Ahearn 'oppositional agency is only one of the many forms of agency' (2001b: 117). So she warns against the confusion that may arise from conflating agency with resistance. Rather women may play an active part with a 'complex and ambiguous agency in which they accept, accommodate, ignore, resist or protest, sometimes all at the same time' (McLeod 1992: 534). This observation is also in line with Kabeer's advocating of a 'middle ground' between methodological individualism and methodological structuralism 'in which the agency of individuals can be recognised without losing sight of the constraining structures within which they exercise their agency' (2000: 47).

These recent studies in India accord women (and men) a far greater degree of agency and tend to pay much more attention to people's notion of their own individuality while also acknowledging the importance of local and global processes of socio-economic change in shaping 'modern' selves. For example, in her analysis of middle-class households in Calcutta, Donner (2008) shows how people accommodate notions of personal choice and preference in relation to marriage arrangements even though these are still mostly defined in terms of collective interest. Donner suggests that the counterpositioning of arranged marriages as a vestige of the past and love marriages as a new and modern phenomenon does not do justice to the actual situation. She argues instead for the coexistence of 'new forms of being modern, which include the possibility of falling in love, conducting a self-chosen marriage' (ibid.: 67) with patrilocality, caste endogamy and joint families and a certain degree of 'parental authority over young people's passion' (ibid.: 69). She also acknowldges the role of prolonged girls' education in postponing marriage and favouring the development of mostly platonic premarital relationships conducted by letters. Similarly, Grover's (2009) research in Delhi slums noted an increasing tendency among sections of young people to engage in forms of 'modern courtship', and, quoting Uberoi, talks of 'arranged-love marriages…a style of match making where a romantic choice already made is endorsed post-facto by parental approval and treated thereafter like an arranged marriage'.[16]

This is rarely reflected in the literature on life stages in Bangladesh, not least because the main studies were done some time ago. Much of this remains within the earlier perspective that saw the formation of identity in a process of socialisation as adherence to predetermined roles that unfold in the passage through stages in the life cycle. Aziz and Maloney's study is based on life stories collected from 65 male and female respondents in 1978 in Matlab Thana, Comilla district. Kotalova's ethnography was conducted among a peasant community in the village of Gameranga in Faridpur district in 1983. They partially acknowledge that the actual behaviour of men and women does not always conform to social expectations and norms: for example, premarital sex and extramarital relations were found to occur in their respective study areas. However, they describe the situation as a static one and their picture is one of an integrated, agrarian community where transgressive behaviour reinforces the normative strength of the social rules without challenging them. Moreover, they fail to acknowledge striking evidence from their own interviews: that in most of the cases the girls reporting premarital sex claim to have been forced. This gender violence is not actually discussed in their ethnographies, which rather gives a picture of a harmonious society where the adherence to the prescribed age and gender roles assures stability. Gender relations are depicted in terms of separation and different roles and the imbalance in the distribution of material and symbolic resources (Kabeer 2000) that they imply is completely glossed over. Conflict does not seem to exist in the villages they describe. It is assumed that the socialisation process reproduces the same identities from one generation to the next, and that ascribed social roles such as those of daughter, wife or mother, and of husband or mother-in-law are in some way reproduced through rituals and mechanically executed. Identities are adhered to passively and there seems to be no space for individual agency. Kotalova, for example, quoting Davis (1983: 81) subscribes to the view that 'the individual does not enter into thinking in Bengal' (Kotalova 1993: 69) and argues that the individual's only aspiration is to fit into the group and carry out one's role. This kind of conceptualisation of gender relations as a set of social roles can produce a very dichotomous view of self-identity. For example, Das, analysing Punjabi women, ends up depicting them in some senses, once again, as entrapped in the performance of the social roles where these become like masks that hide their 'true identity'. She thus sees women as split between a true self where emotions are located and the performance of social roles that exclude the manifestation of emotions of attachment and love to husband and children.

REFRAMING INDIVIDUALITY: IDENTITY AND THE SOCIAL

Some points can now be drawn from the above discussion in order to reframe the issue of the applicability to a South Asian context of the concepts developed in the tradition of psychology and psychoanalysis and in relation to the development of selfhood in adolescence. We have seen that according to psychoanalysis and psychology a first process of separation/individuation from the mother occurs during infancy that gives the individual a fundamental sense of self-perception and self-boundedness, and the sense of being a separate individual. The establishment of a sense of 'I', called by Mahler, Pine and Bergman (1975) as 'first individuation', is considered to be a universal feature of individual development and psychic structure by theorists belonging to different psychoanalytic traditions and also by some anthropologists. When Erikson and other Ego psychologists describe the development of the individual self-identity, they refer clearly to a meaning of the term 'self' as being founded on self–other differentiation, on the perception that one's self is bounded and separate from all other persons. This kind of development, whether we call it self–other differentiation (James 1981) or self-awareness and self-reflexivity (Hallowell 1955), is a 'distinguishing feature of the very notion of human nature' (Spiro 1993: 110). As Hallowell, referring to Boas, underlined, all societies uphold the separation between self and other and this is reflected in the use of the three personal pronouns I, Thou and She. Furthermore,

...*if this be accepted we have an unequivocal indication that languages all have a common socio-psychological function. They provide the human individual with a linguistic means of self–other orientation in all contexts of interpersonal verbal communication. A personal existence and sphere of action is defined as a fundamental reference point.* (Hallowell 1955: 89)

For Erikson the experience of autistic children is significant in this regard: 'no one working with autistic children will ever forget the horror of observing how desperately they struggle to grasp the meaning of saying 'I' and 'you' and how impossible it is for them, for language presupposes the experience of a coherent I' (Erikson 1968: 217).

Following these theoreticians we can consider the experience of separateness and self–other differentiation or self-awareness: 'as integral a part of a human socio cultural mode of adaptation as it is of a distinctive human level of psychological structuralization' (Hallowell 1955: 75). It seems, thus, that at this minimal level the psychological understanding of the mechanisms of formation of the individual self can be considered an appropriate interpretation of a universal reality. However, it is more important to insist on the relational character of the self as modelled in many non 'western' anthropological contexts and acknowledged in the psychoanalytic field. For psychoanalysis, a successful self-identification is founded on the introjection of the other. The subject of psychoanalysis is constituted by relation from the start: this individual is never a monad pursuing his/her interest in a social, or indeed historical and cultural vacuum.

I have summarised literatures that see adolescence as a second process of separation/individuation that is qualitatively different from the first one, and emphasised Erikson's analysis, which particularly stresses the importance of the relational/interpersonal dimension. Even if it is difficult to disentangle the psychodynamic/universal aspect from the historical and socially constructed one, in the psychoanalytic theorisation of the process of development in adolescence, the latter seems to weigh more and more as the individual grows up. Both Erikson's self-identity and Blos's character are conceived as resulting from a balance between the self and the other, from a synthesis of a balanced psychic structure (balance between ego, id and superego) and the outer world. Erikson was even more specific about this when in advocating a new conceptualisation of the environment in psychoanalysis he set out the terms of his investigation in these words:

Instead of accepting such instinctual givens as the Oedipus trinity as an irreducible schema for man's irrational conduct, we are exploring the way in which social forms codetermine the structure of the family; for as Freud said towards the end of his life '...what is operating in the superego is not only the personal qualities of these parents but also everything that produced a determining effect upon themselves, the tastes and standards of the social class in which they live and the characteristics and traditions of the race from which they spring. (Erikson 1968: 47)

Erikson's account sees a much greater role for interpersonal relationships in the formation of adolescents' identity than in the first phase of development. As a child, the individual is embedded in social relations that are not of his/her own making and is not autonomous in articulating objectives, interests, life plans. What changes during adolescence is that there is a gradual move towards a different kind of embeddedness, one where the individual is able to play an active part in shaping social relations as much as he/she is shaped by them. 'Self-identity' or, I would say, selfhood are an individual's specific way of being in the world and this implies first of all a sense of self-awareness, of articulating oneself in terms of a firmer 'I'. The adolescent who has successfully overcome the identity crisis, or accomplished the second individuation, is supposed to be able to support him/herself and have in him/herself the source of self-esteem. Moreover, the sense of 'I' presupposes, according to these theorists, a way of acting, a capacity to assert oneself. He/she is supposed to be able to take responsibility and make autonomous choices in conformity with his/her own life project.

This broad approach radically reconfigures the older universal versus culturally-specific debates referred to earlier, but also invites anthropologists to reconsider the cultural content of social relations. In the specific context of rural Bangladesh explored here, social embeddedness means that, apart from the universal way in which the language contains 'I', there is no public recognition of the search for identity as it is conceptualised in accounts of adolescence in the West and by Erikson. Boys and girls are not encouraged to develop their own preferences and to take the initiative in marriage or work; rather the individual is expected to conform to parental and social expectations. I reject the strong Eriksonian version of social identity as a sense of coherence and continuity and I rather view it as something that 'has to be established socially through a set of discourses that are both discoursive and practical' (Moore 1994: 37). Again, following Moore, I argue that 'since all psychic and developmental processes are relational, then the nature of the relaltionship between self and other(s) and the matrix of social relations and symbolic systems within which that relationship is conducted, must play a key role in the development of the self and subjectivity' (ibid.: 31).

This book begins on the premise that we can interpret the work of becoming adult in terms of a gradual process of definition of one's selfhood inside a particular network of social relations. In this perspective, Bangladeshi adolescents of both sexes, no less than their western counterparts, face this developmental challenge. They have to acquire a sense of selfhood and of their social position in a context where the public discourse does not encourage self-assertion, and where their capacity to choose and to act may not be discoursively acknowledged.

In this perspective, in my ethnography, I explore different arenas to search for the footprints of a process of acquisition of selfhood and for manifestation of agency and self-assertion in boys and girls, who in adolescence open up to an extended network of social relations with many significant others in different social domains: school, work, peer group. This perspective is consistent with ethnographies that show that individual intra-psychic autonomy is not in contradiction with a strong level of 'interpersonal engagement' (Ewing 1991; Mines 1988; Roy 1975). It is also consistent with the recent 'agentive turn' in social sciences (Ahearn 2001b) and in South Asian scholarship that tends to emphasise the spaces for agentful behaviour in situations of social embeddedness as against the image of the 'subordinate' as powerless and voiceless. The literature on agency and resistance has rightly stressed that women are not passive enactors of other people's interests and desires and that bargaining, negotiation and conflict are always present in gender relations (Jeffery and Jeffery 1996; Kandijoti 1988; McLeod 1992; Mohanty 1988; Sen 1990; Whitehead 1981).

Considering women as victims of a false consciousness from being fully submerged in a constraining social structure and unable to see where their collective interests lie, or romanticizing their limited resistance while losing sight of the significant structural gender asymmetries, are misguided perspectives that do not take us far. I suggest first that Gramsci's concepts of contradictory consciousness and fragmentation of common sense offer a way forward out of this dichotomy and also a fresh perspective on agency and resistance. Second, I argue that the analysis of the social relations of gender offers a dynamic view of gender relations where individuals, conceptualised as capable of self-reflection, act within the limit set by hierarchical power relations in pursuit of their needs and wishes. If it is true that specific social relations produce a certain type of consciousness and perception of one's well-being delimited by common sense, it is also true that this consciousness is always in a Gramscian sense 'contradictory' and that identity and status are always renegotiated in everyday practices.[17] The incoherence and fragmentation of 'common sense' is what impedes a simple reproduction of the hegemonic social order and allows for change. In Williams's words: 'the reality of any hegemony in the extended political and cultural sense is that while by definition it is always dominant, it is never either total or exclusive' (1977: 113). In fact, in a Gramscian perspective the subordinate groups may develop a 'critical understanding of self' through a struggle of political 'hegemonies and of opposing directions...in order to arrive at the working out of at a higher level of one' s own conception of reality' (Gramsci 1971: 333).[18] But even before the development of a full critical consciousness and of a collective political movement, the subordinates are not merely resistant, rather they can be active even if in a 'weak' and constrained position.

The originality of my approach lies in an attempt to look at the processes of achievement of selfhood and identity where these receive little public recognition or representation, and at the particular kinds of agency expressed by adolescents. I argue that even in the context of social embeddedness of rural Bangladesh life trajectories are not just set down with no room for manoeuvre for young people. I explore the spaces in which these processes are occurring, taking into account the specificity of the developmental phase, shaped in a particular way by the context in transformation.

Identity and selfhood are gendered and classed and the dimensions of gender and class underpin and run through my entire discussion. I look at the extent to which boys and girls belonging to different socio-economic backgrounds have different opportunities to access higher levels of education and different perspectives on their future in terms of work and employment. I also look at how gender differentiates the way puberty, the transition to adulthood, and adult responsibilities and roles are conceptualised, and the actual experience of schooling and marriage. If, on the one hand, hierarchical power relations delimit the choices of both men and women in different domains and boys are no less subordinated than girls in generational relationships, girls are more constrained particularly in relation to marriage choices, for example, in so far as in the hegemonic cultural repertoire values of honour and shame discursively sustain their subordinate position in familial relations.

My research is based on fieldwork to explore the social and cultural aspects of young people's experience of 'adolescence'. I have not used research methods developed in the psychological or psychoanalytic field and my ethnographic methodology has not and was not intended to give me access to intra-psychic dynamics. Nevertheless, the interpretation of my field data is informed by the psychoanalytic approaches I have discussed above and I use them particularly to identify some key questions that guide my analysis.

Initial questions concern the changing nature of Bangladeshi 'adolescence' brought about by those socio-economic changes that, more than anything else, contribute to the creation of social and temporal spaces between childhood and adulthood. Questions can be asked about what the hegemonic view is on puberty and the transition to adulthood, and the extent to which this is challenged by competing discourses and whether or not a sense of 'adolescence' as a social stage is emerging and in what terms. To what extent can some of the categories developed by Erikson and the theorists of adolescence be applied to the interpretation of Bangladeshi young people's experience of adolescence? What sense of selfhood emerges from young people's discourses and behaviour? What coheres around the notion of 'I' and what kind of self is being envisaged? In the process of identity formation that characterises adolescence, parental figures are supposed to play a significant role along with peers, school mates and friends. What are the spaces for socialising outside the boundaries of the family, the neighbourhood and thé village, and how are these spaces gendered? What spaces are there for independent decision making in the context of hierarchical intergenerational relationships? Is there any evidence of distantiation of adolescent boys and girls from the network of relations that characterised their childhood? Although these questions guide the analysis, they do not structure my argument directly, which instead is set around the examination of three main bodies of empirical material central to young people's experience of adolescence.

Chapter 5 explores the extent to which higher secondary education provides in ideal and practical terms a privileged space for living adolescence, focusing on the perceptions and experiences of college students, both boys and girls. It explores the extent to which studying and postponing marriage open spaces for a different type of consciousness about one's position and entitlements in family and society.

Chapter 6 considers other sides of the discourses about the self, those dealing with the expressions of emotions and the domain of 'love' relationships and intimacies between adolescent boys and girls. It explores how the diffusion of the media, TV, video and DVDs contribute to a cultural change in the way people talk about love, sex and relationships. Media representations of a model of romantic love seem to be significant in younger and older adolescents' imaginary and provide them with a language to express their feelings through love letters and other ways of communication. The chapter looks at how young people experience and express feelings of cross-gender attraction and attachment in relation to the model of romantic love spread through the media, and explores their understanding of friendship, love and sexuality.

Chapter 7 focuses on marriage practices and on the experiences and perceptions of young women about this significant turning point in their lives. Marriage is a basic social institution; it secures for women, and to a lesser extent for men, the passage to adulthood and it is a central arena in relation to my questions. The aim of the chapter will thus be to explore how girls assert themselves in this critical moment of their lives and what spaces there are for manifestations of self-assertion and agency in a context where the capacity to act autonomously is quite limited. These central chapters are preceded by three critical chapters setting the context.

In chapters 2 and 3 I define the economic and socio-cultural contexts of rural Bangladesh, and also discuss the nature of social embeddedness. I look at the material context of the relations of production and how they are intertwined with cultural values and representations. Chapter 2 describes patterns of production and distribution of material resources and discusses the criteria according to which some socio-economic categories can be identified according to different levels of poverty/well-being. The chapter discusses the importance of social networks and interdependence in ensuring survival to all, but especially to the most vulnerable households. Chapter 3 describes the context of hegemonic values, norms and cultural counters that are intertwined with the basic structure of economic relations as important material forces that sustain and reproduce the same relations. It looks at the terms under which categories of prestige, honour and respect constitute the foundations of an hegemonic world view, where hierarchy and rank define the social position and the entitlements of individuals and groups.

Some authors have identified education as one of the most significant factors in the emerging of adolescence as a social stage in different countries. Chapter 4 attempts to assess the role that primary and secondary education play in postponing marriages of girls and boys in order to define the modalities of the changing transition to adulthood and the emergence of 'adolescence' in my research area, setting the scene for the themes that will be ethnographically developed in the subsequent chapters.

In the concluding chapter, I discuss extensively the context and meaning of the emergence of adolescence in rural Bangladesh in the light of my ethnography. I draw my conclusions using some observations and reflections about acid violence.

Notes

1. Maheen, after being attacked, became an activist in Naripokkho. She was a vocal leader in the campaign against acid violence organised by Naripokkho between 1997 and 2000. Many other women survivors were also active agents in this campaign which succeded in bringing the issue of acid attacks to the fore and in obtaining legislative changes (Del Franco, 1999; Chowdhury, 2005).

2. Nasreen Huq died in an accident in Dhaka on 24 April 2006. She was the director of the Action Aid Bangladesh for whom she had worked since 2002. She was one of the founders of the feminist organisation Naripokkho and was an active member for 20 years. With this organisation she led the national campaign in the late 1990s against acid violence, and helped many survivors get support and justice.

3. From March 1994 to March 1996 I worked in Jessore with a local NGO and I lived in Dhaka for a few days every month with a group of male intermediate college students.

4. I refer here to intermediate college students, between ages 17 and 19 approximately.

5. Whiting and Whiting started the cross-cultural 'Harvard Adolescence Project' in 1978. Field studies were conducted in the Canadian Arctic, Morocco, Nigeria, Thailand, Australia and Romania in the 1980s and resulted in the publication of several papers and four monographies (Burbank 1988; Condon 1987; Davis and Davis 1989; Hollos and Leis 1989). These authors (Burbank 1995; Condon 1995; Davis 1995; Hollos and Leis 1995), together with others and Schlegel, contributed in 1995 to a special issue of the periodical *Ethos*, on adolescence.

6. The school of Ego Psychology to which Erikson belongs does not represent the only interpretation of Freudian thought. Ego psychologists focus on the study of the so-called realistic Ego or self, an agency that mediates between antisocial endogenous sexual impulses and the demand of reality. Psychotherapy's goal in this perspective consist in helping the analysand to form a strong, masterful, autonomous Ego.

7. In the processes that occur in the first stages of psychological growth, it is well recognised in the psychological and psychoanalytic discourse the fundamental role played by the dyadic relation mother/infant.

Marcia (1993: 103) talks of this relation as 'the most important for future relational development' as recognised by 'every psychoanalytic theorist, whether drive oriented, object-relations oriented or self oriented'. The introjection by the infant of the image of the mother, his/her first love object, is the first step in a process that continues with all the other childhood identifications as the primary means by which the self is structured.

8. To synthesise, briefly, object relation theory: 'people react to and interact with not only the actual other but also an internal other, a psychic representation of a person which in itself has the power to influence both the individual's affective states and his overt behavioural reactions' (Greenberg and Mitchell 1983: 10).

9. Grootevant and Cooper (1986) quoted in Coleman and Hendry (1999: 76).

10. See Moore (1994), chapter 2 for a detailed discussion.

11. A person can maintain, improve or worsen personal substance through interactions with others and exchanges, for example, of food. This explains the strict code of behaviour that forbids certain kind of contact with members of inferior castes. Even if Dumont and Marriott discuss mainly the Hindu caste ideology, they consider the logic of hierarchy and rank as informing both Hindu and Muslim communities in the subcontinent.

12. Marriott (1990: 2) quoted in Jeffery and Jeffery (1996:13).

13. Spiro's article is one of a series of articles that appeared in the periodical *Ethos* that challenge the monolithic version of the western self, as egocentric or independent. Murray (1993) does this showing that western philosophy, western psychology and western religion don't present the same conception of the self. Ewing (1991) argues that there are different sites of self-production and popular discourses are an important site as well as religious and philosophical texts.

14. Another point is worth making that contributes to attenuate Dumont's interpretation of Hindu caste society as a system where there is no space for the individual. The concept of a unique individuality is actually culturally present in the figure of the ascetic 'renouncer' who pursues self-realisation in positioning himself outside the caste system and the 'social'. Werbner (1996) argues that the same is true for the Sufi Muslim saint.

15. The historians associated with the subaltern studies school have given particular emphasis to 'the alternative discourses' of women

and peasants and explored forms of resistance by the 'subalterns'.

16. Uberoi (1998: 306) quoted in Grover (2009).

17. In a Gramscian perspective, hegemony is established when a dominant class can maintain and exercise a sort of legitimate power based on consent via civil society and social practices. 'A simple experience and its signification via common sense can be constitutive and constituting the operations of hegemony' (Holub 1992: 104). Hegemony as the 'discoursive face of power' can be seen as 'the power to establish the common sense or doxa of a society (Fraser 1992: 53). But hegemony is never complete because common sense is: 'not a conception that even in the brain of each individual is fragmentary incoherent and inconsequential in conformity with the social position of the masses whose philosophy it is' (Gramsci 1971: 326).

18. The 'resisting' individual is for Gramsci a phase in a process: 'if yesterday (the subaltern element) was not responsible, because resisting a will external to itself, now it feels itself to be responsible because it is no longer resisting but an agent necessarily active and taking the initiative' (Gramsci 1971: 337). Resistance for Gramsci presupposes limited awareness and responsibility, and a sort of passive reaction; it presupposes not a false but a contradictory consciousness. Agency is, on the one hand, a transformatory phenomenon that implies a collective will, a political action in the perspective of changing the structures of subordination. Does this mean that outside of structural transformatory change, there is only mere reactive resistance for Gramsci? Not quite, for Gramsci continues the same passage saying: 'but even yesterday was it mere resistance, a mere thing, mere non responsibility? Certainly not. Indeed one should emphasize how fatalism is nothing other than the clothing worn by real and active will when in a weak position' (ibid.).

TWO

The Village and the Area
Livelihoods and Economic Relations

'Telo matae dalo tel, sukno matae bhango bel.'
(Give oil to the oiled heads; break a wood apple on the
dry ones.)

I often heard the above proverb from young and mature people
belonging to poor, vulnerable households as an expression of the terms
of their relationship with the well off. The meaning of the proverb
was explained to me as follows: 'people will give only to those who
can give something back; they do not bother about those who have
nothing to return'. Everyone, male and female, in rural Bangladesh uses
oil to keep their hair shiny and healthy. Oil does not cost much and
even the poor households can usually afford it. When asked about the
character of their husbands, women tend to evaluate it by their ability
to provide essentials such as food, clothes and hair oil. Women and men
whose hair is dry and reddish are usually identified as very poor and of
a very low status. Untreated hair thus symbolises a condition of social
marginality associated with having nothing valuable to exchange. In
what follows I elaborate further the meaning of this popular saying
by exploring the terms of the relation between *gorib* (the poor) and
borolok (the rich) in the village where I conducted my fieldwork.

I begin by describing the main economic activities and sources
of livelihood in the area and the village. This description is based on
data collected through a household survey during the first months
of my fieldwork. I then explore the socio-economic characteristic of

households west of the village, referring to the views of the villagers themselves and the criteria that they value as indicators of poverty/ well-being. The chapter then develops a case study that throws light on the dynamics of the relationships between households of different socio-economic conditions and on the strategies that the rich and poor employ to maximise their advantage and well-being. Particular attention is given to the strategic importance of securing effective social relationships. As the proverb expresses, people will give only to those who have something to exchange, establishing in the process a relationship of interdependence. This resonates strongly with Devine's argument that 'making relationships function' is an important condition for survival (Devine 1999: 87).

THE AREA AND THE VILLAGE

The village Tarapur belongs to Tala sub-district, one of the seven administrative units of Satkhira district in south-west Bangladesh. Tala is almost a rural sub-district in its own right, as it consists of 228 villages. However, it also covers an urban area that has government offices, the police station, the headquarters of a number of local NGOs, a permanent market and some educational institutions. This urban area is also called Tala. In Satkhira, as in other south-western districts of Bangladesh, there is a higher percentage of Hindus than in other parts of the country. According to the 2001 census (BBS 2003), at the time, 89.6 per cent of the population was Muslim, 9.3 per cent Hindu and the remaining 1 per cent comprised Christians, Buddhists and groups classified as tribal communities. According to the same census, about 78 per cent of the population in Satkhira district were Muslims and more than 21 per cent Hindu. The district also has three other groups that can be considered ethnic minorities and do not belong either to the Muslim or to the Hindu communities. These are the Bhagobhenes or Bhagobanias, the Bunos or Mundas, and the Kaiputras or Kaoras (Bhumijo 1996).[1] In the census they are all classified as tribal populations and none of them can be found in Tarapur.

Among the Hindu population in Satkhira district and in Tala sub-district, the most numerous group is that of the Rishi, a group

of Hindu outcastes.[2] The ascribed occupation of the Rishi is locally
reported as the main reason for their extremely low status and their
ritual exclusion from the Hindu community. Most of the Rishi
in Bangladesh inhabit the three districts of Jessore, Khulna and
Satkhira. According to a local survey, in the three sub-districts of
Dumuria (Khulna), Tala and Debhata (Satkhira) there were in 1996
about 3,500 Rishi households in 91 villages (Bhumijo 1996). The
'traditional' occupation of this caste consists of processing leather
to make shoes and drums, an occupation that is considered impure.
Moreover, and to make matters worse, the Rishi are often accused of
killing cows deliberately in order to obtain the hides in addition to
a range of other devious practices such as lying, cheating and trouble
making. Most of the Rishi who live in south-west Bangladesh have
converted either to Catholicism or to the Baptist Church. The
Rishi neighbourhoods are characterised by a very high percentage
of landless and functionally landless families and very low levels of
income and education. Among the Muslims of Satkhira, there are
also a few groups such as the Beharas, the Dai and the Roshua,
with extremely low status. These again are considered to have impure
occupations and they are prohibited from entering the mosque. Also,
they do not intermarry with other Muslim groups.

In order to understand the characteristcs of livelihoods and the
socio-economic differentiation in Tarapur it is important to consider
some of the economic characteristics of the district and the broader
area to which Tala sub-district belongs. Three recent World Bank
studies (Sharma and Zaman 2009; Shilpi 2008; World Bank 2008a)
point out that there is a significant east/west divide in terms of
economic growth and incidence of poverty in Bangladesh. This is due
in part to the geographical characteristics of the country: the course
of the two main rivers, the Padma and the Jamuna split the country
in three parts creating a natural border that divides the east, where
the two main industrial poles of Dhaka and Chittagong are located,
and the West. The three studies mentioned agree in saying that the
eastern region has benefited greatly from being integrated with Dhaka
and Chittagong whereas the west and the south-west in particular are
much more isolated from the two important growth poles.

A spillover effect from Dhaka district, that has had historically the lowest poverty incidence, has made the surrounding areas able to attract higher return economic activities resulting in large differences in the economic structure of the two regions (World Bank 2008a). The south-western districts, on the other hand, have more difficult access to bigger markets, are less developed from the point of view of infrastructure, such as electrification, and are more prone to natural disasters. The statistics account also for a comparatively smaller number of urban households engaged in non-agricultural self-employment in the south-west. Between 2000 and 2005, a large decline in poverty levels occurred for Dhaka, Chittagong and Syleth divisions, whereas little changed in Barisal and Khulna divisions. Between the east and the west there is also a significant difference in terms of remittances received: while in Chittagong division (in the eastern region) 24.2 per cent of households received remittances from abroad, in Khulna division they were only 3.9 per cent. The percentage of remittances from domestic migration is however similar at around 25 per cent (World Bank 2008s: 41). It is also found that in non-migrant households the incidence of poverty is 42 per cent compared to 17 per cent, and while domestic remittances are received by both poor and rich households, foreign remittances appear to go mostly to rich ones (World Bank 2008a).

Tala belongs to the less prosperous western region. According to the updated poverty maps obtained from the Household Income and Expenditure Survey (HIES) 2005 (BBS 2008a), Satkhira district on the whole is among the poorest in Bangladesh but the incidence of poverty in Tala *upazila* is not so high as in the southern sub-districts closer to the delta: the percentage of population whose per capita household expenditure is below the upper poverty line is between 38 per cent and 48 per cent (more than 60 per cent in the poorest upazilas and less than 20 per cent in the richest). The percentage of poor population however is between 45 and 55 per cent, more than 55 per cent being the highest.

The 2001 population census suggests that the majority (74.34 per cent) of the households in Tala sub-district depended on agriculture as the main source of income against a national average of 31.13 per cent and more then 50 per cent are engaged in daily agricultural labour against a national average of about 31 per cent (BBS 2008b). The majority of both landless and landowning households carry out some form of *bebsha* (business). It is possible to distinguish *boro* (big) and *choto* (small) bebsha: the former includes highly profitable activities such as large-scale trade and commerce and the latter different kinds of petty trade that range from repairing goods to buying and selling small quantities of rice and vegetables. Some landless labourers drive bicycles with an attached cart (called *van*) for the transport of goods and people. A particular source of employment in the sub-district of Tala and in the village derives from educational institutions and NGOs. The latter have increased exponentially in numbers since the 1980s; there were more than 20 such organisations when I conducted my research, which employed approximately 500 people. Both the colleges where I carried out fieldwork are situated in the Tala urban centre. There was also a third college, which was located in the urban area but unlike the other two colleges, was completely funded by the government.

The village of Tarapur is very typical of the area in its demographic and physical characteristics. The majority of the population is Muslim and the only Hindus in the village are the Karmokar, an artisan caste. All the households of the Rishi neighbourhood converted to Christianity and belong to the Baptist Church. Among the Muslims there is a group called the Roshua, which has as low a social status as the outcaste Hindus. The village is situated a few miles north of Tala urban centre and about 6 miles south of a crossroad that heads west to Satkhira town, and east to Chadnagar village and eventually to the towns of Jessore and Khulna. While 20 years ago Chadnagar could be reached from Tarapur only by foot, now there are buses running every 20 minutes. There is a local permanent market with small wooden stalls and brick constructions scattered along the two sides of the road that connects Tala with the crossroad to Satkhira.

The housing pattern of the 259 households of the village is very similar to others in south-west rural Bangladesh. Most of the houses are mud huts composed of one big room used for storing goods. This is where the children also sleep at night. Most of the daily activities take place outside the house, in a courtyard that is usually shared by

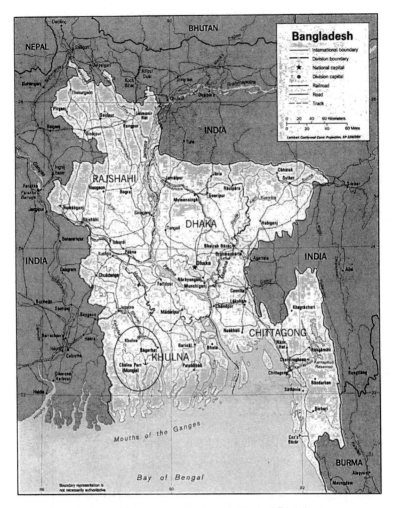

Figure 2.1: Bangladesh and Khulna Division

Source: http://www.lib.utexas.edu/maps/middle_east_and_asia/bangladesh_pol96.jpg, downloaded 29 June 2006.

related families. Like all the other villages of the area, Tarapur is divided into neighbourhoods called *para*. A *para* is more than simply a set of contingent residencies. Its constituent households are families that are socially linked. In the case of Muslims these households belong to the

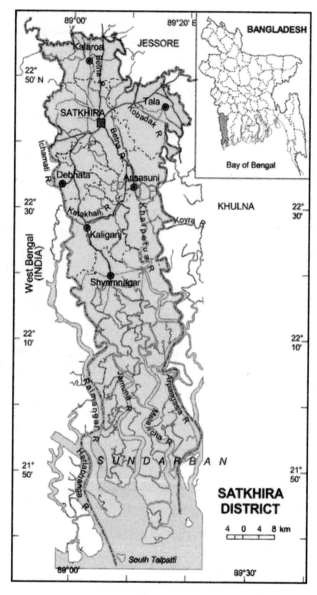

Figure 2.2: Map of Satkhira District

Source: http://mapofbangladesh.blogspot.it/2011/09/satkhira-district.html, downloaded 20 October 2012.

same descent (*bongsho*), in the case of Hindus they belong to the same caste (*jati*). The Tarapur Rishi para contains Christian households.

Amongst the NGOs present in the district only one extends its activities to the other sub-districts of Satkhira and outside in the district of Khulna. This can be considered a significant actor in the area, and in Tarapur in particular. The director of this NGO is a native of the western part of the village and in the early 1980s, when the NGO was established, the organisation's main office was located there. The NGO runs an integrated development programme whose main components are functional education for adults and drop-out children, training for income-generating activities and microcredit, legal aid, basic health and hygiene and agriculture extension. The NGO's basic unit of intervention is the *samiti* (group) comprised of about 20 beneficiaries/clients, usually belonging to the same para. In Tarapur, there is a samiti in almost every para. The director of the NGO is Muslim, but the organisation employs personnel from all three main religious communities of the area. The NGO was founded with economic assistance from the Catholic missionaries active in the area, and with whom the NGO has always had a good rapport. The NGO had on various occasions taken a decisive public secularist stance and this provoked the strong opposition of local supporters of Islamic organisations.

LANDOWNERSHIP IN TARAPUR

In Tarapur, land is perceived to be an essential asset in terms of ensuring economic security and a certain degree of status and it is one of the most important indicators of well-being in both poor and rich people's discourses. Although my research overall considered and involved people and relationships that extend beyond the boundaries of Tarapur, I conducted a survey of the 259 households of the village for the purpose of collecting quantitative information on the ownership and control of land, the forms of employment and the main sources of income. Tarapur village consists of eleven para: Roshua, Kha, Sheikh, Sardar, Karmokar, Mahmud, Biswas/Karikar, Morol, Fakir, Mollah, Rishi. On the basis of the survey, I divided Tarapur's households into five groups according to landownership. The findings are reported in Table 2.1:

Table 2.1: Landownership in Tarapur by para

Landholding in bigha*	0 to 1.5	1.6 to 5.9	6 to12	Over 12	Over 20	Total
Name of para						
Roshua	18	2	/	/	/	20
Kha	5	4	1	2	/	12
Sheikh	9	5	4	/	2	20
Sardar	9	1	/	/	/	10
Karmokar	5	1	1	2	2	11
Mahmud	4	/	/	/	/	4
Biswas/Karikar	76	18	7	3	/	104
Morol	4	1	4		3	12
Fakir	15	6	1	/	/	22
Mollah	12	1	/	/	/	13
Rishi	20	7	4			31
Total	177 68.3%	46 17.7%	22 8.4%	7 2.7%	7 2.7%	259 100%

Note: *A bigha corresponds officially to 0.33 acres but in some regions of Bangladesh this may vary. The Bangladesh Bureau of Statistics (BBS) and the Bangladesh Institute of Development Studies (BIDS) classify those who own less than 1.5 bighas of land as functionally landless.

It is immediately apparent from Table 2.1 that about two-thirds of the households are landless or functionally landless. There is a considerable spread in the size of landholding for the other households with only a small minority (5.4 per cent) of families eligible to be classified as big landowners.

A key question about the landholding pattern is what it means in terms of household livelihoods. Many sources suggest that self-sufficiency in rice production is one of the key ways in which people assess their household's well-being in rural Bangladesh (Nabi et al. 1999). People interviewed in Tarapur distinguished between rich and poor households on the basis of the quantity of land owned and whether this was enough to ensure self-sufficiency in food. A medium sized family owning 1.5 bighas was considered to be able to eat their own staple for approximately two months. 5-6 bighas of land was considered the minimum amount for a family of four to five persons to be self-reliant for food for the whole year. In stressing the importance of this criterion, Jansen has underlined that 'the degree of self sufficiency in rice production can be used as a measure in understanding the nature of the strategies the households pursue and the economic relationships they enter' (Jansen 1986: 6). Members of poor and extremely poor households in Tarapur associated well-being to eating three meals a day and considered the ownership or possession of land as the most secure way of ensuring it. On these bases the 177 households who are reported in Table 2.1 to own less than 1.5 bighas of land do not have enough land to be self-reliant in rice, pulses and vegetables (the main components of a rural family diet), let alone in fish and meat, which are considered a luxury.

The occupations of the 177 landless or functionally landless households are given in Table 2.2.

Table 2.2: Main occupation of landless households

Main Occupation	No.	Percentage
Cultivating as sharecroppers	2	1.1%
Cultivating as sharecroppers and daily labourers	33	18.6%
Cultivating as daily labourers	46	25.9%
Cultivating and sharecroppers plus petty business/trade	18	10.1%
Cultivating as daily labourers plus petty business/trade	14	7.9%
Petty business, van driving, begging...	64	36.1%
Total	177	100%

The majority (63.8 per cent) of the landless or functionally landless households depends largely on agricultural daily labour and on taking land to sharecrop. Some of them are also engaged in petty and not very profitable trade and, in the case of the Hindus, in the 'traditional' caste occupation. The other 64 households are not involved in direct land cultivation. Most of them are engaged in business or trade. In the case of landless households, bebsha is usually on a very small scale (choto) and is easily distinguished from boro (big) bebsha done by richer families. Choto bebsha includes petty trade of betel nuts, fish, vegetables, pan leaf, rice or paddy. Paddy trade is more profitable if the trader does not need cash and can afford to wait and sell his goods when the price is higher. The Hindus belonging to the Karmokar caste work as blacksmiths, the 'traditional' caste occupation. The Hindus belonging to the Rishi group are traditionally leather workers and shoemakers although nowadays, due to the stigma attached to this work, they have turned to making baskets and carpets with bamboo. As in other villages of the area, the Rishi do not consider themselves agriculturists and, unless they own some land, they are not keen to engage in agricultural employment. For 18 households the main source of income is van driving together with occasional agricultural labour. Beside choto bebsha and van driving, some of the 64 households who are not involved in land cultivation earn a living from activities such as carpentry, mechanics, traditional healing, clothes making and shopkeeping. Finally, five households in this category make a living by begging.

Landowning Households

Most of landowning households do not actually own very much: 17.7 per cent of households own from 1.6 to 5.9 bighas. This puts them in a less vulnerable situation, but they need to secure other income besides cultivating their own land. The households belonging to this group may combine different activities and their main advantage over the landless lies in the fact that even a small amount of land can be the base from which to branch out into other activities. Among this group of households, the vast majority cultivate their own land, at least in part, and approximately one-third of them are also sharecropping tenants. The possibility of obtaining land to sharecrop depends on cattle ownership and availability of labour. A poor household could be forced to sharecrop out even a small plot of land if they do not have bullocks and a plough to farm it themselves. Equally, they could be prevented from taking land in sharecropping because they are not able to afford the inputs and the labour costs. Out of 46 households, 14 are in this condition and give land in sharecropping, while working as daily agricultural labourers. The more male members there are in a household, the more land can be taken in sharecropping without incurring the expense of hiring labourers during peak season. Households who own some land and can count on their own labour force thus have more choices and can diversify their strategies more easily. Income earned from this diversification often gives them the possibility of investing cash in other income generating activities such as small shops in the village or at the bazaar, petty trade and small business.

Most of the 22 medium landowners (owning between 6 and 12 bighas of land) cultivate only some of their land and sharecrop out the rest. Only two households take additional land to sharecrop and do not engage in any other work besides land cultivation. All the remaining households carry out other profitable activities in trade or business, or run shops on a larger scale. These households can easily borrow or lend money against the land and all of them have either taken or given land in mortgage.

Most of the 14 big landowning households (owning more than 12 bighas of land) sharecrop out the vast part of it. These households are more likely to be extended families where some of the members administer the family land without being directly involved in its cultivation. Other members of the family are usually employed as government officers, NGO directive staff, teachers, or run other businesses. Some of them are big traders of rice while others are engaged mainly in activities that have no connection to agriculture. These households invest significantly in education with most of the older male members educated up to college or degree level and the younger generation (both males and females) likely to continue studying up to the tertiary level.

Sharecropping: Wage Labour and Mortgage

As this discussion suggests, the basic arrangements based on land are
sharecropping, mortgage and daily labour. The literature in Bangladesh
more generally (Adnan 1990; Arens and van Beurden 1977; Jannuzi
and Peach 1980; Jansen 1986; White 1992) suggests that the prevailing
form of tenancy all over Bangladesh is sharecropping. The most
common sharecropping agreement is one in which the tenant bears
all the costs and responsibilities while the crop is divided equally with
the landowner. This system is in operation in Tarapur. Locally, the
sharecropping contract is known as *baghe kora* which means 'splitting
into two parts'. *Borga*, the term used often in other areas of Bangladesh,
is less frequently used. According to baghe kora, the tenant has to
provide the means of production: bullocks and plough, fertilizers and
pesticides. He may also be required to hire labourers for the peak
season if the plot is too big for the family labour force.[3] Other scholars
have noted the progressive shortening of the duration of this contract
over time (Adnan 1990). At present, in Tarapur, the contracts are oral
and last between one and five years, or even simply for one season.
Sometimes the landowner and the tenant are linked by kinship but
this is not common. Often they are neighbours or belong to different
villages. What is common to all arrangements are sets of obligations
and responsibilities entailing labour, loans and land. The higher the
level of interdependence between landowner and tenant the more the
landless household will be able to count on a stable relationship and
feel secure.

Rates for daily agricultural labour can vary by age, skill and sex.
Tarapur's women, especially those involved in NGO activities and
the poorest, work in the fields without incurring social disapproval
even if this implies a partial transgression of purdah and even if there
is a very low status attached to wage labour in agriculture for both
men and women. Most are engaged in post-harvesting operations and
are employed on exploitative terms for very low piece work rate or
food or clothes. Wives or daughters of landless labourers, divorced or
abandoned women, may also work as domestic servants and are paid
in kind with rice. Women may also tend other families' animals. In this

case they get milk or eggs or part of the profit if the animal is sold. They are also entitled to receive saris or other gifts as *zakat* (ritual charity) on the occasion of important religious festivities. During the survey when asked about the occupation and income generating activities of each family member, the interviewees always classified wives and daughters who were not going to school as housewives, even if many of them were actually contributing directly to the household income. A household with only one earning member, a situation that is common in Tarapur, can hardly cover the basic expenses for food. During slack season, when employment is not regular, all these households are bound to suffer some form of starvation.

Mortgage of land is also common in Tarapur and concerns wealthy as well as poor households because it is a relatively easy way of getting a loan and it is also one of the means through which land changes hands. Health emergencies, weddings, a sudden death of an earning member are some of the main reasons that motivate households to give land in mortgage. This type of exchange happens even among poor peasants. Among the 177 landless or functionally landless households, at the time of the survey, four had mortgaged some land out in exchange for cash while 41 had taken some land in mortgage, mostly with the earnings of small trade and business. Among those that own between 1.6 and 5.9 bighas of land, 12 households have mortgaged land out and eight have mortgaged in. Half of the households that own from 6 to 12 bighas had taken land in mortgage while the other half had given land in mortgage.

In Tarapur, the difference between rich and poor households is striking in terms of assets, capacity for coping with health or other emergencies, income and the satisfaction of basic needs. Apart from the data just discussed, these differences are evident in the way people dress, the quality of housing, the levels of education and people's physical build. In trying to assess the level of well-being of a household and to classify households according to ownership and possession of commodities and assets, ownership of land is an important element because, as stated earlier, it is considered the base for ensuring food security. Landownership can also be a source of economic and social power as it corresponds to a dominant position in class relations.

Economic and social distinctions based on wealth and status are undeniable and these distinctions imply dynamics of power and inequality. Big landowners command labour and enter sharecropping and mortgage agreements on dominant terms. They can engage in profitable trade and have access to cash, which in turns allows other kinds of investment.

Classifying peasants according to land ownership, however, is only a very limited approach to socio-economic differentiation. Households that own the same amount of land may employ different strategies to survive or improve. Particular strategies depend on several crucial factors and contingencies. As we have seen, human resources are important to allow a household to cultivate its own land and to take more by sharecropping. If a household lacks male members they may have to give out their own land in sharecropping and resort to daily labour. The availability of cash may encourage a household to lend money in exchange for land and this mortgage may guarantee another household the availability of cash through mortgage for a wedding, or health emergency or for investment. All these exchanges of land, money and labour link households in a complex network. While all households are involved in these networks, the ability to use them strategically has a clear influence on the household's survival and well-being possibilities.

A Tarapur Conversation about Gorib and Borolok

Studies on poverty have advanced significantly by focusing on local perceptions of poverty and wealth. These are very critical in order to understand the local processes and mechanisms that sustain and reproduce socio-economic differentiation. As early as 1970, P.J. Bertocci, in a village study of Bangladesh, underlined the importance of looking at people's interpretation of their own reality (Bertocci 1970: 35). In what follows, I try to explore how villagers in Tarapur perceived their own situation and valued different types of resources. My evaluation is inspired mainly by a long conversation that took place in my house with a small group of poor people comprising Halima, a middle-aged woman who used to work as a cook for a local

NGO; Siraj, a landless man who worked mainly as an agricultural daily labourer; Bina, a young woman who lived with her mother after the death of her husband; and Ma,[4] Bina's mother. The conversation started from a question that I posed regarding what it means to be poor and who can be defined as such. I told them that during conversations with people of different social and economic backgrounds, I noticed that people would refer to themselves as gorib (poor) as this was the best way to describe their position in relation to mine. As the conversation proceeded, more categories referring to socio-economic differentiation were introduced and I asked further questions to elucidate what they meant. All the people mentioned in what follows lived in the western part of Tarapur that comprises four Muslim para (Morol, Sheikh, Fakir and Mollah) and the Rishi para.

Didi[5] (myself): *How many sorts of 'poor' are there? When you say for example 'khub gorib' (very poor) what do you mean? and 'alka gorib' (slightly poor), what do you mean?*

Halima: *You want to know how it can be understood.....*

Didi: *Yes, for example, what do you mean by 'khub gorib?*

Siraj: *Didi, it means the 'poorest', someone who has no land to produce food. He is landless and his family depends on daily labour. Then there are poor who have 4 or 5 katha of land or a few sothok.[6] Then there are those who have, for example, 2 bigha of land and the family can manage to look after themselves. But even those with land will call themselves poor. And then there are those who have a lot of land such as 7 or 8 bigha and a big family of 9 or 10 persons…they also will be poor, but they are not really so poor…. For example, if someone has at least two bigha, he will harvest rice. It is possible to have up to three yields. A family of five could live with five bigha of land for some part of the year and then they will have also to work.*

Didi: *So do you mean that with at least 5 bigha in some way or another a family can manage?*

Siraj: *Yes, it would work for five people more or less.*

Didi: *And they could eat three times a day and they would not have much problem…*

Siraj:	*Yes, yes.*
Didi:	*And would they need any loans?*
Siraj:	*No. The more land they have the better it would be; they could earn more and eventually get some more land in mortgage.*
Didi:	*And those who do not have anything, how do they survive?*
Siraj:	*Working...for others. For example, today I worked and I earned Tk 30. What can you do with Tk 30? There are five in my family. We need at least 2 kg of rice every day. Two kg of rice cost Tk 26. How is it possible to manage?....Am I poor or not?*

In the words of Siraj, the poorest are those who do not own land and ownership of land is related to the capacity of being self-reliant in the production of food. Not owning land and relying on daily agricultural labour is associated with dependence especially if it is the only source of income for a household. In fact, wage labour is never assured because workers are employed seasonally or daily and the salary is very low. A few katha or sothok of land is a very small amount, but could be used for gardening and fruit plants. This can be a seasonal source of income. 2 bighas may be enough to manage in the sense that it can provide food for a family for about four or five months. 5 bighas can produce enough rice and vegetables to support a family for the whole year if income from wage labour can cover some of the expenses. 7 or 8 bighas are just a bit more than what can be considered enough for a family of five to survive. Other villagers have included households who own 7 or 8 bighas of land in the category of *majhari* (middle). Siraj, who owns no land at all except his homestead, considers 7 or 8 bighas as 'a lot'. He sold everything over the last four years to treat, unsuccessfully, one of his sons who suffered from a liver disease. It is mainly poor people who stress the importance of land for self-subsistence. This was confirmed again when I asked what is the main criteria to discriminate between poor and rich. Women, who would not normally work in the fields as daily labourers, stressed instead the importance of having cattle together with land.

Didi:	*So, what are the main criteria to understand who is poor and who isn't? What is the most important thing?*

Halima: *If one has land he will get some crops, paddy, wheat, mustard oil.*
            He can sell vegetables, he will be able to buy rice and he will not
            lack anything.
Didi: *And what else is important?*
Bina: *Cows, for milk. For example, my mother, when she feels weak she*
            will not be able to work. But if she had two cows she could sell the
            milk.
Didi: *And what else?*
Ma: *Goats…then from the land it is possible to earn money, it is possible*
            to improve…to build a house…to have a motorbike.
Didi: *So, who are the real poor in your opinion?*
Siraj: *For example, there are people like me and your ma (Bina's mother,*
            who I also used to address as mother) who have absolutely nothing.
            They are like beggars, they beg and eat. Sometimes they work daily
            if work is available. These people will go to a shop and tell the
            shop owner to give them something for the family…at least to eat
            something. The shop owner will give some oil, garlic, brinjal…in
            this way, your ma (Bina's ma) runs her family, she does not have a
            husband or sons.
Didi: *This is what you identify as bhikka gorib (begging-poor)?*
Siraj: *Yes, here in Bangladesh.*
Didi: *And in this area among Morol, Fakir, Mollah, how many bhikka*
            gorib are there?
Siraj and Bina's mum: *Nobody like us, there are people who eat more than*
            us, rice, everything, they have land in mortgage ….For example,
            there is someone who has four sons…what will they lack? Each of
            the sons can earn Tk 30 per day.
Didi: *So do you mean that if there are sons in a family, the household*
            will not lack anything?
Halima: *Yes, if there are sons a family will not lack anything.*

Here we see that Siraj and Bina's mother presented themselves as the
poorest and at the same time they offered some insights into what
extreme poverty consists of. There are actually other households in
Tarapur's western part that are as poor as they are, but the claim to be
the 'poorest' is a common feature in the discourse of Tarapur's poor

villagers. To put oneself in the most needy position is a way of claiming an interlocutor's help.

There is a category of 'extremely poor' that depends exclusively or almost exclusively on the assistance and charity of others. These are the people who cannot count on a regular income from daily labour and have to beg to survive. Usually, very old women or men who do not have a place to stay or any relatives, these beggars wander from village to village to collect a few handfuls of rice. But there are also households in the village that get the occasional help from wealthy families or shopkeepers in the form of food, clothes or work. Ma and Bina are examples of this latter group.

Extreme poor, bhikka gorib, are households where there are no male members to earn a living, not even with the worst kind of daily labour employment. Most of the households that have been defined as bhikka gorib are either female headed households or families whose male members suffer from some disability or are too old to work. As we have seen, there are households in Tarapur that combine begging with occasional wage labour or other activities. In this sense, the presence of sons rather than daughters is an important asset and a family with four sons is presented as an example of a household that will not lack basic commodities.

Didi: *A lot of people here say, 'I do not have anyone' ('amar keu ney'),
         what does it mean exactly?*

Siraj: *It means they do not have parents, relatives (attiyo swajan),
         friends.*

Didi: *So does it mean that they do not have anyone whom they can ask
         for help?*

Siraj: *Yes, they can't ask for help from anyone, they do not have anyone
         like that.*

Didi: *But look at ma…she always says that she does not have anyone
         but actually she gets help from a lot of people.*

Bina: *Yes we get a lot of help from a lot of people.*

Siraj: *It means she does not have sons, uncles, father or mother.*

Didi: *So having nobody means having no 'men'?*

Ma: *It means…no son who can earn money, no land.*

Beside defining themselves as gorib, in an attempt to make me understand what they meant and sometimes while asking for help, many villagers added that they did not have anything ('amar kicchu ney'). In some cases, women who did not have a male or a senior in the household, also expressed a condition of extreme need saying 'I have no-one' ('amar keu ney'). Devine argues that while 'amar kichu ney' 'indicates a state of serious material poverty', 'amar keu ney' expresses 'a deeper state of entrenched powerlessness and helplessness' and that this expression can be interpreted as underlying the importance of social relationships in a context of material poverty (Devine 1999: 82). Bina's mother frequently uses the same expression, amar keu ney, to mean that she does not have a husband, father or son to take care of her; because she is poor, old and a woman, she has no means to earn money and she can count only on charity. She is sometimes employed daily for processing rice but this is not enough to make her feel protected and secure, because these forms of employment are nowadays more and more occasional.

Didi: *And what do you mean by borolok?*
Halima: *Borolok means, for example, our Razzak, Shirin's father…*
Bina: *He is a doctor* (he has a pharmacy).
Halima: *He has 60–70 bighas and a shop. He has a shop and a motorbike. These are borolok.*
Didi: *Does this mean that the difference between poor and rich is only in terms of how much money they earn, how much land they own? Aren't there any other things that matter, for example, education?*
Halima: *Yes, those who are poor, they have no job, they cannot study…for example, my uncle has sons and can he send them to school? He cannot earn money.*

Beside owning land, rich people usually also run businesses. Indicators of well-being usually cited include possessing motorbikes, a brick house, regular paid employment and the possibility of studying. The term borolok (literally big people) is slightly different from *dhoni* (literally wealthy). Borolok are not only materially wealthy, they also have high status and command respect. In short, they are powerful. The fact that all the dhoni are often called borolok suggests that power, status and material assets are associated.

Didi: *So, if Shirin's father is the richest and you are the poorest, who is in the middle?*

All together: *Mujib's family, Jalil's family, Noju, Moen…*

Didi: *And why do you put them in the middle?*

Siraj: *Because they have a position ('tader obosthan ache'). They have some land, this is why they are in the middle. For example, Moen and Nasir, Shahana's uncle have more or less 10 bighas of land. They also have fruit plants, cows, money and a shop at the bazaar. Nasir is a trader/shop owner and runs a business ('bebsha kore'). So what do they lack? And then Mujib, his family has land in sharecropping, they can harvest rice and they have money. Mujib's father has some land, runs a business and the family are all employed.*

Didi: *But Mujib does not own much land.*

Siraj: *No they have 4 bighas and they get the rest in sharecropping from a very rich family. And Mujib has got some land in mortgage… thanks to his job. Among us poor, no-one is employed. We are not educated, we can't get a job.*

Didi: *So it seems that a household can survive better with sons than with daughters, why?*

Halima: *They are not educated!*

Didi: *Can't girls study?*

Halima: *They do not have money, how can they study!!?? For example, her sister (Bina's sister) couldn't study, so her mother gave her in marriage, so how could she study?*

Between poor and extreme poor on the one hand and borolok on the other, a fourth category has been identified. Most of my informants referred to this group as *majhari* or *majamaji*, meaning those who are in the middle. The immediate reason for considering some households majhari is that they have a position (*obhostan*). This means that they are secure, stable, not vulnerable like those that depend only on others to get employment, or land to cultivate. Majhari have land, fruit plants, animals and some of them run businesses (boro bebsha). One of them,

Mujib and his family, has land in sharecropping. Not all the households that have been identified as majhari have the same kinds of material resources. Mujib's household is characterised by a great diversification of economic activities. Mujib works for the local NGO, as does one of his brothers, while his father and his elder brother cultivate their own land and take land in sharecropping. They also have land in mortgage so that they have cash at their disposal. Others have been included in this 'middle' category on the basis that they have the security of land and work that assures them yearly subsistence.

Didi: *And then who else is in the middle?*

Halima: *Abnur Kashir is the most well off in Mollah para, the others are all poor. They don't have much intelligence while Tanjila's father (Abnur Kashir)…even if he is not economically well off ('arthik na takle'), he is intelligent ('buddhi shatti kori'), has a machine and takes Enamul's land in sharecropping. With all this buddhi (intelligence) he can eat…in this way he can be considered a majhari even if he doesn't have land of his own.*

Abnur Kashir's household is a key one in terms of thinking about this category. He is considered majhari even though he has no land because he has secured the land of a powerful person in sharecropping. Also, he is considered an intelligent man and has nurtured good social relations. Abnur Kashir lives next to the Mollah para, but actually his family belongs to the Morol bongsho, the same bongsho to which the landowner from whom he takes the land in sharecropping belongs. Moreover, all the members of his family are involved in agricultural work despite having only daughters. Mujib's household referred to above is an interesting example of upward mobility, so much so that Halima ended up describing them as borolok. They also sharecrop the land of a wealthy family on good terms. Mujib was the first driver to be employed 13 years ago when the NGO was set up and he recounts with pride all the trips to the nearby town that he did with the NGO's director. In 2001, he was offered a job in Dhaka by an international donor agency. The job offered a better salary than the one he received from the NGO. He refused the job saying: 'The director is very attached to me, I am one of the first to work for him, the NGO is like a family to me'. If only land and other material assets were taken into account Abnur Kashir would not be considered a majhari and Mujib's family would not be associated with borolok. Their good connections with powerful families is what facilitates their security.

This conversation, which began by trying to examine the local categories that people use to describe socio-economic differences, is very rich. It reveals, among other themes, that people distinguish four categories of people according to their level of poverty/well-being. These are borolok, majhari, gorib, and bhikka gorib. These categories are significant in their own right and I wanted to use them to rank the households belonging to the western part of Tarapur, which was the part of the village closest to where I was living. Some of my best informants come from its five para: Morol, Sheikh, Fakir, Mollah and Rishi. I was also interested in this part of the village because of the presence of the Rishi, a group about which I conducted research in the past (Del Franco 1983). Focusing on a smaller number of households allowed me to understand the dynamics of the relationship between the three borolok households belonging to the Morol bongsho and some of the poor and extremely poor households belonging to the other three. The three Morol households that own more than 30 bighas of land are linked by kinship.

In order to rank all the households residing in this part of the village, I conducted a participatory session in each of the five para. I told the participants that other villagers had used the four categories and asked them to put each household of their para in one of the groups. Table 2.3 summarises the results of this exercise.

Table 2.3: Classification of west Tarapur's households according to the ranking exercise based on villagers' categories

	bhikka gorib	gorib	majhari	borolok	bhikka gorib/ gorib	gorib/ majhari	majhari/ borolok	Total
Morol		3	2	3			4	12
Sheikh	1	2				2		5
Fakir		9	8		1			18

Mollah	1	10			1			12
Rishi	16	9	5	1	1			32
Total	18	33	15	4	3	2	4	79

In placing the single households into the four categories, there was almost unanimous consent among Tarapur villagers about who had to be placed in the category of the extremely poor (bhikka gorib) and that of the rich (borolok). Much debate and disagreement characterised the middle categories and it was in many cases very difficult to draw a clear line between the poor and majhari, and sometimes also between the poor and the extreme poor. It was not possible to reach an agreement about nine households so I put them under mixed categories: bhikka gorib/gorib, gorib/majhari, majhari/borolok. Some informants placed four Morol households in the majhari group because they own only 6 bighas of land. Others instead put the same households in the borolok category because of the stable position they enjoyed through kinship links with the other three Morol. All of this reveals a dynamic and complex picture. In the language of poverty analysis households can experience many kinds of shock. It is very easy for a poor household to fall into a situation of extreme poverty for different reasons such as illness, lack of employment, and so forth. Amongst the majhari who do not own much land, economic security depends very much on their ability to keep good relationships with landowning families that can offer land to sharecrop. But even for this group the cost of a wedding could cause indebtedness and a severe cash crisis. It is in a way possible to divide each category into two: an upper group of households that are in a stable secure position and a lower group of more vulnerable families that could easily fall into lower positions.

What has emerged so far from this discussion reflects the perspectives of the poor. Students and educated people adopted the same criteria when identifying indicators of poverty and well-being. However, they also introduced some differences and tended to use a more formal language to identify the categories. The categories they used were:

- *Uchu bittho* (upper class): 'They can have what they want. They have assets *(dhon, shompod)* and money. Some of them are permanently employed *(chakri kore)* or run businesses and trade (bebsha) or are big landowners. They live in three/four storied buildings/houses. They do not lack anything. They have land up to 100–150 bighas.'

- *Madhyo uchu bittho* (upper middle class): 'They own 50 bighas of land. They have a lot of money and they eat well.'
- *Nimno uchu bittho* (lower middle class): 'They do not own much land: 10 to 20 bighas.'
- *Nimno bittho* (lower class): 'They eat on the basis of what they earn daily. The male children do not study more than five or six years and the girls are married off early. They run small businesses such as buying a cow on credit and selling it later on. They cannot afford extra expenses unless they sell something'.
- *Ekkibare gorib* (absolutely poor): 'They live by begging *(bhikka kore kae)*. They wander around looking for some work in the fields, asking for money. They can't eat three times a day, they get rice out of begging but they do not have anything to eat with it'.

What appears from this classification is that the well off and educated have a slightly different perspective in terms of the amount of assets, in particular land, which is needed to locate people in different classes. For poor men and women the ownership of 5–6 bighas of land is enough to be considered majhari, while 12–20 bighas makes people borolok; those who are better off speak in terms of bigger plots of land. The middle category is divided into two groups and this is in some way consistent with the debate that emerged during the ranking of west Tarapur households. The middle category is more difficult to define and within it there seems to be a wide range of situations.

It is now possible to draw some summary points from what has been discussed so far. The long conversation with Siraj Bina, Ma and Halima confirms that land is an important material asset in terms of household survival and economic security and it is the base on which a household's economic strategy can be built. The cases of Abnur Kashir and Mujib show that tenancy in the form of sharecropping is valued only if the agreement is a long term one, reinforced by a personal relationship with the landowner. When sharecropping does not imply a stable link with a more powerful family it is considered an insecure form of livelihood '*porer kaj kora*' (working for others). Even more, *jon dewa* (selling one's labour for wages) and not having other sources of income, represents an extreme form of dependence on others and is associated with vulnerability and insecurity.

Landownership and surplus production are seen as the basis for investment in profitable business and trade; while landless, almost landless families and sharecroppers can only afford to engage in small-scale business and trade and artisan activities. With the diffusion of schooling and the increasing value attributed to education as a means of acquiring skills and qualifications, a very desirable form of employment is constituted by *chakri* (permanent white collar job in state offices or NGOs). Chakri is sharply contrasted with daily agricultural labour to the point that students find it very degrading to work in the fields, even occasionally, to finance their own study. Households that live on daily agricultural labour, however, seem to be more secure than households whose members have to beg for a living or who survive thanks to the occasional assistance of others.

There are different kinds of poor households according to their level of vulnerability and security. The extreme poor, bhikka gorib, have to resort to begging or to find occasional daily labour in order to survive. They do not have land or other assets and they also lack the human resources in terms of labour force that would allow them to enter stable wage labour relationships. Daily labourers and sharecroppers are considered slightly better off, but still they depend on others for a living and thus they are a step below those who can obtain stable sharecropping contracts or possess enough land to be self-reliant in food production. 'Porer kaj kora' defines a condition of dependence with a negative connotation unless the owner of the land taken in sharecropping is perceived as reliable and the contract is stable.

As an answer to the initial questions of who are the poor and why are they poor, I would suggest that poor households are those that have scarce material resources, but also lack the human resources and the kind of connections (*jogajog*) with the wealthiest that can ensure stable help and protection in case of need. A condition of material vulnerability can be compensated for by a good relationship with a wealthy family and thus the position of a household is perceived to depend very much on its relational resources as well its material ones. This is powerfully expressed in the saying '*amar keu ney*' that people use to express the extreme vulnerability that comes from lacking relational resources. Claiming to be gorib is employed as a strategy to seek the help of an interlocutor who is perceived as superior and more powerful.

PATRONS, CLIENTS AND *MAN SHONMAN*

Tarapur's villagers use complex gradations and make the kinds of distinctions discussed above to identify different levels of poverty and well-being. At the same time, they want to claim gorib status and their discourses around vulnerability and around the relations between these categories are often about dependency and social relations. As White (1992: 37) argues: 'the key to understanding social and economic inequalities is to grasp the relations through which they are reproduced' rather than trying to identify fixed categories. I now look more closely at an aspect of rural social relations in Bangladesh around which there has been a substantial debate in the literature.[7] The essence of this debate is whether or not the socio-economic differentiation in rural Bangladesh is best understood in class terms or whether the dominance of patronage relationships means that the experience of inequality does not take a class form.

Jafrul and Razzak

The last night of my stay in Tarapur I went to say goodbye to Prodip's family. Prodip, a 17-year-old college student, was one of my closest acquaintances in Tarapur and one of my best informants. While saying goodbye, his father, Jafrul, asked me to remember them, saying with a mix of bitterness and pride: 'I managed to survive all these years with my family because every time I was mistreated (slapped on my face) I never reacted. I just said "please do it again" (I offered the other cheek)'.

Jafrul is now approximately 55 years old. His parents were not originally from Tarapur and did not have any relatives in the village. So when they died, Jafrul, who was then still a child, was brought up by a rich landowning household of the village and took their lineage name, that of Morol. He worked for them in the fields since he was little and slowly he became a trustworthy, de facto caretaker of their land. When Jafrul married he continued living with his wife and children in his landlord's house while working for him. Before he died, the landlord promised Jafrul that some of his land would be registered in his name and instructed his son, Razzak, to do this. Razzak, however, did not follow his father's will. Initially he did register a few bighas of land in Jafrul's name, but then he cancelled the registration and gave Jafrul and his family only a couple of mango trees and a few sothok of land where they could build their own mud hut. In Jafrul's words:

I could have taken him to court to claim my rights on that land but I did not because I did not want to spoil the relationship. After all I have to live here so I knew that it would have been better for me not to stand against him.

One evening I had visited Prodip's family and saw Razzak's uncle, who was over 80 years old, leaving his house and asking for Jafrul, who was hiding behind a tree and feeding his cows. Jafrul's wife whispered to me: 'I told him that my husband is not here because he comes for no reason and just wastes my husband's time'. After a while the visitor managed to find Jafrul and the two of them sat on the veranda of Jafrul's house chatting and smoking together like old friends. Later, I was told that the old man needed someone to take care of him during the night so Jafrul frequently slept in his house in exchange for the evening meal.

Prodip and his parents address Razzak's wife as *bhabi* (elder brother's wife) and his daughters Shirin, Rotna and Reka as cousins. Prodip served at the wedding ceremony of one of Shirin's cousins, and gave private tuition to Shirin and her younger sister Reka. On Friday afternoons, Jafrul's wife and son watch TV in Razzak's house together with other servants and Razzak's daughters. Once, when a group of college students came to Tarapur, Prodip pointed to Shirin's house and indicated it as his own. When I asked him why he had pretended to live there he said: 'That is where I have been brought up and I consider them as my family'. Despite the attachment he has for some members of Razzak's family, Prodip recounts his family's relationship with Razzak and Razzak's uncle and cousins as a troublesome and conflictual one. He acknowledges the help that his family has received from them over the years but, unlike his father, he also criticises them openly.

Listen, for example, what happened when my middle sister, after two divorces, got married to a man she had loved since she was young. Their marriage was a 'love' one ('premer biye') but 'they' (Razzak's uncle and his sons) were not happy about it. They thought that the man would not suit my sister because his family was borolok and we were too poor. They opposed the marriage but my father did not listen to them and the marriage took place. For some years after this my father and mother could not get any work in their fields and my father had to search for work in other villages. At that time my family went through a particularly difficult time because my other sisters were still unmarried and we were so poor that we couldn't afford to eat every day. I remember I once asked Shirin's mother (Razzak's wife) to give me the rice leftovers to eat and she said: 'If I give that to you what are my cows going to eat?' I felt so humiliated...

After the temporary crisis following his daughter's marriage, the patronage link between Jafrul and Razzak's family and relatives was re-established. Jafrul still works regularly for them as a daily labourer for Tk 30 and two meals a day. When he can afford the cost of fertilizers he takes 1 bigha of their land in sharecropping. His wife continues to work as a maid in Razzak's house for 0.5 to 1 kg of rice per day.

Clearly, the relationship between Jafrul and his employers has been a long term one and cannot be understood mainly in terms of an impersonal contractual relation. Other members of Jafrul's household have also been involved in different ways with members of Razzak's family and the families of Razzak's cousins. These relationships clearly entail an intimate dimension and many types of exchange besides those focusing on labour and money. The interference by Razzak's cousins in the wedding of Prodip's sister and what followed is not an exceptional event in the context of what is a fairly unequal relationship and was a considerable exercise of power. Jafrul copes with all this by accepting and adapting to the status quo.

Razzak's family presents the relationships differently. Aminur (one of Razzak' s cousins) told me:

Prodip had been helped by me and my brothers otherwise he would not have been able to study at college. I gave his father Tk 5,000 once and he wasted it to marry off one of his daughters for the third time. She left all her previous husbands because she did not like them and she wanted to marry her first love. She has to be blamed for the failure of her previous marriages because she did not dare to tell her father that she actually loved someone else. Prodip's father has been working for us for years because we have always trusted him. He gets Tk 900 per month but we also give him three meals a day. Now we give him dinner because he assists my father. If we hadn't land and rice in excess we would not be able to help him in this way. Prodip is a good student, our NGO, the one founded by Aminur's younger brother, will employ him in the future.

The director of the NGO had this to say:

Prodip would not have achieved what he has if it wasn't for the help that he and his family have received from us. We always tried to give good advice to them and to other needy people in the village but sometimes they do not listen to us.

The attitude of Jafrul's employers is clearly a patronising one. This is evident also from how they talked about Jafrul's household. They come across as proud of the role they played in Prodip's education and blame his family for not having always complied with their will. They consider themselves good patrons and tend to conform to this image. High ranking, wealthy people are supposed to be indulgent and treat with *daya* (grace-blessing) those who show them respect and serve them.

The condition of Jafrul's household has actually always been one of vulnerability and precariousness and the relationship with some powerful households has enabled them to survive. They were described as khub gorib (very poor) by other villagers, on the basis that they do not have any assets. In the slack season when there is less work in the fields, Jafrul cannot ensure his family three meals a day. The precariousness of the situation is exemplified by the fact that he regularly resorts to small loans or buys food on credit. Recently, Jafrul took out a loan to buy two cows for ploughing. This allows him to earn a bit more than if he sold only his labour. However, he still cannot refuse his services to his patrons. On Eid, he walked the full distance from Tarapur to Khulna (approximately 33 miles) to take a cow to one of Razzak's cousins for a wage of Tk 100.

The relationship with the most affluent family belonging to the Morol lineage is the biggest asset of Jafrul's family. Assuming their lineage name, he has become one of them and this more or less ensures him their support, even if on clearly unequal terms. Jafrul acknowledges that he and his family would not have survived without Razzak and his relatives. The price he has had to pay for protection was to give up the claim to some bigha of land that would have granted his family some economic independence. But claiming the land would have put his family in a risky position for it would have entailed losing a borolok family's support. Jafrul is bitter about this because he is aware of his subordinate position, but is proud for having kept his man shonman (honour) and atta morjada (self-esteem) intact. The other big asset of the family is the only son who is expected to provide for the whole family in the future and has already assumed a sort of leading role in the family because of his level of education. His qualities as a bright, intelligent student have made Prodip valuable to the family of his father's patrons as a trustworthy teacher for his daughters as well. As stated above, he is expected to accept in the near future a job in the local NGO.

Prodip, unlike his father, seems willing to break the relationship with the patron family. While his father has never angrily complained about Razzak's or Aminur's family, Prodip expresses an ambiguous attitude towards them. Sometime he acknowledges the help received from some members of the household and the long-term co-operation between his family and Razzak's. However most of the time, he emphasises that his father has always been exploited by the patron family. He plans to leave the village and complete his studies in town and views this as the only chance of escaping what he perceives as the patronising/arrogant attitude of Razzak and his cousins. Hierarchy and a relation of subordination is expressed in everyday life by simple indicators like dress. A young poor man would not for example wear 'modern' pants instead of the traditional *lungi*, or expensive accessories, like a watch, at home or when moving around the neighbourhood. This would be judged as showing off and as a lack of respect for elders and rich neighbours. Prodip is used to being reproached for small transgressions like keeping his hair too long, or wearing jeans that are considered too 'modern' for the son of a poor landless worker. Once I was present at a discussion between Prodip and a woman who works for a local small NGO. She warned him that even if he was educated he was still the son of a poor man. As such he should stay in his place and not challenge the borolok, at least as long as he lived in the village.

Poor people in Tarapur have a very precise perception of their unequal relationship with the borolok and this relationship is well expressed by what Prodip's father said at the beginning of our last encounter, as well as by the proverb quoted at the beginning of this chapter. Prodip himself, as others have done, has interpreted the relationship in terms of *do ut des*: people will help only those who can give something in return, they would not give anything to those that have nothing to exchange, those that are not full members of society. The exchange is not between equals and it is not perceived as such.

The proverb '*tel matae dalo tel, sukno matae bhango bel*' expresses the kind of unequal interdependence and exchange typical of a patron-client relationship as discussed by Devine (1999). Drawing from Wood (1994: 104), he argues that 'the context of Bangladesh represents a case where class and patronage are not mutually exclusive realities but mutually defining ones' (Devine 1999: 90) The exploitation and subordination typical of class relations is expressed through mechanisms and processes of patronage. The relationship between Jafrul and his patrons is captured by Scott's (1972) definition of patronage as implying two main points. First, the exchange between patron and client is between actors of different rank and the relationship is reciprocal and instrumental. While the client can access credit, employment, protection, charity, the patron secures cheaper labour, favourable sharecropping agreements, and political support for himself. Thus 'the patronage relationship, not only allows for the exchange of goods, services and labour, it also operates as a mechanism which reflects and reinforces the allocation of social power and status'

(Devine 1999: 91). As Boissevain (1966) highlights, the way patronage operates, its mechanisms and dynamics vary from country to country. Devine stresses how in Bangladesh interdependence is an important feature of the patron-client relationship and that to work properly and in the interest of both parties, patron-client relations should be 'open' and interlinked. 'Ideally then, what happens is that from a single stranded economic transaction, both patron and clients try to build multi stranded relationships. As the economic relation slips into a social one, the actors involved may even create a fictive kinship bond with each other' (Devine 1999: 92).

Finally, this reciprocal interdependence between households does not only characterise the relationships between borolok households and gorib ones. As Devine argues: 'it indicates a multiplicity of relations, which permeates and intersects with each other...in this way all the patrons become clients to someone else and many clients are in turn patrons to others' (ibid.: 91). This is evident if we consider for example that even small landowners can sharecrop land out and even poor people may lend or borrow money through mortgage. Credit in the past was provided mainly by so called *mahajons*, well known rich people who could also be consulted like the *matobars* (village leaders) in cases of disputes. I have been told that nowadays these people are losing their power and this is due in part to the microcredit programmes being implemented by the NGOs that are being used increasingly by people to avoid the high interest rates. I also noticed the diffusion of microcredit amongst the poor. A poor household can resort to relatives (women to brothers and vice versa) or neighbours for small amounts of money with minimum or no interest charged. The loan in these cases is part of a network of reciprocal exchange and mutual help that links two or more households. It is also very common to buy food or other commodities on credit. Every six months, when shopkeepers want to balance their books, they decorate their shops for a sort of special festivity called *alkata*. During this time, all debts are expected to be resolved. Actually, this system of small loans is what ensures survival for many poor households. As in Kurmipur 'with sharecropping and labour relations, the market for credit is far from perfect: it is deeply entwined in people's other social relationships' (White 1992: 63) and it is very difficult, as with mortgage, to identify a group more dependent on it than another. In some way the only ones to be cut off from this unequal system of exchanges are those who do not have anything to offer, not even their labour. For example, those who cannot even afford to buy some oil for their hair, and have to resort to begging for charity. These are the ones who can with some justification say 'amar keu ney' because their extreme state of need and lack of material and human resources make it impossible for them to be part of any system of exchange.

From this perspective it is now clear why people of different socio-economic backgrounds tend to define and introduce themselves as gorib, irrespective of their objective situation. According to Maloney (1988: 7):

...what a Bangladeshi means by the word (gorib) is to set up a relationship of inequality between himself and the person addressed in anticipation of possible patronage or at least in a statement of the moral social order which he needs to make the relationship function.

Thus, what actually matters is not only the 'economic' domain of the possession of material tangible assets. Claiming to be gorib does not necessarily mean asking for immediate economic help, but rather to put oneself within an asymmetrical relation as client to a patron who has the social and moral duty to give in exchange for loyalty and gratitude. It is not only those who cannot count on material resources who refer to themselves as gorib, but also those who own land and other assets.

From the beginning of my stay in Tarapur, local residents identified me with the local NGO, whose guest house I was occupying. As a consequence, they also identified me with the family of the NGO director. After a few weeks, I had my own small group of 'clients'. As I made myself available to put people in contact with a Catholic mission where poor people were given free medical assistance, I quickly gained a reputation as someone to turn to in times of need. Siraj and Bina's mother would insist during our conversations on their vulnerability, saying: 'we do not have anything' or 'we do not have anyone'. This was a way of reminding me of my obligation to 'help' them by giving money, medicines or food. But the wealthy headmaster of the local high school would also claim to be gorib in front of me and would ask me to help nurture good connections (jogajog) with foreign organisations and donor agencies to fund the school and get special economic assistance for the poorest students. While saying goodbye to some of my neighbours at the end of my first stay in Tarapur, the NGO director observed that they were showing me a lot of 'devotion' (bhakti). Interestingly bhakti is a word that is used to signify the attitude of devotion that children have towards their parents and in general expresses a form of hierarchical love (cf. Inden 1976) of an inferior towards a superior and thus also of a poor client towards his rich and powerful patron.

FROM PATRONAGE TO HIERARCHY AND STATUS

This chapter started with a description of livelihoods and of the economic context of the area where I conducted my research. From the discussion of the ethnographic material it emerged that classifying people into fixed categories and ranking them according to their material possessions is not enough to understand the full extent of socio-economic differentiation among villagers. Human resources and intangible resources also play an important role and people are linked by a complex network of relationships that are a fundamental part of the survival strategies of the poor. These relationships are characterised by interdependence and are best understood through the idiom of patron-client relations.

In Bangladesh, over the years there has been a progressive impoverishment of the lower strata due to the increase in landlessness. The size of landholdings has been decreasing and the proportion of rural families owning any land has declined too (Caldwell 1998; BBS 2008b). While the number of chronic and extreme poor is generally decreasing, the gap between the rich and the poor is becoming bigger (Sen and Hulme 2004). Moreover, while in the eastern part of Bangladesh there has been a movement to more remunerative jobs and salaried employment, in the south-west most of the households continue to depend on low productivity jobs in agriculture. This process has reinforced the dependence of the rural poor on richer patrons. Since fostering stable relationships with a reliable patron is paramount to the poor, the possibilities of establishing horizontal solidarities among the poor remains distant.

The story of Jafrul and the relationship between the members of his household and his powerful patrons show that patronage includes moral and social dimensions as well as economic ones. Along with the need for economic security, people's behaviour and choices may be driven by a need to preserve one's honour or prestige. This emanates from and serves to reinforce a strong hierarchical mode of thinking and behaviour. Before I look at the significance of this for young people at the micro level of interpersonal relations in everyday practices, I intend to explore more closely a wider macro perspective on these forms of inequality. I do this in the next chapter, looking at the specific and complex cultural framework within which these relationships are experienced. This will entail an exploration of the ways in which people in rural Bangladesh make sense of their everyday life through cultural ideas and structural features which are long lasting and broad based, and which impinge very strongly on the micro level.

NOTES

1. The Bhagobhenes refused to identify themselves as either Muslim or Hindu in the 1991 census and professed themselves as Bhagobhenes by religion. The physical features of the Bunos/Munda reveal a Dravidan origin. They were classified as a tribal for the first time in the 1991 census. The Kaiputras, a nomadic group, have been engaged in pig rearing for centuries.

2. I use the term 'outcaste' to identify groups that are otherwise called 'untouchables', or Harijan (in the Gandhian tradition), or Dalit (the more politicised way of identifying them). Outcaste is the term that best translates the local term in Bengali which is *antaj* (which literally means 'the last ones').

3. Arens and van Beurden (1977) found two types of agreement in Jhagrapur: *bagh* and *tikka*. The latter however involved only 10 per cent of households.

4. I used to address Bina's mother as 'ma' which means 'mum'. Addressing her as 'mother' meant acknowledging her age and paying her due respect. She in turn would also call me 'ma', implying that I had a sort of duty to help and protect her.

5. *Didi*, a Hindu kin term, is commonly used in Tarapur also by Muslims. It means 'elder sister'. I was commonly addressed as didi by adult people.

6. 1 khata corresponds to 1/20 bigha while 1 sothok corresponds to 1/30th of a bigha.

7. In the 1970s a number of village studies tried to interpret the socio-economic structure of Bangladeshi villages in terms of class and class exploitation. See BRAC (1986), originally published in 1980, and Wood (1994), originally published in 1976 and 1981. Also see, Arens and van Beurden (1977), Hartmann and Boyce (1983), Jahangir (1978), and Thorp (1978)). White (1992: 36–37) drawing from Van Schendel (1981), Wood (1981), Jahangir (1978) and their discussion about the opportunity to use the category 'class' to understand social stratification in rural Bangladesh agrees with Jahangir (1978) that the most significant objection to the use of a class terminology for rural Bangladesh is the 'dominance of patronage relationships' and the difficulty of identifying a 'class for itself' ready for class struggle. As Scott, adopting a Gramscian perspective, maintains 'class' may be a useful concept to define 'class in itself in relation to the means of production' but such 'objective *structural determinations*' may not be echoed in people's consciousness. Kinship, neighbourhood, faction or other kinds of belonging may well count more than a sense of class belonging as a space for social action (1985: 43).

THREE

'Let Life Go, Preserve Your Honour'
Hierarchy Status and Power in Tarapur

'Pran chole jak, man tak, jak jan, rok man.'
(Let life go, preserve your honour.)

INTRODUCTION ·

In this chapter I explore the larger context of meaning and structure within which the relationships of patronage and interdependence, on which I focused in the previous chapter, are played out. I do this because the cultural framework and the idiom within which these relationships are experienced impinge strongly on the micro level of people's practices and everyday life. Before discussing how groups and individuals are ranked and the many dimensions that hierarchy takes, as well as its implications for defining a moral and social order, it is necessary to outline and explain some key concepts. The concepts of man shonman, samaj, dharma, jat, far from belonging to the domain of a distant and monolithic Hindu or Muslim tradition, are lived cultural counters that people rework continuously in their everyday practices. These cultural counters shape the interpersonal relationships of young people and adults and they are the reference points of an hegemonic worldview that dominant groups are interested in upholding and that subordinate groups only partially contest. They are nonetheless reinterpreted and given new meanings in use.

In the first part of the chapter, as an entry point to a broader discussion of hierarchy, I explore the concept of man shonman (honour or prestige) and some of the contexts in which it is used at the individual and group level. The proverb cited at the start of this chapter introduces these themes well. Man shonman underpins hierarchy, one aspect of which is the ordering of groups, such as Muslim lineages and Hindu castes, in a hierarchical sequence that is of great importance, for example, in marriage choices. This kind of ranking, partially expressed through the idiom of caste, raises the issue of the cultural identity of Bengali Muslims and the complexity of the '*Bengali jat*' (Bengali nation) cultural background.

In the second part of the chapter I deal with the individual dimension of rank and hierarchy in Tarapur, and look at how status considerations determine people's reciprocal attitudes, behaviour and choices, and what are the referents that contribute to an individual's social worth. As shown in the previous chapter, there is a strong element of hierarchy in the patron-client relation were gorib and borolok are opposed but interlinked categories. It is important for individuals to preserve their honour and their reputation. Keeping a respectable social position and avoiding being given a *durnam* (bad reputation) are priorities for men and women, with the samaj charged with maintaining social control. Village leaders (matobar), elders (*murobbhi*), wealthy people (borolok), and members of high-ranking lineages and castes command deference and respect because they have a higher man shonman and in this sense they represent the samaj and exercise a legitimate power. In this chapter I also argue that an aspect of this power is precisely that of establishing a hegemonic representation of what is in conformity with a shared code of conduct (dharma) that allows the reproduction of the social order. Kinship is the hierarchical domain that I consider, introducing a discussion about distinctions based on age that I develop more extensively in the next chapters where I focus on intergenerational relationships.

MAN SHONMAN, THE CULTURAL IDENTITY OF BENGALI MUSLIMS AND 'CASTE MENTALITY'

Before exploring the lived cultural meanings of man shonman, a brief discussion of the word's etymology is necessary. '*Man*' derives from the

Sanskrit *mana* which means dignity, honour, prestige; 'shonman' (from the Sanskrit *sanmana*) is composed by *sho*, which means self and man. The two words together express, more forcefully, the same concept of man alone. In Tala sub-district, and also in the Khulna district area, man shonman is conceptualised in a wide social and moral sense: it is an attribute of the person, a subjective sense of moral value and virtue, and at the same time it is an objective quality of an individual belonging to a certain group, depending on the group's position in the social hierarchy. Prestige can be gained or lost according to the extent to which one's behaviour conforms to the hegemonic norms. Man shonman gives to every individual and group a sense of social identity and self-worth, an idea captured succinctly in the proverb: 'it is better to lose one's life (*pran*) than one's honour/prestige (man). Man shonman carries the same complex meaning as the Arabic word *ijjat* which is used in other areas of Bangladesh (Aziz and Maloney 1985; Bertocci 1972; Kotalova 1993). When I asked about the meaning of, and the difference between, the two words, I was told, amid embarrassed smiles, that ijjat is a shameful term used mainly in relation to the sexual domain and linked to women's chastity.

It is interesting that the most commonly used word to denote honour and prestige in Tarapur is not ijjat but one that derives from the Sankrit and that can be referred to the caste system. In fact, according to Inden, the different castes (jati) are considered 'high' or 'low' in the hierarchy according to the level of honour (sanmana) they command and in terms of their relative qualities (Inden 1976: 21). This raises the issue of the co-existence and mixing in rural Bangladesh of Muslim and Hindu cultural aspects, of an apparently egalitarian Islam with the hierarchy implied in the caste system. Here, I want to explore the multiple contexts in which man shonman is invoked to explain social behaviour. Many examples concern the domain of gender relations where the prestige/honour of a household is measured against the degree of honour attributed to its women. To explain the proverb with which I began this chapter, Niloy, a young Hindu, referred to poor women who may have to choose between working as daily labourers in the fields and starving. He said that ideally it would be preferable for a woman to die rather than damage her own and her family's man shonman by working outside home and breaking purdah. Prestige was also mentioned to explain the spreading of dowry, a Hindu custom, even amongst Muslims. 'When a bride arrives at her in-laws, they have to show that she brought expensive and precious gifts to safeguard their prestige in the neighbourhood'. Cases of acid violence against adolescent girls who reject marriage or 'love' proposals are understood as an extreme defensive reaction by a suitor whose prestige has been threatened. It seems that the consequences of such a gesture for the attacker (in some cases the death penalty) are preferable to a perceived loss of honour.

Marriage is also a domain where many choices are explained in terms of preserving and possibly enhancing a household's social position. A father told me that it is mainly for prestige that it is mandatory for parents to choose the marriage partner for their children even if this means going against their will and their preferences.

We have coped with so much hardship for them and they owe us respect, it is a question of prestige (man shonman), that is more important than their satisfaction, we would lose it if they chose on their own, the people would disapprove (lok kharap bolbe).

It is clear, in this case, that honour depends also very much on public recognition. The importance of maintaining a positive social image is much greater than the realisation of an individual preference or desire. Finally, shame (*lojja*) is also connected to losing one's social image through laughable or reproachable behaviour. As some students stated: 'lojja means to be considered choto (small) in terms of man shonman.'

Thus the opening proverb expresses powerfully the importance of maintaining one's social identity and social position even at the expense of one's physical survival. The latter is not valued much if it is not accompanied by social existence and social recognition. Poverty, economic hardship and the daily struggle for survival are such a present and constant reality in the life of most households in Tarapur that a state of precariousness and insecurity seem almost taken for granted and accepted as destiny even if not with resignation and passivity. People manifest this sense of hardship saying: 'Poor people have to work hard to eat'. Words like *dukkho* (grief), *somosha* (problem), *oshubida* (trouble) are recurrent expressions in the complaint discourse of the more vulnerable ones (Wilce 1998). It is said of women: 'there is no happiness in women's fate, only grief'; and of poor people: 'the poor have to bear a lot of hardship'. While the struggle to survive is considered part of life, what is perceived as really dangerous is the prospect of poverty also spoiling one's moral character and thus the loss of social respect. This is expressed by another saying: '*obhab hole shobhab nosto hoy*' (when there is nothing to eat the nature of the person gets spoiled). Man shonman in terms of self-respect and self-esteem is linked to a person's moral qualities and moral nature, and can be kept intact by behaviour that conforms to the perceived social hierarchy and moral order, as we have seen in the case of Jafrul in the previous chapter.

Some categories of people embody man shonman as an objective quality of the group they belong to. Man shonman, an important element of a person's or group status, highlights the significance of hierarchy as the organising principle of social relationships. Hierarchy structures every domain of life and entails different aspects and values. Thus individuals and groups are ranked and categorised so that their respective position is always clear at least in public and the social world is neatly ordered. For example, there are *uchu* (upper) and *nimno* (lower), bongsho (patrilineage) and jati (caste); boro (big) or *bhaddhro* (honourable) and choto (small) people. Nobody is equal to anybody: either he or she is a step up or a step down and everyone knows which individual is above or below him or her and which group is higher or lower in the hierarchy, especially when important choices, such as marriage, are at stake.

Ranking the Muslim Groups

Lineage and caste are important terrains for the discussion on rank and hierarchy. Each Muslim para usually comprises of households of the same patrilineage (bongsho)[1], whereas each Hindu para comprises of households belonging to the same caste (jati). As elsewhere in

Bangladesh, the names of the different bongsho in Tarapur reflect either occupational, ethnic or religious origins. So, for example, in Tarapur, Sheikh refers to spiritual leaders, Mollah to ritual specialists, Karmokar to blacksmiths, and Morol to village leaders.

Mannan (2002) describes the historical process through which bongsho became status groups in British India, by examining the opposition between Ashraf and Ailaf. The Ashraf were Muslims of foreign origin and can be further divided into four categories: Sayeed, Sheikh, Moghul and Pathan. The Ailaf were low status, converted Muslims. According to Mannan, the opposition between Ashraf and Ailaf was born when the impoverished, powerless non-Bengali Muslims started claiming noble origin and inclusion rights within the Ashraf group. Nowadays, in Bangladesh, the distinction between Ashraf and Ailaf has almost completely lost its significance as a measure of the relative status of each group. However bongsho are still categorised as uchu (high), madhyo (middle), and nichu (low). My informants in Tarapur distinguished some middle status Muslim bongsho that can be classified as cashcia (cultivators).[2] For example, Biswas/Karikar, Morol, Sheikh and Sordar belong to this group, but both Biswas and Sordar could also be names of a Hindu outcaste group. Respondents identified as high status bongsho Sheikh, Syed, Kazi and Mir, as corresponding more or less to the groups that traditionally belong to the Ashraf category. Finally, they identified low status bongsho like the Behara.

Apart from these approximations, there is no clearly defined hierarchy between the different bongsho in Tarapur. For example, Morol and Sheikh were placed in the highest group and Karikar and Behara in the lowest but no one was able to rank all the other bongsho. This seem to be consistent with what Mannan says about the historical evolution of the Ashraf-Ailaf classification: 'because there was no well defined principle of status delineation, through mutable structures of bongsho and rapid economic mobility, people were able to change or hide their low bongsho origin in a generation or two' (Mannan 2002: 253). Moreover, the economic condition of the households belonging to the same bongsho is not homogeneous. For example, among the Morol in Tarapur, there are three households that are definitely wealthy and powerful and four other households that have been included in the poor category and whose members work as daily labourers or sharecroppers for the rich. This means that even if all the Morol can claim to belong to a high bongsho their actual socio-economic opportunities differ.

Although my informants were not able to agree on ranking the bongsho, their ideas appeared to be much clearer when they had to decide about marriage arrangements. In this case the status of the bongsho in itself is taken into account, and if it is low, a good economic situation may or may not be enough to compensate for it. Towards the lowest groups this is even more accentuated and a high status and wealthy family would never give its daughter to a wealthy but very low status household. A Morol girl told me that she could never marry a Karikar boy even if his family's economic condition was good. Thus, even if the economic condition of a household is undoubtedly important, 'blood' counts as well in defining a bongsho as low or middle or high, especially in arranging marriage matches. I would like to suggest that a sort of 'jati thinking'[3] is at work even among Muslims. Mujib, a Muslim young man who was discussing with me his attempts to identify a suitable wife, told me that one of the criteria that he had to consider was the jati. This is more evident at the lower end of the ladder, where there are groups like the Behara and the Dai who, despite being Muslim, are in some areas prohibited from accessing the mosque. Their status seems to resemble that of a Hindu outcaste group.

Ranking Among the Hindus

The group of Rishi living in the western part of Tarapur next to the Muslim Mollah para, constitute an interesting case for the study of hierarchy and social mobility in rural Bangladesh. An exhaustive analysis of the condition of this caste is out of the scope of this research, but some aspects of their present and past situation are worth considering. As mentioned earlier, some of the Rishi living in south-west Bangladesh no longer belong to the Hindu community, with part of them converting to Catholicism and part of them belonging to the Baptist Church. All the Rishi households in Tarapur are Baptist. Although today only a minority of the Rishi is engaged in the 'traditional' occupation of processing leather, while the majority are pursuing diverse strategies to secure a better standard of living, the status of the caste remains stubbornly very low. The majority of the communities have adopted forms of 'Sanskritization' (Srinivas 1952) by trying to conform to Brahmanic standards and abandoning the most impure aspects of their occupation like the skinning of cows. They have turned to agriculture, cane and bamboo work and have adopted the new name Rishi (a reference to the early rishi/muni ascetics who according to tradition wrote the sacred Vedas) instead of the original one, Muchi.[4] Conversion to Christianity can be interpreted as one of the strategies the group used in the past to ensure patronage and economic support from either the Baptist or the Catholic Church. From the socio-economic survey that I conducted in Tarapur's Rishi para, it appears that only a few households are still engaged in the traditional occupation, while most of them now make baskets and carpets with bamboo. However, in comparison with other para, there is a higher percentage of 'poor' and 'extremely poor' households in the Rishi para. A very high percentage of landless and functionally landless families and a very low level of income and education also characterise other Rishi para of the area according to a survey conducted in 1996 by Bhumijo, a local NGO. In Chadnagar, a few kilometres from Tala, lives another big community of Rishi.

Twenty years ago, the Rishi living in Chadnagar and in the villages of Tala sub-district were subjected to many forms of discrimination, not only by the other Hindu castes but also by most of the rich and poor Muslim households. According to my field research (Del Franco 1983) in 1981 in Chadnagar to study the social relations between the Rishi of Chadnagar and the other bongsho and jati of the village, no other Muslim or Hindu group would accept food (cooked or raw) from the Rishi and none would offer them any food. The Rishi therefore had to bring their own cups and plates if they wanted to be served tea or food at the bazaar. The members of the four Hindu jati present in Chadnagar had nothing but contempt towards the Rishi. I was once quoted the following proverb: 'Like when you crush a fly you will stain your hand, the same with a Muchi'. The Muslim in Chadnagar despised the Rishi because of their dietary habits (eating pork meat) and because they were well known for smoking *ganja* (drugs) and drinking alcohol. However, the Rishi constituted for them a cheap labour force, appreciated for their submissive and humble attitude. They were useful as daily labourers. The Rishi lived and still live next to Muslim *para* and this has favoured the establishment of patronage relationships with Muslim households. To resolve some internal disputes the Rishi even turned to a Muslim *matobar* whose authority was more recognised than that of their own leader.

The situation has undoubtedly changed over the last 30 years, but the change has been more significant for single individuals than for the caste as a whole in terms of the enhancement of social prestige and economic improvement. A Catholic missionary congregation has been working with the Rishi community since the 1960s and has had a base in the village of Chadnagar, in Khulna district, since the end of the 1970s. Over the last 25 years, the work of the missionaries with the Rishi of Khulna and Satkhira districts has been mainly targeted at the social and economic advancement of the group. Particular attention has been paid to the promotion of primary and secondary education and general 'awareness raising'. As a result of this work, literacy has spread and the level of education increased in most of the communities. Since the early 1990s, some of the missionaries have also been involved in the formation and establishment of local NGOs that are now active in the area. Some of these NGOs consider the issue of caste discrimination as a fundamental part of their development agenda and seek to raise the problem in public meetings and campaigns as a human rights issue. In most cases, the directive staff of the larger organisations come from wealthy and affluent families, many of whom are also Muslim. Ownership of a movement against caste discrimination is therefore problematic as the Rishi themselves are usually marginal in terms of decision making. Recently, two new organisations have emerged that seek to address the question of ownership, in that they are run by members of the Rishi community. However, both organisations, for different reasons, are still too weak to constitute the beginning of a collective 'Dalit'[5] movement.

Being a Rishi is still a stigma even if the commensal form of ritual discrimination towards the group has weakened, in some areas. If a

Rishi commits some form of reproachable behaviour, it invites a typical response: 'He/she is a Muchi, what can you expect?' A discriminatory attitude has been noticed paradoxically even inside the local Catholic Church and its organisations where the priests who come from the Rishi groups are considered in some way inferior to those who come from other groups or descend from the Christians converted by the Portuguese (Paggi, 2002).

Cases of individual mobility and improvement of status are linked to personal help received from the Church or local organisations. The only man belonging to the Tarapur Rishi para who obtained a masters degree and then found employment in a college achieved his position because of the personal help he received from an NGO director. As a teacher, he now commands respect but his relatives and neighbours are still called Muchi whenever something untoward occurs. A friend of mine who now works in Dhaka as a lawyer comes from the Rishi group. His family was one of the poorest of their village and from his time in primary school the missionaries offered him considerable help. He is now well known in Tala area as a reliable and capable lawyer and his clients come from every religious group and socio-economic background. He is cited as an example of how individuals are able to 'progress' through education and good social connections. It is interesting to note however that his personal choices in life have been influenced by his origin. His marriage has been a particularly complicated matter because of a sort of double identity and 'double consciousness' (Osella and Osella 2000: 235).[6] Because he is a lawyer he has received over the years several marriage proposals from wealthy families but since he is a Hindu belonging to a low status caste he was afraid to accept any of them. First, he suspected that the proposal would have been withdrawn as soon as he revealed his village and caste of origin. Second, he was unsure how his origins would have affected his relationship and his actual position and consideration inside the group of new in-laws. He once told me that if he married into too high a status family he would risk being treated as choto (small or inferior) and his in-laws would feel they had the right to decide on his behalf and guide his life.

A small number of boys from Kanpur, a village situated a few kilometres from Tala, who have studied thanks again to the support of the church, have also achieved high levels of education and currently live and work in Dhaka. The following statement illustrates the considerable value they place on education:

> ... and thanks to the level of education we have achieved, people at Tala respect us more, even if we come from a Hindu low caste. Now if anyone from Kanpur needs to come to Dhaka they will come to our place because they know that we can help, because we know the city and because now we have a nice flat to stay.

The role of education as a status enhancer will be discussed more extensively in the following chapters. Here, I simply want to highlight some points from this description of the similarities between the socio-economic position of the Rishi and the social differentiation between Muslim bongsho. To do this a discussion of the meaning and concept of jati/jat is necessary.

The word jat derives from a Sanskrit word meaning species or kind or variety (Stirrat 1982: 11) and it is used in Bangladesh as well as in the Indian subcontinent with a multiplicity of meanings. It can designate the two genders, 'female and male jat'; a national group like the 'Bengali jat'; a religious group, like Hindus or Muslims and it is also the most commonly used South Asian word to identify caste. Jat are distinguished and ranked according to their substance, and their essence and nature defines their behaviour. According to Inden (1976) each differentiated set of substances and beings, and thus each jat, shares a kind of bio-moral substance[7] as well as having an inherent code of conduct (dharma) within it.

> When realized through actual conduct, a code for conduct is believed to bring about the well-being and good fortune or prosperity of its genus. Taken in this sense dharma is not simply a code for conduct; it is the highest of the three goals of man as an embodied being, taking proper precedence over the enjoyment of desires and the acquisition of wealth. As a goal dharma is the 'proper order' of things that brings about the good of the whole world, a goal that is achieved only by the constant striving of people. (ibid.: 19)

As we have seen, prestige (man shonman) is, in this perspective, a quality of each jat and of every individual belonging to a certain jat. It can be maintained and enhanced by acting in a way that respects the social order that is conceived as moral, social and natural.

Inden's interpretation of jat is consistent with how both Muslims and Hindus in Tarapur talk of it. Jat is important in defining the status of each Hindu group and also of each Muslim bongsho, described extensively earlier. It is definitely linked to an idea of 'nature' and 'bio-moral substance' exemplified in the discrimination the Rishi are subjected to and associated with their spoiled nature and corrupted character. But amongst the Muslims too there are bongsho that are denied access to the mosque because they are considered 'dirty'. Jat belonging is also taken into account for marriage purposes. As in Hindu north India, it is desirable for a girl to marry up the social hierarchy with someone from a higher lineage or caste, while marrying down is not acceptable. Some Tarapur villagers argued that the fact that even Muslims consider this criterion when arranging marriages, is proof of a widespread, hierarchical 'caste mentality' that has managed to penetrate Muslim orthodoxy. This raises again interesting questions concerning the cultural discourses of hierarchy in contexts of Muslim–Hindu co-residence.

Hierarchy and 'Bengali Culture'

In order to understand the coexistence of a hierarchical mode of thinking with Islamic egalitarianism, the issue of the cultural identity of the Bengali Muslims needs to be taken into account.[8] It is well known that up till the end of the 19th century in Bengal, the Bengali Muslims were integrated in the Hindu socio-economic order and were considered a caste amongst others. Locally, it was the Hindu elites who collected taxes, administered land and justice inside a hierarchical structure that consisted of Persian-speaking Muslim rulers of foreign origin at the top of the pyramid, Hindu zamindars at the middle level, and Muslim and Hindu peasantry at the bottom. According to Zannini (1991), quoting Bhattacharya (1991: 29–66), the consequence of a strongly influential Hindu Aryan tradition in the Indian subcontinent is that a particular system of castes has emerged even among Muslims. This also includes lineage endogamy.

Although there was a succession of Buddhist, Hindu and Muslim rulers, the peasantry retained beliefs and practices that had little to do with the abstract and metaphysical doctrines of the religions of the rulers. Instead, they incorporated aspects of the successive civilisations into their 'spiritual worlds' (Blanchet 1984: 10). During Muslim rule, the cult of local village gods and spirits (mostly of tribal origin) diffused through the *pirs* (saints) was more important to the Bengali peasants than the Koran and the preaching of the ulema, who used Urdu or Arabic. The Sufi tradition which has influenced all spheres of life of Bangladesh society also supported the popular Islamic religiosity with its typical Bengali syncretistic attitude (Haq 1975; Roy 1983).

The political movement that started in 1870 and which led to the creation of two separate states in 1947 was characterised also by an attempt by Bengali Muslims to purify the Bengali language and culture from its Hindu aspects and non-Islamic practices. However, this effort affected mostly the elite. For the rural peasants, the formal adoption of Islamic orthodoxy did not substantially displace the old beliefs and practices. Thus it can be argued that the world view of the peasantry 'reflects...levels, layers compartments, parallel juxtaposition of religious systems, more or less loosely articulated with one another' (Blanchet 1984: 14).[9] Kotalova observes, for example, that in Gameranga the ideal form of marriage entails rituals that stem from the Vedic sources: the word for marriage is *biye* and not *nika* as in the Islamic orthodoxy. She comments that 'the Brahmanic ideal of prepubescent marriage set out in the Vedic texts still lingers in the way gender morality is constructed' in the village she studied (Kotalova 1993: 195). Her informants however always referred to Islam whenever they invoked dharma authority to explain or justify a belief, norm or practice. I observed similar practices among most of my Muslim informants. In some cases, what they reported as an Islamic dictate actually could be referred to the Hindu tradition.

Naomi Hossain in her recent work argues, referring to Bertocci (1970)[10] and Ahmed (1981), that caste-like distinctions are just 'remnants' that 'have been popularly rejected' and that 'Bangladesh society is comparatively mobile, unlike most of South Asia because of the absence of strict social hierarchies like caste' (Hossain 2003: 23). It is true that at the macro political level caste is not an issue in Bangladesh. The caste system does not exist formally among the Muslims and in some areas of rural Bangladesh the only Hindus present belong to the lowest groups. So it could be argued that even within the Hindu society, caste is not as strict as it is in India. However, as we have seen, this does not mean that hierarchy between groups and categories is absent. There are also some instances in which rank is partially expressed in the language of caste purity. Illustrations of this are the Rishi who cannot eat from the same plates as others because of their 'impure' nature, and the low status Muslim bongsho who are denied access to the mosque on the basis of their 'dirtiness'. The fact that Muslim lineages are sometimes referred to as jati instead of bongsho and that the word jat is used are significant in the light of what Bertocci himself asserts:

caste as an organizing principle of rural society is not significant' but *'given the persistence of certain low ranked, endogamous Muslim occupational groups....jati thinking' as Gould (1969) has put it certainly forms part and parcel of the ideology of social relations held by most cultivators'.*(Bertocci 1972: 32)

It is not surprising then that many of my informants used the expression 'caste mentality' to explain the importance of status and rank in marriage arrangements. Social ranking, classification and categorisation are endemic in Bangladeshi society. Complex rules of respect and deference regulate social relations not only in the traditional spaces of the village, the neighbourhood and descent group, but also inside government offices, NGOs, colleges and 'modern' spaces in general. There are cultural elements that are shared by Hindus and Muslims and are best understood as an illustration of syncretistic 'Bengali culture' (Zannini 1991:1 41) rather than a specific attribute of either religious group. Finally, in south-western Bangladesh, Hindus are more numerous than in other districts, so it may well be that social differentiation and hierarchy are represented more often through the language of caste. The use of the word dharma by both Hindus and Muslims is also significant here. The term 'dharma' derives from the Sanskrit root '*dhr*' (literally 'to sustain') and is normally translated as religion but assumes a wider meaning for both Muslims and Hindus in

Bengal (Kotalova 1993). In this wider sense, it can be translated as code of conduct. In Tarapur, dharma is used by Hindu and Muslims alike as a synonym for culture and for social norms, rather than in the sense of 'religion'. In this sense, Hindus and Muslims invoke the same core cultural background when they identify themselves independently from any religious community as 'Bengali people' or the 'Bengali nation' (*bangali* jat). In this perspective, the authority that ensures the respect of dharma as a common code of behaviour, in a pragmatic rather than in a transcendental sense, is not a religious authority (the maulana/imam for the Muslims or the Brahmin priest for the Hindus), but the samaj and those who have the authority to speak in its name. Borolok, rich/powerful and above all high status people have the power to create and sustain but also, I would argue, to manipulate moral and social norms. What is *dharmik* (in accordance with dharma), I suggest, is continuously adapted, reformulated and reinforced.

This chapter has so far explored mainly how a hierarchical mode of thinking is the basis of ranking categories and groups. I want now to turn to the micro level of individuals and look at how hierarchy is reinforced or contested in personal relationships in the village.

RANKING INDIVIDUALS AND HOUSEHOLDS

The most common terms to express a sense of the relative inferiority/ superiority of two individuals or two groups are nichu and uchu or choto and boro. Differences of status expressed by the use of these adjectives are applied in Tarapur first of all in two opposite categories, borolok and gorib.[11] Agricultural labour, such as cultivating one's own land or working in the fields as a daily labourer, is typical of poor people of low status, whereas the ownership of land not directly cultivated confers prestige. It is significant, for example, that all the students I talked to complained of the scarce opportunities for part-time employment that would permit them to self-finance their study. However, they also absolutely ruled out doing physical labour, such as working as daily agricultural workers or helping their fathers in the fields, as a means of earning money. Working in the mud, under the sun, under the direction of someone else is considered degrading and incompatible with the prestige associated with education. Poor people are also considered ignorant and not able 'to understand', as are children, youth and women without men. Some of my interlocutors belonging to the poor or extreme poor category used to say to justify their own low position: '*amra gorip amra ki kichu bujhi?*' ('We are poor, do we understand anything?')

The mechanisms of hierarchy and of challenges to it can be understood through the observation of personal interactions (Osella and Osella, 2000: 226). Poor people are aware of their inferior position in terms of status and power and this is underlined by indicators such as gestures, dress and the way they address each other. As we have seen in the previous chapter, wearing skirts and pants, and 'modern' accessories like sunglasses or a watch, characterise a borolok. While people of lower status cannot in general afford to buy these items, they would in any case avoid showing them off in public because this would be perceived as a lack of respect. No one would smoke a cigarette in front of someone who is perceived as being of higher status. The use of the personal pronouns of Bengali *apni* (formal you), *tumi* (familiar you) and *tui* (either very familiar, or very derogative you) is also significant. The third form (tui) in particular shows intimacy and affection between children and adults, but when used with subordinates underlines their inferiority. Some kinds of food, like *chapati* made of wheat flour, are associated with a diet typical of the poor who sometimes cannot afford three rice meals a day. Borolok on the other hand can afford to invite people and offer meat and good quality rice. One day, while I was travelling with the brother of an NGO director, I received an invitation from him for lunch at his place on Eid day. I turned his invitation down saying that I had already accepted an invitation to eat with the driver's family. I immediately realised that I had said something wrong and offensive. The driver quickly intervened saying that I always liked to joke and of course I would accept the director's invitation. Accepting food acknowledges the equal or superior status of the giver, as in the Hindu tradition where high-caste people would give food to the lowest groups, but would never accept food from a lower status individual.

Public Deference and Off-stage Behaviour

Poor people always maintain a deferential attitude towards borolok in public and sometime this is accompanied by verbal expressions of gratitude towards those who are perceived as good patrons. *Bhakti kora* (to express devotion) is the verb used to identify manifestations of esteem and affection towards superiors. I often heard people express their appreciation towards the directive staff of the local NGO, especially if they had received credit, a free distribution of latrines and other services from the NGO. More significantly, many seemed to appreciate the personal help they obtained from the director, as opposed to that they receive generally from the NGO itself. Halima, Siraj and others stressed many times how available the director was towards the poorer neighbours. But as soon as the powerful do not fulfil expectations placed upon them, opinion changes: contempt and blame replace respect and deference in the 'off stage' (Scott 1985) conversations among the poor.

During my fieldwork, the NGO experienced some liquidity problems, and, under pressure from the donors, some jobs had to be cut, starting with the so-called 'service staff' comprising cooks (all women) and peons. Halima and others perceived this as an act of betrayal. 'We have been working for them for so long, for so many hours a day, we have given our lives for them and now they want to fire us. This is unfair'. The NGO's director was blamed and in private conversations was accused of wasting money and paying excessive salaries to the directive staff that 'do not really do any hard work'. After being dismissed, Halima was employed to cook for one day on the occasion of a big gathering of the NGO personnel. When she claimed her daily fee, she was refused the payment on the ground that the NGO considered her work a voluntary act. When she came back from the office she angrily commented on her treatment saying: '*borolok shudo shashon kore, age borolok chilo ekhon Seva*' ('The rich, they just want to command and keep you down, before we were subjected to borolok, now we are subjected to Seva'). Seva, the NGO in question, has in some senses become a new patron in the expectations of its beneficiaries and lower staff: replacing the rich as providers of work and protection. However, just as for the rich, the NGO deserves to be blamed if it does not fulfil its patron role.[12] Halima said she was fully aware of her subordinate position, but this awareness was rarely expressed in forms of open contestation, let alone in collective actions of resistance.

Another episode can illustrate how the NGO is perceived by some of its beneficiaries/clients. Seva, like many other development organisations, offers legal assistance to women victims of violence. When Zobeida, a relative of Halima, wanted to file a case against her husband for domestic violence, I suggested she seek the help of the NGO. I ended up accompanying her and Halima to the office because they were both afraid that the NGO would never listen to them without my intervention. 'We are poor and they don't listen to poor people'. As soon as I explained the situation to the director we were promptly directed to one of their lawyers who assured us that he would file a case at the district court. One year later, the case had still not been heard and the two women again requested my intervention:

The lawyer won't do anything if you do not tell him, they will listen to you but not to us, ...now that the NGO has some financial difficulties they will not follow up the case unless you put pressure on them. What has been done wouldn't have happened if you had not come with us from the beginning.

As this example illustrates, Halima and Zobeida did not dare to claim legal assistance from the NGO as a right, but rather expected it as a favour, with a much greater chance of getting it if I acted as intermediary. Gorib people try to use their connections (jogajog) in order to obtain what they want, while formally and publicly the system of rank and gradation is observed and enforced.

Those in higher positions consider it part of their social responsibility to stress their social role and position, for example, with particular gestures, attitudes and behaviour, and expect deference and respect from their inferiors. However, as Scott argues and the above examples illustrate, such public expressions of deference are sometimes 'false': 'the rich, while they may be relatively immune to material sanctions, cannot escape symbolic sanctions: slander, gossip, character assassination'. They maintain control of the public stage: 'the public symbolic order is maintained through outward deference, to which there is no open challenge' (Scott 1985: 25).

The 'Samaj' and the Force of 'What People would Say'

Prestige can also be seen as linked to having a 'good name' and keeping a good reputation. People of different socio-economic backgrounds and age expressed preoccupations with what 'people' would say and with the judgement of 'others' using expressions such as: 'lok or manush/manshi kharap bolbe' (people will speak badly), 'manush/manshi kharap choke dekbe' (people would look at this with bad eyes). Kotalova (1993: 42) argues that the reference to lok (people) or manush (human beings) is typical of women's vernacular and that when it implies a coercive social sanction, samaj means 'the society of men'. It is true that traditionally the samaj as a structured village institution was composed only of male members. However, now women can also participate in informal judgements, especially those arranged by the NGOs. Thus in Tarapur the expression 'lok kharap choke dekbe', or its equivalent was used by men and women alike. Both young people and adults referred frequently to the lok, and samaj as sources of approval or disapproval and to the necessity of keeping one's man shonman intact in order to reinforce one's sense of belonging to the samaj. Losing one's reputation in front of society/samaj implies the risk of being excluded from it.

Samaj is a word with shifting meaning. Depending on the context it may indicate one's family and relatives, the religious community, the village, the ethnic group, the nation and, in general, also the 'Bengali community'. The word can be translated as society or community. In the anthropological literature on rural Bangladesh, samaj is often described as a formal institution whose membership is reserved for males and is a constituent part of the power structure of a village or a locality. Adnan (1990: 169) while reviewing village studies undertaken in East and West Bengal between 1942 and 1988, notices the difference between the normative concept of samaj as 'a group of member households, forming a distinct and exclusive group, which had reciprocal obligations to each other' and the actual functioning of samaj organisation which over time 'departed considerably from these ideals' (ibid.: 172).

Rozario (1992) found that in Doria samaj was defined by a religious boundary. In the village she studied there were five para but only three samaj corresponding to the three religious groups (Muslim, Christian and Hindu) present in the village. Membership reflected religious affiliation. Members of the three samaj were involved in all the important rituals. However, there was also a kind of secular samaj involving the entire village that could be called to regulate inter-village disputes and which was led by leaders of the three religious groups.

Siddiqui (2000) describes samaj in Jagatpur as an informal institution whose function traditionally was to regulate the personal and social conduct of the members of the community in accordance with religious and customary norms, as well as to manage the practices connected with socio-religious festivals and rites, such as funerals and marriages. In this context, membership was restricted to males. Each Hindu para of the village had, in 1977, its own samaj whereas in the Muslim para, samaj was coterminous to political factions (that is, *dal*). Siddiqui notices that 'over the years not only had the extent of various samaj shrunk, but also that samaj control over the conduct of its members had loosened considerably' (ibid.: 284). In 1997, 'there were no more samaj and samaj leaders but only factions and faction leaders' (ibid.: 285). The same fate occurred to the village *shalish*, which are informal village courts for the resolution of different kind of disputes, where the same prominent village leaders (matobars) who acted as samaj leaders were involved as mediators.

In Tarapur, at present, samaj does not exist as a structured institution formed by permanent identifiable members. When people refer to samaj as a source of norms and control, it is the same as referring to lok or manshi. However, the power of samaj goes beyond merely labelling people, women in most cases, as having a bad reputation (durnam). It has the power also to materially sanction people so that acquiring a durnam can significantly hamper a girl's future. When I asked some female college students whose judgement they feared most, they mentioned the elders (murobbhi) and the leaders (matobars) of the samaj. In the past, every para had its own leader or leaders who could

decide informal dispute settlements through shalish.[13] Ramesh, who is
from a village not far from Tarapur, described the process of becoming
a recognised matobar:

*Suppose that you have a problem and I live in the same village. I helped you solve
your problem. Some time after this somebody else gets into trouble and I intervene
again to help. After some time it happens that I have actually helped a lot of people
and if any of them fall into trouble again they ask me for help. In this way I end
up being a point of reference for say 10 households or more. If there are problems
between them and with other households in the village I am on their side and they
will listen to what I say. I might also help them economically. Matobars should be
educated and aged; they are experienced. So I can give help to 10 households, giving
advice, and some other matobar will help another 10 households. Those who do this
become matobars, and if in the village there is a big problem that involves everybody
these matobars are called and everybody has to do what they say.*

But he also underlined the fact that this reality is changing:

*However, nowadays it may happen that matobars are not obeyed. If a judgment
is against you, you might not listen to it and not accept it and the case ends up in
court. At present I think matobars are not listened to. It may be because they do not
do their work correctly or they take bribes. This is why nowadays village people do
not like them much. This is what happens, they look only after their own interests,
they support those they think they can get something in return from.*

Even in Tarapur, the role of the matobars seems to on the decline.
Some villagers told me that the matobars do not have much power
now and nobody really listens to them. Other new figures of authority
are emerging. The power structure in the village is much more open
to external influences and dynamics. Political and urban connections,
education and wealth are all factors that make a person or a household
really powerful. The presence of a strong NGO in the village has probably
influenced the system of village judgements, as it also organises and
manages shalish where even women can sit and participate as judges.
This does not mean that there are no acknowledged leaders in the
village. The father of the director of a local NGO was, and in part still
is, a recognised matobar, but his power is exercised within the borders

of the village. The NGO director and his brothers and sisters, most of whom have urban connections and state jobs, are taking over.

Even if the traditional representatives of the samaj authority, at least in Tarapur, have lost influence and power, the samaj is still a powerful entity that exerts influence over people's choices and represents a powerful source of norms. Prestige, samaj, the importance of a good reputation, are all linked in a context that is captured by Scott's notion of 'symbolic equilibrium' (Scott 1985: 24) where both rich and poor 'forgo their immediate material interest in order to protect their reputation'. As Scott rightly underlines, the cost of a bad name depends very much on who you are. Thus, the 'rich have the social power generally to impose their vision of seemly behaviour on the poor, while the poor are rarely in the position of imposing their vision on the rich' (ibid.: 24). This is reflected nicely in Halima's words: '*Borolok bhalo lok kharap korte pare and kharap lok bhalo korte pare*' ('Borolok can make good people seem bad and bad people seem good').

Samaj thus refers to a moral order which represents the enforced rules related to social life. I conclude this discussion drawing on Kotalova's interpretation of the role and nature of samaj: 'the maintenance of the proper, natural and moral order of society is the ultimate justification of samaj intervention in the individual and household sphere. It is ultimately a moral community. Every social group of Bangladesh belongs to a moral society called samaj (Kotalova 1993: 42).

Age Hierarchy and Intergenerational Relations

In this section I introduce another dimension of hierarchy that I develop more extensively when discussing intergenerational relations and adolescents in the next chapter. The same deference that has to be shown towards those who belong to a higher bongsho, caste or class is also due to elders and to older relatives. Age is an important determinant of status and regulates reciprocal behaviour and attitudes, the way people address each other, and what can or cannot be discussed. Man shonman is clearly a relative, relational concept. Thus every individual owes respect and deference to those who are older than him/her and in turn is due respect from those who are younger.

It is well acknowledged that family and kin relationships constitute an important hierarchical domain. Inden and Nicholas (1977), analysing kinship in Bengali culture, provide a detailed analysis of the different forms of love between members of a group of related people defined as *jnati kutumba* (one's own people) and two smaller solidary units, bongsho and parivar (family). One's jnati kutumba comprises individuals that are related by blood and by law. Within a jnati kutumba there are similarities generated by birth, as between siblings, as well as differences generated by birth, as between parents and children. The similarities generate a pattern of equalitarian love, an example of which is the fraternal love that unites brothers or sisters, while the differences generate a pattern of hierarchical love. Within the family, the egalitarian love that siblings have for each other is supposed to be subordinated to hierarchical love, based upon the differences in their ages. Thus older siblings are like parents in relation to younger siblings. The love that unites juniors with elders is thus a form of hierarchical love expressed as bhakti or devotion and it entails expressions of respect and deference (ibid.).

In Tarapur I never heard any reference to jnati kutumba; however people used to mention frequently another category, that of attiyo swajan. According to Inden and Nicholas this also means one's own people but in a wider unrestricted sense. In Tarapur, an individual's attiyo swajan can include members of the same bongsho, the same caste, neighbours, people living in the same or different village, people attending the same school or working in the same office, and even people of a different caste or religion. It seems therefore that almost anyone can become a member of one's attiyo swajan group. All members of an attiyo swajan group are addressed in kinship terms even if there is no affinity or consanguinity. As it is considered very impolite to address anyone by name, people refer to and address others of the same age as 'brother' or 'sister', and older men/women as 'father' and 'mother', and so on. So an individual may have innumerable brothers and sisters, cousins, in-laws, mothers and fathers. A 15-year-old boy who was working as a cook for a local NGO used to address a member of the directive staff coming from the same village as *kaku* (uncle) and the director as *boro bhai* (elder brother). Halima used to address a neighbour as brother-in-law, but her husband was actually the only son of her father-in-law. When I asked for an explanation, she said: 'he is my attiyo swajan'. This is consistent with Inden and Nicholas' account: 'almost anyone could under appropriate circumstances, be considered one's own person' (ibid.: 4).

The category of attiyo swajan, as used in Tarapur, has some analogies in terms of meaning and practice with the category of *apon jon* (one's own people) as used in the Dhaka slum studied by Ahmed (2004). In Monipur, 'people are more inclined to develop relationships depending on the level of daily interaction. Apon jon is the category they want to have interaction with. People who would do things to help them and make them feel closer' (ibid.: 121). Ahmed finds that the process of 'adopting' people related neither by blood nor law is linked to the experience of poverty and vulnerability. 'Kinship idiom links and helps people to build material and obligatory relationships to carry out household tasks as well as cope with poverty' (ibid.: 121). The creation of reciprocal obligations through the use of a kinship terminology is also important in Tarapur. Moreover, I suggest, the use of a kinship terminology for those included in the attiyo swajan group can serve to establish a hierarchical relation between a superior and an inferior inside a relation of patronage. So, for example, the bhakti due to parents and to older siblings implies a sort of hierarchical love where children expect protection and the fulfilment of their needs from parents in exchange for respect and loyalty. I was also 'adopted' by the people with whom I interacted daily into their own group of attiyo swajan. So I was didi (elder sister) to some adult women and men, and 'aunt' to children. Another dimension of this use of kinship terminology is that it allows people to address unrelated men and women in a way which desexualizes the relationship (Huq 2005). Addressing someone by a kin term eliminates any possible ambiguities about the nature of rapport between unrelated men and women and makes clear what is the position occupied by an individual in the social hierarchy. So the use of a kinship terminology has a double utility: it defines clearly the nature of a relation and the respective position of two individuals; it also legitimises and makes socially acceptable contact and relations between unrelated men and women. Finally, as

Ahearn (2001a) following Trawick (1992) underlines, 'the mere use of particular terms is often enough to trigger behaviours or sentiments appropriate to them' (Ahearn 2001a: 29).

CONCLUSION

This chapter attempts to delineate a map of concepts and categories that make up the social and moral world of the villagers in Tarapur. I wanted to show how this set of interrelated cultural referents is organically linked with certain aspects of the economic structure, and the extent to which rural social relations are relations of power in which the idea of prestige as man shonman plays a pivotal role. In this respect I find the Gramscian concept of prestige/hegemony particularly relevant for grasping the working of power relations in rural Bangladesh where the concept of honour/prestige 'man' or 'man shonman' has a central place in structuring class, gender and age social relations. In a well-known and much commented upon passage in the notebook on 'intellectuals', Gramsci explains the concept of hegemony in reference with civil society as follows:

.....*spontaneous consent given by the great masses of the population to the general direction imposed on social life by the dominant fundamental group; this consent is historically caused by the prestige (and consequent confidence) which the dominant group enjoys because of its position and function in the world of production'.* (Gramsci 1971: 12)

The association between hegemony and prestige can also be found in other passages of the notebooks where the concept of prestige is used to explain or to substitute that of hegemony. Gramsci talks of 'prestige and ideological pressure' exercised by the well organised, big landowners in Sicily as the source of their power over peasants (Gramsci 1934, Q19: 35–102).[14] In the articles published in the periodical *L'ordine Nuovo*, prestige belongs to the same semantic area of the subsequently developed concept of hegemony and is associated to 'ethico-cultural leadership' (*direzione etico-culturale*) and legitimate power (Lo Piparo 1979). The Gramscian concept of hegemony suggests that we have to look beyond the material level of the relations of property and production to the moral and political sphere and understand how this is intertwined and is 'organic' with a particular set of economic relations. There are, in a Gramscian sense, 'hegemonic' values, norms, cultural representations and ideologies that shape actors' self-consciousness, their sense of identity and their perception of their needs and interests. They ultimately inform their views and conceptions of life and society, in Gramscian terms, their 'common sense'. In rural Jatpur the sense of prestige (man shonman) ingrained in a profoundly hierarchical social structure is undoubtedly a powerful 'material force' in reproducing and reinforcing unequal social relations and a key element of common sense. The preoccupation with ranking and status, sometimes expressed in the language of caste, is linked to a way of life in which prestige and hierarchy are underpinned by particular kinds of economic and political relations.

In its discussion of dharma and samaj this chapter also describes the hegemonic definition of the moral standards, that is, what is just and legitimate. I have attempted to illustrate that poor and powerless people buy into the elite vision of the social order in as much as this shapes their consciousness and their common sense, but that they do not completely adhere to it. In what I have described, there are examples of poor people's perception of their subordination as both material and symbolic through the opposition of prestige and bad reputation. Halima's words are worth repeating here: 'rich people can make bad people good and good people bad'. Although there are no signs of open collective resistance, people at the individual level try to manipulate their surroundings to their advantage. This can be interpreted as close to the Gramscian notion of 'contradictory consciousness', in which subordinate people are seen as capable of resisting hegemony. Rather than victims of a 'false consciousness', they have an awareness of their own position but only a limited one. This makes them agentful even if in a 'weak' and constrained position.

Perhaps the most significant point that has emerged from this chapter and the previous one is the strong social embeddedness that characterises Bangladeshi rural society as a whole. From the next chapter I address the core themes of my research and contextualise issues of power and social control, prestige and economic differentiation, looking at the way they impinge upon adolescence and adolescents, their individual and collective agency and their maturation and passage to adulthood.

NOTES

1. A bongsho can be defined as a lineage that refers to ancestors of a distant past without a clearly drawn genealogical linkage. The term derives from the Sankrit word *vamsa* and according to Inden (1976) was used in Bengal to refer, as jati was, to shared bodily substance—in this case the semen of its males. Sometimes bongsho is used interchangeably with *gusti* but the latter is actually only a segment of a bongsho covering up to three generations. Both bongsho and gusti comprise agnatically related descendants with the exception of in-marrying wives and out-marrying daughters. According to Mannan (2002), it would be more correct to call the localised group of households bearing the same title and living in the same para as gusti while bongsho should be considered a cultural category. However, in Tarapur I seldom heard the word gusti. The more common term to identify a group of households residing together is bongsho.

2. *Chas kora* means to cultivate.

3. See Gould (1969).

4. They are still called Muchi, especially when a derogatory objective is intended. Henceforth, I identify this group exclusively as Rishi.

5. Dalit is the politicised term used in Bangladesh and in India for the outcastes.

6. Osella and Osella argue that Izhavas: 'appear sometimes to suffer under a form of double consciousness in which other communities' negative judgement form part of their own self assessment'. I found this relevant for the Rishi too and I would add that this might translate in some cases also into low-level psychological self-esteem.

7. According to Marriott (1976) and Inden (1976), the so-called ethno sociologists, a caste is conceptualised in Hindu thought as a group characterised by a particular bio-moral substance that can be preserved and even improved if the members of the caste properly observe caste rules regarding marriage and the interaction with others groups. The fact that interactions between castes may

affect their bio-moral substance explains the rules regarding the exchange of food and women between castes of different status. Purity and power, in Marriott and Inden's analysis, are not separated as in Dumont's interpretation; they are rather aspects of 'a unitary Indian concept of superior value—power understood as vital energy, substance code of subtle, homogeneous quality and high, consistent transactional status or rank' (Marriott 1976: 137).

8. Blanchet (1984) deals with issues linked to Bengali Muslim identity in the introduction of her book 'Meanings and Rituals of Birth in Rural Bangladesh' to argue that it is especially in the cultural world of rural women in Bangladesh where traditions practices and beliefs can be found. These are common to Muslims and Hindus and often clash with the fundamental Islamic positions.

9. In the constitution approved in 1971, Bangladesh was made a secular republic where each religious group had the same rights. In 1977, the article was changed. In 1982, the weekly holiday was changed from Sunday to Friday, and in 1988 President Ershad officially proclaimed Islam as the state religion despite the fact that there were negative reactions from several sections of the population and even from Islamic movements. This indicates a process of Islamisation within Bangladesh that is supported by the Arab nations.

10. Bertocci (1972) however says that in Comilla 'there exist caste groupings among Bengali Muslims' even if 'they are not widely distributed as corporate groups and concrete structural units of local villages' (p. 32).

11. Rich are also defined as dhoni when material wealth is underlined. Bhaddhrolok means gentlefolk and it points to landownership but also to some kind of noble origin. I have seldom heard this word in Tarapur. Chotolok is another way to designate poor people. It means literally small people and when I asked my informants why I hadn't heard this term much they said that in Tarapur there are no chotolok in the sense of very low status people.

12. See Devine (1999) for an extensive discussion of NGO policies and relationships with clients/beneficiaries in Bangladesh.

13. The words shalish and bichar are used interchangeably to indicate informal village courts and their judgements. However, to be precise shalish refers to the court and bichar to the judgement.

14. Italian edition of the prison notebooks: Quaderni del Carcere. Edizione Critica dell' Instituto Gramsci a cura di V. Gerratana, voll.4 Torino 1975.

FOUR

The Changing Transition to Adulthood and the Emergence of Adolescence

'kurite, buri'
(A woman at 20 is old.)
'kurite buri noe....kurir niche bie noe'
(A woman at 20 is not old...no marriage before 20.)

INTRODUCTION

There is a multiplicity of discourses in Tarapur area about the proper age of marriage for girls. The first proverb reflects the hegemonic view that girls marry as soon as possible after puberty, and that at the age of 20 a woman would be considered already old. The second is a slogan frequently quoted by NGO members and beneficiaries during meetings, demonstrations and campaigns against early marriage. Both statements capture part of the reality that I explore in this chapter. I discuss some aspects of the economic and socio-cultural changes that are linked to the emergence of adolescence as a social stage in the life of girls as well as boys in Bangladesh, taking into account its significant gender and class dimensions. There are different sites and places where the modalities of a changing transition to adulthood can be explored. Education plays a significant role in this process. However, a distinction has to be made between secondary and higher secondary schooling[1] to understand it properly. There are a greater number of girls now who attend high school (grades 6 to 10, ages 11 to 16) until they are at least 14, 15 or 16 (grades 8, 9 or 10) instead of getting married, but marriage is still the main referent for the formation of their adult identity because such a short time span does not allow them to develop alternative expectations. I suggest that it is only for those girls who pass the matriculation exam and enrol at college with a view to proceed further that education may potentially open significant alternative life trajectories. Boys who enrol at college, unlike those who stop studying to join their fathers' businesses or because their families cannot afford the costs of their education, postpone the assumption of adult responsibilities and assume the status of students. Ultimately, therefore, it is for college students of both sexes that education opens up real spaces to think and pursue different life trajectories. There is also a strong class dimension in the way people experience adolescence and this is most evident for girls. Girls who belong to richer households are more likely to proceed to higher studies and delay marriage. In Tarapur, poor parents are more willing to invest in a son's higher education in view of better employment opportunities; they are less likely to invest in a daughter, especially if she can be more conveniently married.

LIFE STAGES AND THE TRANSITION TO ADULTHOOD

Two studies (Aziz and Maloney 1985; Kotalova 1993) quoted in the first chapter[2] deal explicitly with the conceptualisation of life stages and the transition to adulthood in rural Bangladesh. Both the ethnographies describe inter alia the different life stages and the way purdah informs the process of socialisation of boys and girls into adult life. This process appeared to be strongly gender differentiated. According to the authors, women were socialised to structure their identity around the concept of lojja (shame and modesty) and men around that of ijjat (honour and social prestige). Lojja developed as submissiveness, modesty and shyness and was clearly expressed through body language. As girls grew up they were gradually separated from boys, and with puberty purdah was strictly enforced so that if they did not go to school their physical world was further restricted to the household and the immediate area surrounding it. Puberty was characterised by biological and physical changes connected with the emergence of strong and socially dangerous sexual impulses.[3]

According to Aziz and Maloney's ethnography, it was commonly acknowledged that boys and girls have strong sexual feelings and fantasies and as such needed to be kept under surveillance. 'Young people find it difficult to control passion'. Girls thought of marriage as the ultimate objective of their life. 'Females dream of a husband and appreciate their parents' effort to find one' (Aziz and Maloney 1985:54). Interviews conducted by Aziz and Maloney show that there was strong social pressure to marry pubescent girls in order to ensure that they did not have premarital sexual relations and that they did not develop emotional bonds before marriage. Sexual desire was constructed as a destructive force, a strong impulse that had to be controlled and repressed. For a woman, the ideal stage for getting married was *kisori*, which broadly corresponds to early adolescence. For a man it was acceptable to remain unmarried through the *kisor* (early adolescence) and *nabajauban* (young adulthood) phases. The nabajauban stage of life applied de facto only to men because girls were married during early adolescence. Adulthood for a woman was achieved by getting married and girls who married in their teens took up de facto adult roles, even if they did so in a subordinate position. In fact, as young brides they were subjected to the authority of both the husband and the in-laws. When they gave birth, women acquired a more secure and established position inside the family, but it was only as mothers-in-law and with middle age that they became more powerful and visible. Then they could disregard some of the obligations of purdah, such as limited mobility and wearing the veil.

Post puberty, boys were not subjected to any restriction in their movements. For them, becoming adult was connected mainly with being able to economically support their own family. During the nabajauban stage, however, young adult males were submissive to the authority of their fathers and elders. There were few opportunities to rebel against them. Students had a somewhat more troubled passage to adulthood because of job uncertainties. Marriage was not seen as based on companionship and shared feelings. The husband's main duty was to provide material and economic support for his wife and children. The word *bibaho* (marriage) comes from the Sanskrit and means 'to support' or 'to sustain'. The word *swami* (husband) also comes from the Sankrit and means 'master' and 'protector'. While marriage was truly a major turning point in the lives of women, most men experienced less change, for they continued to live with their natal families, cultivating family land.

These ethnographies tend to depict integrated communities where conflict does not occur and individuals occupy ascribed roles without questioning social norms. I will return to this criticism at the end of this chapter.

A number of other studies, though not primarily focused on life stages, contain descriptions and analysis of adolescent boys' and girls' activities and status before and after marriage, and stress their different position in gender relations. Some are older village studies that testify to a situation where purdah was strictly observed, with girls being inevitably withdrawn from school after puberty to be married off, so that they would not go further than grades four or five (Abdullah and Zeidenstein 1982; Arens and van Beurden 1977). More recent studies (Rozario 1992, 2002, 2009; White 1992) describe a more nuanced situation but still one where girls' status and identity are very much defined in relation to the categories of purdah, shame and honour and where 'women's only source of socially approved status is through marriage and motherhood' (Rozario 2002: 43). Policy-oriented studies dealing with demographic issues, such as age of marriage, fertility and reproductive health concerns (Amin et al. 1998; Huq and Khan 1990; Jahan 1994; Khan 1997, 2000; MOHFW 1998; Rashid and Michaud 2000), once again stress girls' subordination and dependence on adults. They describe early adolescence, in particular, as a period of great hardship because of ignorance on the one hand and also because of the pressure girls experience in having to conform to adults' prescriptions. They highlight physical and psychological problems linked with the onset of menstruation in situations where information and assistance are inadequate and also the psychological distress that girls suffer because they are continuously reminded of their vulnerable status. Girls are constantly reminded that they are responsible for their future and their marriages and that these can be spoiled by behaviour that can elicit disapproval and ruin their reputations.

EDUCATION AND THE CHANGING AGE OF MARRIAGE

In these descriptions, there is no social, temporal or subjective space for adolescence in rural Bangladesh and, correspondingly, no socially recognised life stage between childhood and adulthood for girls. For boys there is a recognised temporal stage of young adulthood, but this is seen either as a period of gradual acquisition of working skills, or as a period dedicated to study in function of acquiring qualifications for future employment. In both scenarios, boys remain submissive to parents and elders. However, in Bangladesh today, the modalities of the transition to adulthood are changing. First, the number of people employed in agriculture is on the decline. This is accompanied by a rapid increase in both boys and girls occupying places in schools and colleges; this was particularly true during the 1990s. The literacy rate has been rising: 56 per cent in 2005-10 compared to 24 per cent in 1991 (EIU 2005), while the disparity in the level of schooling between rural and urban areas and between men and women has been narrowing. The passage to adulthood for boys is not so smooth nowadays as it was in the past when in the rural reality of the extended family they would inherit an occupation straight from their fathers and earn a living cultivating family land. The proportion of rural families owning any land has declined and the number of people employed in agriculture has also been decreasing since the mid-1970s, with a shift from low return agricultural labour to non-farm employment, more accentuated in the eastern part of the country (Caldwell 1998; World Bank 2008a). The national accounts indicate that the share of agriculture in the GDP decreased from 25 per cent to 19 per cent between 2000 and 2005, while in 2005 the services sector accounted for more than 50 per cent and industry for 26 per cent with the Ready Made Garments (RMG) sector being the main source of manufacturing growth. The urban population is growing at a rate three times the national average due to migration from the rural areas to the main cities, especially to Dhaka and Chittagong where daily wage labourers in agriculture can get employment in the services and informal sector. International migration to the Middle East, South-east Asia and Europe has also become an important employment option for many young people (World Bank 2008a).[4]

In this situation the demand for education for boys is understandable in relation to their and their parents' aspirations for better paid non-farm employment. On the other hand, as some research indicates, education is not such an attractive option for boys who belong to poorer households especially in the richer eastern parts of the country where there are increasing opportunities of children employment in both rural and urban areas (Tariquzzaman and Hossain 2009). Here, migration is also present as an alternative remunerative option for boys belonging to better-off households. Overall, young males have to face a longer period after puberty before being able to earn enough to marry and assume full adult responsibilities.

The more significant progress in educational attainment concerns girls. Gender parity was achieved in primary school enrolment in 1999 (Campe 2000). From 1992–93 to 1995–97, the increase in the number of secondary school students in rural areas was mainly due to an increase in the number of female students (BANBEIS 1998). By the end of the 1990s, two-thirds of the total group of 11–15-year-old girls were in school, but this was differentiated by socio-economic class, with 73 per cent of non-poor girls compared to 52 per cent of poor girls at school (UNICEF 1999). Through the 2000s, enrolment rates of poor boys at the secondary level have been declining and there is a growing reverse gender gap. In 2005 there were more girls than boys enrolled in grades 6 to 10: 52.8 per cent of girls against 47 per cent of boys (BANBEIS 2006). Some authors have suggested a correlation between the increase in girls' enrolment in primary and secondary education and a trend in postponing marriage (Amin 1996; Amin et al. 1998; Caldwell 1998), and that a temporal stage of adolescence is de facto emerging. The median age at marriage among women aged 20–24 has increased by one year over the past decade, from 14.2 years in 1996–97 to 15.3 years in 2006–7 (NIPORT 2009). The statistics also show that more educated women tend to marry later: those who have completed secondary or higher education marry two years later than those with no education. Residence and economic condition also matter: women from the highest wealth quintile marry two years later than those from the lowest wealth quintile and urban women aged 25–49 tend to marry one year later than their rural counterparts (ibid.). Recent demographic and policy-oriented research have addressed the complex intertwining between girls' education, poverty, marriage and the practices related to marriage, such as dowry, focusing mostly on primary and secondary schooling (up to grade 10) and exploring the rationale behind parents' choices in respect to their children's marriage and education (Amin et al. 2006; Amin and Huq 2008; BRAC 2006; Hossain 2005; Mahmud and Amin 2006; Schuler et al. 2006; World Bank 2008b). These studies show that while on the one hand education seems to play a role in postponing marriage for girls, the imperative of marriage and the social norms that regulate it strongly influence parents' decisions. If it is true that girls' enrolment has significantly increased in the sixth to tenth year of schooling, only a minority of girls sit for the final exams in their tenth year and proceed to intermediate college and university. The national statistics show that the highest drop-out of girls is in grades 9 and 10 (respectively 35.5 per cent and 47.41 per cent) and that only a minority go on to higher secondary education at intermediate colleges. In 2005, the gross enrolment rate in grades 6 to 8 was 67.52, it was 40.53 in grades 9 and 10, and in grades 11 and 12 at intermediate colleges it was as low as 11.37 (BANBEIS 2007). The tertiary enrolment rate for males and females was 6 per cent in 2005, of which 24 per cent were females (UNESCO 2009).

EMERGING ADOLESCENCE IN TARAPUR

In Tarapur, the strongly prevailing view is that girls should be married as soon as possible after puberty in order to guarantee their own and their parents' respectability. In this sense there is an ideal correspondence between puberty, marriage and the acquisition of adulthood. For boys, the situation is quite different. Adulthood and marriage are postponed until they are able to economically support their own family, either sharing their fathers' economic resources or through separate income sources. However, competing discourses and practices are emerging and education seems to have a fundamental role to play in this process.

Adolescents or teenagers are not commonly considered a social category in Bangladesh. The girls that remain unmarried after puberty are *meye* (girl) and are mostly, at least formally, enrolled in school. For those who are more successful in their studies, life is dictated by their daily routine and duties as students. If they successfully pass the matriculation exam at the end of high school they are likely to study up to higher secondary or university level. This delays marriage until at least the ages of 18 to 19. For others, full-time involvement in helping parents in the field or in domestic chores leaves little time for study. They may be enrolled at school but their identity as students is transient and provisional until their parents find them a suitable husband. For boys, even in the past it was expected that they would remain unmarried until they were able to support their own family. Puberty as such did not constitute as much a turning point as it did for women. In Tarapur, most unmarried teenage boys attend school or college at least formally. Those coming from rich or majhari families that are successful in their studies are likely to remain unmarried at least until 25 years of age or longer, and are expected to leave the village after college to study at universities in Dhaka or in Khulna. The poorest or those who are not successful in their studies are given in marriage earlier and tend to join the family business or work as agricultural labourers.

I faced some difficulty at the beginning trying to explain to adults and young people in my study area the main themes of my research. As there is not a precise Bengali term that corresponds to what we would intend for adolescence, a few educated people understood what I was talking about only when I said that I wanted to study 'teenagers'. With others I used the Bengali word kisor/kisori to explain which social group I was interested in because according to Aziz and Maloney (1985) this term can be translated as early adolescence. I noticed, however, that actually the stages[5] listed and described by Aziz and Maloney in their classic study are only partially understood in Tarapur and never used in casual conversations. Different people gave[6] me different meanings for each of them. The same has been observed by Blanchet (1996) and Ahmed (2004) in their study areas. To make clear the subject of my research I had to resort to examples and long explanations, especially in order to include married adolescents in the category of my interest. Otherwise they would have been excluded because they are commonly considered adults.

Thus, I could not isolate adolescents in Tarapur as a social category with a specific culturally recognised status or as a homogeneous group defined by a certain age or by a particular set of entitlements and obligations that distinguished them from children and from adults. However, I would argue that different types of 'adolescence' are emerging. In practice, enrolment in education is linked to the opening of new spaces like the high school itself and the college that imply the development of new ideas and discourses about young people, gender and intergenerational relationships and friendship. There is thus on the one hand a kind of continuity in what people think about the nature of young people and their proper behaviour; at the same time, key changes are underway in how some cultural counters like modesty and honour are understood and lived. Many of the terms that circumscribe and shape young people's personal and social growth are still the same but their content is changing subtly. In what follows I discuss this in three significant arenas: the nature of young people and the proper way of dealing with their strong emotionality and sexual desires, the acquisition of maturity as capacity 'to understand', and the interpretation of 'shame'.

Young People are Prone to Passion (*Abeg Probon*)

Puberty is understood in Tarapur as a turning point in terms of biological and sexual maturation for both boys and girls. The 'highly emotional nature of Bengalis' was repeatedly stressed by adults and young people as a kind of natural inclination attributed at times to the hot tropical climate. On top of this, the time from puberty onwards is commonly considered a phase of particularly strong emotionality. Young people, irrespective of gender, are considered to be abeg probon (prone to passion), even more so than adults. They are said to be exceptionally *gorom* (hot), to have hot blood[7] and this is deemed to depend on being sexually mature. The word 'probon' can also be translated as 'addicted' and the expression 'abeg probon' conveys also a sense of weakness, dependency and incapacity of control. Falling in love is also associated with being weak. When I asked a student in his twenties what his feelings towards his girlfriend were, he said: '*tar pothi ami durbol*', an expression that can be translated as '*I have a soft spot for her*' but where 'durbol' literally means 'weak'. People of different backgrounds expressed the fear and conviction that adolescents would not be able to control their sexuality, their instinctive feelings and their unstable emotionality and that they would be always prone to the temptation of engaging in sexual relationships before marriage and thus 'make mistakes'.

Adults underline the need to control and repress young people's strong emotionality. For example, the best way to avoid 'mistakes', and to prevent abuses against girls that would seriously jeopardize their marriage, is to keep boys and girls separate. This is a concern that village people share with 'educated' people and development workers. A Bangladesh Rural Advancement Committee (BRAC) officer, whom I met in Dhaka, involved in a programme for adolescents had this to offer as a solution to prevent boys from abusing girls:

The boys have to learn to stay away and the girls have to know that they cannot get involved in any relationship before turning 18 which is the legal age for marriage. Between boys and girls of the same age there cannot be friendship because when they are teenagers their sexual desires and passions are too strong and they are bound to make mistakes.

There is a strong gender dimension in the way social control is exercised on young people. Adolescent girls, more than boys, have to withdraw from social spaces and have to be extremely careful not to express their feelings and emotions in improper ways and with strangers. They are considered emotionally fragile and unable to make the right choices for themselves. Moreover, the consequences of a transgression are for girls more serious and lasting than for boys. As one male informant told me, for girls it is not only a matter of bad reputation but also of real difficulties in getting married.

Because in Bangladesh if it is known that a girl has an affair with someone, no-one else will marry her…Girls are in more trouble. Boys won't have such problems. They will get a bad name (durnam) but this is something that only in Bangladesh matters. In another country it doesn't. In Bangladesh they will think that a boy having affairs has taken a bad path, is not good, is being spoiled.

Girls will get a bad reputation but they will also have trouble in getting married because in the future if a possible husband knows about the affair, he will not marry the girl…so what kind of life is she going to have?

The tone of this statement is consistent with findings on the nature of young people in earlier ethnographies. However, modernity and the way it is perceived add new meanings and dimensions to the definition of youth as too passionate and emotionally inconsistent. A common complaint in rural Bangladesh is that the *adhunik jug* (literally, the modern era) exerts a negative influence on boys, thus spoiling even more their nature and character. Young unemployed males who spend most of their time at the bazaar 'hanging around' are a matter of concern for parents of girls who attend local schools and colleges. They are considered in some senses the product of the evils of modernity. 'Corrupted' by *kharap* (bad) TV programmes and cinema movies that present misguided and false models of easy life, where everything can be attained without effort, these young men are likely to rebel against the authority of their parents and elders and are prone to bad habits like smoking and drinking and harassing girls who are seen in public spaces. All this may constitute a further reason for controlling girls' mobility and social interaction because it is taken for granted that increased visibility of women triggers male *loobh* (desire or greed). Girls are usually blamed for provoking men.

All this explains and reinforces the necessity for women to behave according to the code of purdah from puberty onwards. Puberty is lived by girls as an important turning point in terms of new obligations and restrictions they are expected to observe. Their mobility is curtailed after their first menstruation and some activities are forbidden as they are considered improper for grown ups. In general, it is considered shameful for girls to play with boys or indeed in public. It is desirable that girls leave the village only to go to school or college; occasionally they may go to the bazaar to attend *melas* (fairs) or to visit friends. In these latter cases, however, they are always accompanied by others or at least by younger siblings. An attitude of modesty and shame must be expressed by the way they behave and dress. I was informed that it is easy for everyone in a neighbourhood to know when a girl attains maturity or becomes mature (*shekna* or *shabalika*). From that moment onwards, she is treated differently. Her dress code changes and her parents become more concerned about her personal safety and her chastity. During a long conversation with a group of girls attending Tarapur's high school I learnt the following:

We did not understand why, we hadn't been given any explanation but after we had our first menstruation we couldn't go out like we did before. Our parents and relatives were always checking where we were and what we were doing, we couldn't play anymore in the field…and every month our mother used to check if our period had come.

Marriage is commonly perceived as the only way to channel sexuality and desire into an appropriate set of social relations. Older married women confirmed that in the past (I refer to women who married approximately 35 to 45 years ago) puberty coincided with marriage. All the middle-aged women I talked to in the village reported having been given in marriage (*biye dewa*) before or soon after menarche. They also recalled that in the past puberty was celebrated with a simple ritual that involved the girl and her husband's family, because in most cases the onset of puberty followed marriage. Today no such ceremony takes place. Parents prefer instead to hide the moment of puberty of their unmarried daughters partly because sexual matters are an object of shame (lojja), but mostly because of the persistent belief that a *boyoshko* (aged) girl shouldn't be kept at the *baper bari* (parental house) too long. Both adults and adolescents talk commonly of pubescent girls as boyoshko, which is the most generic term to identify grown ups. Implicitly 'grown-up' girls are also thought to be ready for marriage because as people say 'they have come to age' ('*boyosh hoye gyeche*'). Ideally, thus, puberty, adulthood and marriage are collapsed together. Parents' anxiety about the future of their daughters cuts across community and class, even if empirically it can be shown that well-off parents are actually in a stronger position with respect to the pressure of samaj. A local NGO's officer admitted: 'Even the most "advanced" parents do not hesitate to marry off their daughters as soon as they can to avoid problems and to prevent them from falling in love with someone. They do not want to risk missing a good occasion.'

There are also discourses about the proper age of marriage that sustain and reinforce the stronger position of the husband's family. The respective age of husband and wife is a very important element in making it desirable that girls do not wait too long before getting married. It is common conviction that the bride has to be 6 to 10 years younger than the husband (there are some older couples where the difference is more). A number of reasons are given for this. First, men live longer and so they need a younger bride who will be able to take care of them in their old age. Paradoxically, however, it is usually the case that when the husband dies the wife is still young, but as a widow she will not be able to remarry and there will be nobody to support her. Second, it is commonly believed, even by young people, that a woman in her thirties is no longer sexually active and able to satisfy her husband who will be forced to find someone else. On the other hand, a woman in her twenties is considered to be much more sexually active than a man of the same age. Some youths quoted the example of a couple, both of whom were about 45 years old. They said that soon after their marriage the husband fell severely sick and everyone attributed this to the excessive sexual urges of the wife. Another reason reported as an explanation of the age difference between husband and wife is that a young bride can be more easily controlled because her character is more susceptible and she can therefore adjust to her new family setting. The age difference is also determined by material considerations; the younger the bride, the lesser the dowry.

Alongside these hegemonic discourses, other competing discourses emerge that reflect different practices. Educated parents from majhari and borolok households express a different view. Although they have to face the anxiety of opposing the elders and the matobars, and sometimes to cope with the fear of transgressing a religious norm, they tend to believe that for girls a suitable age for marriage is between 16 and 17 years. This corresponds to the end of the compulsory ten years of schooling. The actual power to choose the timing of one's daughter's marriage depends very much on the socio-economic position of the household. As the following example shows, the risk of durnam (bad reputation) impinges more upon less powerful households and groups.

Shopon, a Hindu college teacher, recounted his family experience to me. He wanted to stress how village power relations determine which social norms are enforced, and that this usually works to the disadvantage of the weakest groups, including his own (that is, Hindu). His sister, a good-looking college student, had to endure a neighbour who used to harass her on her way to school and then spread lies about her that eventually damaged her reputation. The man she was engaged to left her and she remained unmarried. Following this experience, the family sent the other sister far away from home to study so that the same did not happen to her. Shopon commented that a nice girl belonging to a powerless family with no connections is always in danger and has to be much more careful than others not to attract a durnam.

Some poorer parents, especially those with contact with the local NGOs, would publicly acknowledge early marriages of daughters as evil. Also, they would again argue publicly that, according to the law, 18 years is the right age for girls to marry and 21 years for boys. However, in practice, the same parents would give their daughters in marriage well before they reached 18 years of age. The reason for this is that if they do otherwise 'people will talk badly' and being poor they 'have no real alternative'. I asked women beneficiaries of NGO programmes why they married their daughters at such an early age despite having been 'made aware' that it is prohibited by law and also harmful for health. The following is a typical response:

We couldn't keep her at home, she was too grown up, people would have said bad things about her. They would have said that we did not perform our duty as parents, which is to marry our daughters off. And then when they are grown up they get interested in boys, wander around more and they could do something wrong with them.

In the past, a strictly marked age never constituted a way of measuring an individual's maturity and development, as Bangladesh did not have a system of compulsory birth registration, although Christian parishes do have registrations of births. As a consequence, the majority of rural people over a certain age do not know their precise age. With schooling, however, boys and girls are asked to declare their ages, a detail that has to appear in the SSC (Secondary School Certificate) obtained after 10 years of schooling. In general, more attention is now paid by parents to recording the birth of their children.[8] For girls, the legal minimum age for marriage is 18 while for boys it is 21. People are generally aware of this legal requirement, especially since NGOs have campaigned strongly against the practice of 'child marriage'. These legal norms are however rarely taken into account and the officials in charge of marriage registrations rarely enquire too much into the age of the bride.

The Capacity to Understand (Bujha)

The acquisition of adulthood in terms of the capacity to assume adult responsibilities is often linked to a capacity 'to understand' (bujha). This expression is used in different contexts and situations in Tarapur. The first time I paid attention to it was when Pia, a young NGO officer, said: 'Now the tendency is to marry off girls when they are adult, that means post puberty but also when they "understand", which means at least after matriculation (10th year of school)'. Here Pia identifies schooling as a parameter to evaluate one's ability to 'understand'. In some situations, I observed that bujha can be understood as the knowledge that derives from experience and the consequent ability to perform one's duties correctly. If during my conversations with married women I asked specifically about their married life, they would often cut short the discussion by saying 'apni bujte parben na' ('You cannot understand') or 'biye korle bujhben' ('You will understand when you are married'). On many occasions, for example, Halima, a married woman, justified her protective attitude towards me by saying that I was still choto (young) and as such I needed someone to tell me how to behave properly. When I protested mentioning my age, she would say 'You aren't married, that's why you are still a meye (girl)'.

'Understanding' is also linked to gender and economic position. In Tarapur, a poor widow who lives with a widowed daughter once told me during a conversation that 'amar shami ney, saval ney, bhai ney' ('I do not have husband, brothers or children'). She then asked herself a rhetorical question: '*ami ki kicchu bujhi?*' ('Do I understand anything?'). With this question she was relating to two episodes in her life when she was cheated and lost quite a lot money.[9] She explained her losses by her incapacity 'to understand'—a capacity denied her because she was a poor woman with no man in her family. Poor people share with children and women the same condition. Siraj, a poor peasant, linked the capacity to understand to being rich and educated.

On the other hand, some women who have received loans to invest in income generating activities from a local NGO stated that the greatest benefit they received from the NGO is that their capacity to 'understand' has been enhanced. In other words, they can now better manage their household economy and are more aware of their own social and familial situation. They also stated that their increased understanding helped them get work at more convenient rates because they had acquired buddhi (intelligence) and they could bargain and avoid being cheated.

All this is consistent with what Blanchet (1996) and Ahmed (2004) observed. The capacity to understand is contextual and according to Ahmed depends on the capacity of children to respond to adult demands. Renu, a 14-year-old girl, explained to me that she had started feeling ashamed about talking with her mother about certain matters when she started 'understanding' things. Once again she linked this moment to when she started attending high school, at around 12 to 13 years of age.

Kotalova (1993), Blanchet (1996) and White (2002), all three argue that what distinguishes adults from non-adults is not their age but rather their capacity to 'understand' and thus to be subject to different 'entitlements and types, levels of responsibility' (White 2002: 728). There are thus different degrees of understanding that do not necessarily correspond to particular ages. It seems that women without a male guardian are always in some sense 'minors', and their capacity to understand is never complete. Exceptions to this are, for example, those women who work for NGOs. These have in effect learnt 'male roles' by becoming contributors to the family income. On the one hand, being able to understand seems to imply conformity: the knowledge and respect of social norms and the capacity to adhere to and behave according to social expectations. On the other hand, when understanding is constructed as related to being educated or to NGO membership, or to being able to bargain for a better salary, it means also to be able to manage one's life and act in one's interests. It presupposes the individual capacity to assume responsibilities in different domains and activities, not necessarily the 'traditional' ones. It is associated then not only with the adherence to social obligations but also to the ability to negotiate them and exercise a degree of agency.

The Meaning of Shame (Lojja)

A more contextualised understanding of the concept of shame might also allow us to challenge, at least partially, the view of Bangladeshi adolescents as the passive victims of a process of socialisation that silences them and makes them invisible. The notion of lojja is at the core of purdah and is a key concept in order to understand the process of children's growing up and their acquisition of moral standards. The word 'lojja' is most commonly translated as shame, but can also be used to express embarrassment and shyness. Lojja is 'felt' especially by children, youth and women, but also by adult men. However, as women are the bearers of the family honour and prestige, shame is a special virtue for them and is assumed to be a component of their gender personality and nature. They are taught, for example, to speak in a low voice, to keep their eyes down, to show modesty and avoid assertiveness. It is said that shame makes a girl or a woman more beautiful. Boys have to maintain a submissive attitude, even in posture, when talking to elders or superiors in general, but for women such an attitude is desirable under any circumstance. As Parish (1994) argues for Nepali Newars, children and youth of both sexes have a greater degree of lojja in their personalities because on most occasions of interaction they are subordinates and have to show respect and deference to superiors. Girls more than boys pay with embarrassment and shame for any behaviour that makes them visible and exposes them to public judgement. This is expressed with the term 'lojja lagbe' (literally, 'shame would occur to me') or 'lojja lagto' (literally, 'shame occurred to me'). Sometimes lojja is what prevents people from acting in particular ways; sometimes it is the consequence of behaviour that has transgressed the norms. Shame also drives people to withhold the public expression of their sentiments, opinions, etc. In other words, it operates as a form of self-control. The description of an episode where I was involved helps illustrate some of the practical consequences of lojja for Tarapur's teenage girls.

I went to visit a newly married girl, Najma, at her house and I found her with her unmarried younger sister, Beauty, Beauty's friend Shahana, and a married cousin, Rotna. They were all neighbours and were chatting and doing some homework together. I knew that in a field nearby there was underway a football match between two local teams. Some of the players were or had been classmates of the girls so I proposed that we go and watch the match together. This would have involved crossing the road and walking for about 100 meters. Initially the girls declined my offer but changed their minds when I explained that most of the people would have been known to them and that it would have been like watching a match in the college courtyard. Their parents allowed us to go because I was going with them as a 'guardian'. I was not aware that unlike school matches, village matches are attended only by males. So when we arrived at the match, the principal of the college and some teachers cleared our way and we were made to seat near the commentator of the match in one corner of the field. This was done to prevent us the embarrassment of sitting on the ground and amongst men. However, our allocated position made us more visible than ever and we ended up attracting more attention than the match itself. After half an hour we left and on the way back the girls were silent and embarrassed. I also felt in some way that I had not been in the right place, in the right moment. Afterwards the girls said that they felt a lot of shame. Disappointed at my naivety, I never tried to repeat the experiment.

This example confirms that girls and women in general feel ashamed whenever they make themselves too visible. Thus riding bicycles or asking the teachers questions in front of male classmates is considered a matter of shame. In these examples lojja seems equivalent to shyness or embarrassment but in fact it also implies something much deeper, that is, the reaction to the awareness of having done something that society would sanction. In this sense shame is a reaction to the fear of the judgement of others. In fact, in some circumstances, lojja is used as a synonym for 'people would speak badly'. So, for example, a girl will not ride a bicycle on her way to school because 'lojja lagbe' ('she will feel ashamed') but also because 'lok kharap bolbe' ('people will speak badly of her'). Equally, a young bride wouldn't wear *salwar kameez* (the dress of unmarried females) in public because 'lojja lagbe' but also because 'lok kharap bolbe'. It seems that shame is used by adolescents and adults in different situations to mean a sense of social impropriety. People of different ages and social backgrounds feel ashamed when they do or say something inappropriate in front of others, or occupy a place that is not theirs, or do something wrong or bad.

Mira, an 18-year-old student, gave me quite an interesting explanation of what shame means. She linked it to the social norms that prevent people from showing their feelings publicly. She said that girls have to show lojja, have to be reserved and show embarrassment in some situations. She illustrated this with the example of a man who had to send his sick wife back to her parents for treatment. He had to do it because if he expressed care and affection and kept his wife with him, he would have felt ashamed. Mira said that lojja is like a '*samajik* purdah', a social curtain, a way of covering up.

This definitely takes us away from an exclusively psychological interpretation of shame as being linked to an interiorized feeling of inadequacy and a devalued image of self. During my time in Bangladesh I came across many self-confident girls who nevertheless experienced embarrassment and unease when they were 'caught' in spaces, situations and attitudes they were not supposed to be in. On the other hand, lojja does not only correspond to a personal feeling and even less to a lack of self-esteem. As Mira said, lojja is a social curtain, something that women (and men alike) may draw around their emotions as a means to accommodate samajik (societal) norms while at the same time protecting their own feelings and thoughts. Scott's (1985) idea of 'on stage' public situations is useful here for it reminds us that when people conform to what is socially required they do not necessarily lose their own feelings, thoughts and emotions. Girls 'understand' and are aware of the fact that there are contexts and channels that allow self-expression, and others that do not. For example, Renu told me that because of lojja, a girl would not tell her mother that she was unhappy with the man chosen to be her husband. However, she would tell her *bhabi* (elder brother's wife) who is then expected to report to the girl's mother. Playing out lojja in attitudes of shyness and embarrassment may allow girls to manipulate situations to their own advantage behind a public façade of passivity and compliance. The same is true for the practice of veiling which, as we will see later, is used by female college students as a means to keep intact their reputation and at the same time be more mobile.

Spaces and Forms of Interaction in the Village

From what has been said it is clear that samaj as a moral community exercises strong social pressure on households and individuals. This is also partly due to the spatial structure of the village itself and the kind of interaction it allows and determines. The way daily life is organised at the village level favours a great deal of interaction between people belonging to the same neighbourhood (para) and influences greatly the modalities of socialisation of children and adolescents. Even if joint families are a minority in Tarapur, the houses of brothers are located close to each other and they often share the same courtyard. Only a few families, who were considered particularly religious, observe purdah strictly and have their courtyards surrounded with a sort of fence made of bamboo and dry leaves to prevent outsiders from looking in.[10] Despite the fact that women's and mature girls' mobility is very limited outside the village, especially *notun bou* (new brides) who rarely leave the para, women actually interact with a lot of people during the day. They perform most of their domestic chores in the courtyard and are constantly under the eyes of their neighbours, who are usually relatives.

As discussed in Chapter 3, those who are not related by blood or affinity are incorporated anyway in a relational network as members of the group of one's attyio swajan (one's own people). People therefore have very little privacy as a family and as individuals in a village. Children and adolescents interact with many adults besides their parents and close relatives. Uncles, aunts, sisters-in-law and neighbours, all exert some control over children and young boys and girls, as they represent the virtual presence of the broader samaj, the moral community, whom every individual belongs to. Everyone knows what happens in the households of the same para and those who for status, age, wealth or work reasons are in a position of hierarchical superiority feel naturally authorised not only to know but to interfere in the 'private' business of their neighbours. This interference may vary from suggesting that is it time to marry a young daughter, to advising about a possible partner, and helping to arrange the marriage or choose a suitable husband. After a few months in the village I realised how much I was constantly 'observed'. In response to my complaint about this I was quoted the following proverb: 'If someone asks you what you have eaten, you have to answer rice and lentils'. Lentils are usually eaten at the end of a meal and in this way you will discourage your interlocutor from posing further questions.

Kin and Intergenerational Relations

In the context described above, children start participating in the social life of the neighbourhood very early and the group of attiyo swajan plays an important role together with the parental family in their upbringing. In the West it is particularly during adolescence that the individual develops significant social relations other than the familial ones, and friends assume a growing importance in daily life and in the process of affective and cognitive growth of boys and girls.

In Tarapur, children and teenagers are socialised to relate to neighbours, relatives, parents and attiyo swajan, but these relationships are not egalitarian. They are shaped by the principles of age hierarchy. These require manifestations of respect to the oldest from the youngest while the youngest expects, as in a patron–client relationship, that his or her needs are taken care of. So parents are credited as knowing where the well-being of their children lies and how to ensure it. This implies that expressions of wishes and preferences by sons and daughters in important life choices, like marriage and work, are regarded as improper. Children of both sexes are not encouraged to develop personal goals that may conflict with their parents' expectations. The principles of hierarchy are part of a moral system where 'acting on one's own views…is regarded as willfullness and a kind of ethical egotism. Ability to submit to the will of elders is similar to selflessness' (Kaviraj 2004: 103). Taking initiative, as in looking for a marriage partner, is equated to a lack of respect for parents and a threat to their man shonman, even in cases where the partner chosen might meet the economic and social criteria expected by the parents. It is the duty of the parents to find partners as they are best placed to know their children's character. I found plenty of examples of this trusting and loyal attitude to parents during conversations with boys and girls about marriage. They expressed complete trust in the choice of their parents because 'they love us and they know what is best for us'. Girls are expected to be more compliant towards their parents than boys. From the cases that I describe in detail in Chapter 7, it appears that conflict between generations over important life choices tends to be managed by both sides in a way that avoids direct confrontation.

Friends and Mates

Besides the hierarchical forms of interaction which characterise the village, attending school favours the establishment of more egalitarian relationships with school or playmates who are identified as friends. The Bengali word for friend is bondhu, literally, 'one who is tied', a term that belonged originally to the domain of kinship. Inden and Nicholas (1977) report that in the sixteenth century bondhu was used in some contexts as a synonym of attiyo swajan. Kaviraj (2004) observes the existence of models of friendship in the traditional Bengali literature as reflecting and inspiring a reality where friends were made 'either in pursuit of a common caste profession or within the circle of friendship'. Caste and hierarchical rules discouraged forms of 'modern sociability' and 'disallowed intimacy and friendships across the boundaries of caste and kin' (ibid.: 110). He argues that in 20th-century Bengal some economic and structural changes occurred that affected mainly the urban upper classes. This led to a loosening of the ties with the paternal family and kin and the emergence of forms of modern sociability. Friendship developed among students, school and classmates, and among professionals and state officers posted away from their natal villages in distant urban locations and in need of new solidarities. Interestingly, Kaviraj sees this process as entailing 'individual differentiation'. While kin do not necessarily share preferences and interests, 'relations with friends are based on similarity of temperament and intellectual inclination', on sharing a similar occupation. In short, on an appreciation of one's individual personality and character (ibid.: 112).

In rural Tarapur, familial and lineage linkages still prevail. I did not hear adults referring to someone as a bondhu, apart from a few cases such as the wealthy and educated principal of the college who referred to his wife as his best 'friend'. He used the term friend to stress the companionship aspect of their relationship. In general, the term bondhu seems to carry a dangerous ambiguity because it can be used to identify a friend but also a boyfriend or a girlfriend, and this raises suspicion of some illicit relationship. I noticed that, especially for adults, the word is so vague that it fails to convey a precise meaning that would allow people to make sense of it. I had a group of friends visiting me for Eid holidays and I was asked by some of my acquaintances in the village the usual question: *'apnar ki hoe?'* (*'Who are they for you or how are they related to you?'*). I was obliged to give a detailed description of the circumstances in which we met, of the reasons that brought them to Bangladesh, and of the nature of the relationship between the two men and the woman that composed the group. This obligation arose because my immediate answer was that they were my friends—a response that was found unconvincing and fuzzy.

The use of the term bondhu is common among adolescents and unmarried youth who use it to identify classmates, neighbours and also boy/girl friends. Often, however, they prefer to use the English word 'friend'. The development of 'friendships' not based on kinship ties (real or fictitious) amongst boys is favoured because they are school or college mates, and because they often meet to play football or cricket, activities that are not usually performed by married men. Girls, as I have stated earlier, have more limited opportunities to leave the neighbourhood and limited access to spaces outside the village. Still, they value the possibility of sharing their *moner kota* (inner thoughts/ feelings) with peers of the same sex, usually relatives, neighbours or school mates. Cross-gender friendship is rarer, even if college students of both sexes boast of having friends of both sexes.This will be discussed more extensively later in describing the spaces for interaction opened up by higher education.The village undoubtedly offers less legitimate and culturally sanctioned spaces for the development of cross-gender friendships or intimacies, even if behind the samajik purdah of lojja both boys and girls engage in a wide range of more or less 'illegal' (as they themselves call them) interactions.

THE CHOICE OF A MARRIAGE PARTNER, EDUCATION AND CLASS

As we have seen, a central point in the 'emergence' of adolescence for girls is the postponement of their marriage. However, the fact that girls marry later is only one aspect of marriage practices worth considering in relation to adolescence. Issues surrounding the choice of a marriage partner, such as the criteria that inform the decisions and the question of who is in charge of deciding, are also important. This is relevant given the emphasis in western approaches to adolescence on the idea that adolescents gradually develop the capacity to assume responsibility for life decisions, such as engaging in affective and intimate relationships and choosing a life partner. In rural Bangladesh, a form of arranged marriage prevails that excludes boys and girls from being involved in the decision of when and whom they marry. Parents are in charge of these decisions and their choices are informed by different considerations and criteria. In what follows I discuss some of the main considerations underlying the importance of the economic background of a household in deciding about their children marriage and education.

As soon as a girl is considered boyoshko, after menarche and sometime even before it, her family may start receiving marriage proposals for her. Poor parents, whose daughters are not attending school, are likely to consider these proposals seriously. Others may refuse them because their daughters are still studying, despite the worries about what people might think: 'the "samaj" will say…such a big girl and still at home, there must be something wrong with her, she must have done something bad…'. Neutralising the pressure and the gossiping is difficult but not impossible as long as a girl is still studying, and this is a justification used by rich and poor parents alike. For a while, parents may want to escape the pressure of the samaj without having to openly contest it, and while waiting for a better suitor for their daughter or to accumulate the money to pay for her dowry. Better off families tend to view their daughters' education as a status enhancer, precisely in relation to marriage, and are willing to postpone marriage until higher qualifications such as HSC or a university degree is obtained.

The case of Shirin exemplifies this. Shirin's household belongs to the group of borolok households of the Morol para. Shirin's mother, besides being busy trying to keep a number of boys away from her daughter, was also very worried about the poor school results of Shirin and her older sister. Once, while discussing this with me, she complained that the family's priority with regard to their daughters' education was to make them get a certificate for the sake of the family's prestige.

I am very worried about the two of them, they do not want to study, we have to force them. All our relatives are educated [then follows a list of relatives and their study achievements]. If they do not manage to get the certificate we will become the last ones.

Throughout 2002 and 2003, Shirin's parents received several marriage offers for Shirin but they dismissed them all. Shirin once told me that her parents had lied, telling everyone that she wasn't shekna (mature) yet.

Conversely, for households of a lower socio-economic background, sending a daughter to high school after the first five years of primary education seems to be a socially acceptable way of delaying her marriage in order to find a better partner for her in the future. Renu was in grade 10 at the local high school. She also had an older sister who had studied up to grade nine before being married because as her brother said: 'Her school results were not so good and then she was growing too old so it was time for her to get married.' Renu did not sit the final SSC exam in 2003. For over a year her brothers had been busy looking for a husband for her and throughout my stay in the village she had been busy working in the fields or helping her mother at home rather than studying. Eventually she was married off in 2004. Although her parents were financially in a position to pay for her study, they no longer felt it worthwhile to invest in her education.

Girls from the more vulnerable households, such as those that have been defined as 'poor' or 'extremely poor' (see Chapter 2), are likely not to attend school for more than a few years because their parents will try to marry them as soon as possible. Normally, in this way a lesser amount of dowry is required. In these cases, the immediate costs of educating girls are directly compared with the costs of a dowry and even if the latter is normally higher, it is considered a more secure investment for the future. It is in these cases where the preference for educating sons becomes more apparent. Raju's mother had to sell a pair of earrings, her last piece of jewellery, to pay the fees for her son's matriculation exam. A girl's parents in the same situation might have found it more convenient to save the money for her dowry.

The socio-economic condition of the family matters a lot with respect to when girls marry and to their level of schooling, especially at the two extremes of the socio-economic ladder. This is not so obvious in the case of boys. Educated and well-off parents have the economic means and enough motivation to encourage their sons' education up to the level of a masters degree. They can usually afford accommodation in town where honours degree courses are available and they often have enough good connections (jogajog) to then secure white collar jobs, or good business jobs for their sons. Poorer parents hope that higher education, at least a simple university degree, would open opportunities of employment in local NGOs, teaching or any other kind of chakri (paid employment). Thus they would be willing to invest in their sons' education, as Prodip's father did, because this would enhance the possibility of improving their own situation. They will not have to pay for their sons' dowry. On the contrary, they will be in a stronger position in premarital negotiations if their sons have a good level of education. Only extremely poor parents will willingly stop their sons' education after a few years to employ them in farming.

It is the groom's family that dictates the terms of the exchange in marriage negotiations, and the respective level of education of the proposed husband and wife is an important element to be considered. It is preferable that the husband's level of education is slightly higher than the girl's, but a similar level is also acceptable. I was told by a group of NGO women members that very poor girls will probably have no other choice but to marry a poor peasant, sharecropper or daily labourer who will very likely be illiterate. In this case, if the bride had some years of schooling, her status would be too high compared to that of her husband and her education could become an obstacle instead of an advantage for her and her family.

This could also partially explain why many girls, like Renu and her sister, are withdrawn from school just before taking the final exam at the end of the first secondary course (this is reflected in the national statistics that show a high drop-out rate at the end of the first secondary course and a lower drop-out rate at higher levels). Obtaining the SSC might make a marriage match more difficult. This was confirmed by a group of college teachers who said that parents try to get their daughters through the secondary school course, or at least up to the 10th year of schooling, because this enhances the possibility of a good marriage. However, most of the girls are withdrawn before they get the final certificate because this could instead be an obstacle to marriage. The final SSC exam is also considered quite difficult to pass and this perception is supported by official national statistics: the pass rate was 35.22 in 2001, 40.66 in 2002 and 35.91 in 2003 (BANBEIS 2007).

They will be able to say and let everybody know that their daughter is studying in class 8 or 9 and they will start receiving interesting marriage proposals. At the same time they will be able to save some money for dowry or for buying some gold ornaments with the stipend[11]. They won't spend so much on books because they · are not actually interested in their daughters' learning. Before the SSC exam they will marry their daughters off because they know that anyway they won't pass the exam. In this way they won't have to pay the exam fee.

The decision to support girls' education, including secondary school, is thus tied in complex ways to finding an appropriate marriage partner. A group of girls attending grade 10 at a high school in Tarapur reported that in grade 6 there were about 40 students in the class, but only 12 had enrolled in grade 10. While a few girls had moved to another school, the majority of those who had left had stopped studying in order to get married.

Among middle and rich households, too, the right timing of a daughter's marriage is an important concern. A woman with graduate or post-graduate degree risks being too old to find a suitable partner, with the probability of finding her a highly educated husband becoming rather low. This is why many intermediate or degree college students are already married; it is usually the woman's husband's choice to allow his wife to continue her studies post marriage. An overeducated daughter-in-law may enhance the status of the husband's family even if their economic condition does not require a new earning member.

Summing up, the growth of girls' education implies that post puberty girls are not always inevitably married off. Their lives follow different trajectories, in the interlinked educational and marriage careers that depend to a great extent, although not exclusively, on the socio-economic background of their families. The experience of female adolescence is therefore far from homogeneous. Most of the girls, as we have seen, stop studying before the matriculation exam and only a minority go on to higher secondary education at intermediate colleges, with a view to continuing their studies up to university. These students are more likely to experience adolescence as a period of transition before adulthood than those who get married before completing the secondary school course. Girls attending the last years of high school with the perspective of stopping their study before or soon after matriculation are aware to a great extent that education is not going to make a significant difference in their lives. During conversations with a group of girls attending grades 8 or 9, I asked them to tell me how they visualised their future. A typical response was 'we will cook at our in laws'. They also confirmed that the main reason why girls stop studying early is mainly samajik (social). In this regard they also drew a clear line between town and village life, presenting them as two different environments and two different worlds. 'In town it would be different but in the village you have to get married soon. If we could study in town, it would be possible for our parents to escape the pressure of the samaj, but in a village this is impossible'. This distinction between village and town reflects another distinction, that between school and college/university, discussed in the next chapter.

THE ARENAS FOR 'ADOLESCENCE' IN TARAPUR

In line with the literature on life stages in Bangladesh, puberty is understood in Tarapur as entailing emotional, physical and sexual changes for both boys and girls. Both genders are considered incapable of controlling their impulses, but girls as well as women are perceived as dangerous sources of sexual temptation. As a consequence, their mobility and visibility must be controlled and constrained. Puberty is experienced by girls as a turning point that signals the beginning of a phase in their life characterised by the need for enhanced social and parental control over their activities. As a result, their social and physical worlds tend to become narrower. Girls are encouraged to withdraw and become less visible. The performance of lojja becomes the virtual curtain that conceals their personalities and individualities as well as their physical bodies.

However, adolescent girls, contrary to the perspective of earlier ethnographies, are not the mute products of a socialisation process. The discussion of the practice of lojja and Mira's comments about it suggest that even younger girls do not simply reproduce passively conventional social roles. They use lojja to show modesty and submissiveness but this does not mean they lack awareness of the situations and channels through which they can more openly express themselves.

In terms of physical development a girl is already considered 'grown up' and ready for adult responsibilities at puberty. For boys, instead, now as in the past, the acquisition of full adult responsibilities is mainly linked to the economic capacity to sustain their own families. For them marriage is postponed until they can demonstrate this capacity. However, for both genders adulthood is not seen as the result of a linear process of growth. Similar to the concept of 'understanding', adulthood is contextual and implies specific kinds of entitlements and the assumption or attribution of responsibilities, which can transcend what is considered the 'traditional' division of labour. So while on the one hand a girl is not considered an adult until she is married, on the other hand even a limited experience at school is deemed to enhance her capacity to 'understand' and as such is part of the process of growing up. Education for boys is also viewed as an asset that enhances their capacity to 'understand'. This leads me to question Kotalova's argument that the capacity to understand is limited simply to being able to 'relate properly to people', which carries overtones of learning in a conformist passive fashion. I would suggest instead that the capacity to understand, from the point of view of the villagers of Tarapur, entails the capacity to 'actively' adapt in the sense that the individual comes to know the contours of the social environment to which he/she belongs and how to negotiate his/her claims and obligations within it. The next chapter discusses this in greater depth, with reference to the importance that college students attribute to education as entitling them to a wider capacity to make choices and to become responsible full members of the samaj.

There is an hegemonic discourse that correlates puberty and marriage and puts strong pressure on girls to conform. However, the reality is changing and other competing views are emerging. Only very poor and vulnerable households marry off their daughters at the onset of puberty (12–13 years of age) after a few years of schooling. For the majority of girls, 16 to 17 years is becoming the new accepted age limit for marriage. A minority of adolescent females continue studying after matriculation and for them college education, as we will see in the chapters that follow, opens more visible spaces for change. For those who get married at 16 to 17, little has changed: the short period between puberty and marriage is intended as a time for learning one's place in society and especially one's future responsibilities as a wife. Purdah circumscribes opportunities for 'experimentation'.

There are thus important areas of continuity with the past, in terms of the dominant view about the proper age of marriage and the transition to adulthood of both boys and girls. The social world of adolescent boys and girls married after a few years of schooling, their experiences, and their sense of selfhood seem to be better understood in relation to a more 'traditional' life direction inside the network of social relations that characterise the village environment. But processes of economic and social change occurring beyond villages are opening up physical and social spaces for different experiences. I would argue that this is particularly evident for boys and girls who attend intermediate college to obtain a degree, and then access better employment opportunities.

Having established that adolescence is emerging in temporal terms with different modalities for boys and girls in rural Bangladesh, in the next three ethnographic chapters I explore how Tarapur's young people experience it, the meanings they attach to these experiences and the ways in which processes of self-definition and acquisition of social identity occur. In the light of the literature discussed in Chapter 1, it makes sense to ask to what extent the delay in marriage and work opens up a stage of adolescence as 'a way of life between childhood and adulthood' (Erikson 1968: 128). This stage represents an arena where young people may distance themselves from the kind of social relations that characterised childhood and occupy wider social spaces. The transition to adulthood is also conceptualised as a period during which girls and boys have to accomplish a series of developmental tasks. These are all oriented towards a gradual definition of who they are and the assumption of social responsibility within their specific context. In this process, adolescents are part of a network of social relations that includes many significant others in different domains, such as the family, school and peers, work and so forth.

There are three main arenas in which to look at these processes and they are what I focus on in the following three chapters. First, in Chapter 5, I examine more closely the life of college students and explore their experiences and perceptions. I look at college as a physical space, which provides new opportunities for contact and interaction, and as a social space, which facilitates the formation of boys' and girls' identities. Education and being a college student may allow boys and girls to develop expectations, dreams and life plans where they see themselves as capable of choice. This may also open new opportunities for peer group relations, which may constitute a challenge to the kind of hierarchical social relations described in Chapter 3.

The second relevant arena concerns adolescents' emotional and affective experiences linked to the development of interest in, and attraction towards, the other sex. In Chapter 6, I look at how different kinds of *somporkkho* (rapport, relationship) are lived by both young and old adolescents, even within limited village boundaries. The diffusion of the media and the way love, marriage and relationships are represented in 'modern' dramas constitute a further element that contributes to the emergence of new discourses and new practices in the field of emotions, love and relationships amongst younger and older teenagers.

In Chapter 7, I focus on marriage arrangements. This is an important terrain for the discussion on the transition to adulthood and the formation of one's social identity. According to the literature discussed in Chapter 1, part of adolescence consists precisely of a gradual development of the capacity to enter into intimate relationships and to choose one's life partner. Few case studies will shed light on some aspects of marriage practices and especially on the choice of when and whom to marry. This will help to explore what, if any, spaces exist in the context of arranged marriages for choice and self-assertion.

NOTES

1.   Primary education comprises grades 1 to 5. Secondary education is divided into first secondary and higher secondary. First secondary education comprises grades 6 to 10. At the end of grade 10, the students have to sit for a final exam; if they pass it they obtain a Secondary School Certificate (SSC). Classes 6 to 10 are attended at so-called high schools. The number of high schools has been increasing in the area, so that the students who attend classes 6 to 10 do not have to cover a great distance to reach them. Higher secondary education comprises grades 11 to 12. At the end of the 12th year, the students have to pass a final exam to get a Higher Secondary Certificate (HSC). Classes 11 to 12 are attended at so-called intermediate colleges. They are less in number and the students usually reach them by bus, or by cycle, or by van (a local substitute of the rickshaw that is used to transport both goods and people). I will refer to classes 6 to 10 as high school and to classes 11 to 12 as

intermediate college. A regular student would start high school (class 6) at the age of approximately 11 to 12 and finish high school at approximately 16 to 17. Intermediate college students are 17 to 19 years old. The two year Intermediate college course corresponds to the sixth form college of the English school system.

2. Aziz and Maloney's study is based on life stories collected from 65 male and female respondents in 1978 in Matlab Thana, Comilla district. Kotalova's ethnography was conducted among a peasant community in the village of Gameranga in Faridpur district, in 1983.

3. The view that adolescence is a time of turmoil and emotionality is also common in India (Verma and Larson 1999).

4. Government statistics on documented migration estimate that 3.7 million Bangladeshis have emigrated during the past 30 years and about 3 million—or 6 per cent of the in-country economically active population—are currently living abroad.

5. *Shisukal* (infancy), *balyakal* (school age), *kaisorer prarambha* (pre-adolescence), *kaisor* (early adolescence), nabajuban (late adolescence), *purnajauban* (young adulthood), *madhyamkal* (middle age), *briddhakal* (old age), and *marankal* (literally, time to die).

6. As explained in Chapter 2, the structure in the labour market in south-west Bangladesh has not changed as much as in the eastern parts of the country. Farming remains an important activity and the share of low-paid daily waged workers is high (World Bank 2008a)

7. Osella and Osella (2002: 119) notice that bodily heat and strong sexual desire are, in Kerala, an attribute of both young males and females, in contrast to what appears from other anthropological sources, where women are depicted as more prone to it.

8. UNICEF and other organisations are currently running a programme for the registration of births.

9. First she was cheated by a boy she trusted as he was her own child. He ran away with the Tk 5,000 she lent him. She subsequently obtained a loan from an NGO but the chickens she bought from that money died of illness. She is now indebted to the organisation for more than Tk 4,000.

10. There are regional variations in this respect. Gardner (1995) gives an account of a much more strict observance of purdah in spatial terms in Sylhet.

11. This refers to the sum paid biannually by the government to girls with good school results up to grade 12.

FIVE

Being a College Student
New Social Spaces and New Forms
of Consciousness

*'Girls are getting educated and they can mix with boys, there is a
lot of change going on for them…'*

Ramesh

*'My biggest hope for the future is to study and grow as a good
human being. It is the same for everyone.'*

Fatima

*'Our appearance can worsen with age but if we get a job, this will
stay.'*

Shompa

INTRODUCTION

In the previous chapter I discussed how a more prolonged transition to
adulthood arises out of the postponement of girls' and boys' marriage,
mainly due to the prolonging of their education. For girls, in particular,
passing the matriculation exam at the end of high school and accessing
higher secondary education constitute a significant life event and a
significant shift in life trajectory. This chapter focuses on teenage boys
and girls enrolled in higher secondary education, and, more precisely,
on those attending intermediate colleges (grades 11 to 12). Unlike
their younger counterparts who stop studying in order to get married,
girls who enrol at college develop more complex and differentiated

expectations for their future and consider education an important instrument of personal growth and self-affirmation. Boys do not marry as early as girls and it is more common for them to proceed to college. Unless they fail the matriculation exams more than once, or unless their parents have an immediate need for an additional source of work or income, they enrol at college with the view to continue studying for a degree or a masters degree. Most boys aspire to acquire qualifications for a white collar job, even if only a few of them achieve such a position. Some of them end up joining their father's activities, or being employed by local NGOs.

In this chapter I explore college as a physical and social gendered space. I also look at the ways in which college opens to boys and girls opportunities to live adolescence not only as a period of preparation for adult roles, but also as one of search for one's direction in life. As students, both boys and girls experience being young differently and this contributes to the enhancement of their self-confidence. It also enlarges their opportunities to exercise more choice in forging their lives in relation to their parents' wishes or social norms.

I begin my discussion with how attending college and the very journey to reach school provide social spaces that favour new same gender and cross-gender encounters and acquaintances. I discuss the development of same-sex friendships among boys and girls and the characteristics of peer group socialisation and activities, underlying how boys and girls occupy private and public spaces differently. Then I explore the effects of being a college student, focusing on the meaning and value given by students to education, their aspirations for the future in terms of occupation and the actual opportunities they have to negotiate relations with parents, peers and the opposite sex. These latter negotiations may or may not be different from the hegemonic ones. I focus particularly on how students conceptualise dependence and independence, and how they view themselves in relation to important life choices.

ATTENDING COLLEGE: NEW AND CONTESTED GENDERED SPACES

Tagore College was founded in 1995 by the director of a local NGO. It is now legally recognised and partly funded by the state. Since its inception, the college has offered a two-year course (11th and 12th year)[1] after which the students obtain an intermediate certificate in arts, science or commerce. Over the years, Tagore college has created for itself a good reputation in terms of teachers' commitment and dedication to work, and for having banned successfully any form of student involvement in politics.[2] Moreover, the college is distinct from other institutions: to motivate the students it offers free textbooks to both boys and girls, and tries to build a close rapport with their families.

Begum Rokeya College, situated in Tala, is a girls college and was also founded as a private institution by a group of teachers. It is now recognised and receives state funding. Like Tagore College, it tries to motivate poor households especially to enrol girls, giving basic textbooks free of charge to the poorest. It has also run a degree course since its inception. In both colleges, low fee supplementary classes, run by the same teachers, allow essential extra tuition even for poor students, who would not be able to afford the widely prevalent system of private tuition.

The students are drawn from throughout Tala sub-district and town, and the vast majority of them take between 20 minutes to an hour and a half to reach the colleges. In October 2001, there were approximately 300 students registered in the first and second years in the mixed college, of which just 30 were female. In the other college there were about 250 girls but most of them, as I was told, did not attend classes regularly and some of them were never present. Around 30 per cent of the girls were married. Out of 150 enrolled in the second year, only 82 filled in the forms to sit for the final exams.

In October 2002, I distributed a questionnaire in the two colleges to assess the socio-economic position of the students.[3] This included a question that asked them to self-assess their situation. Five options were given: (*a*) very poor, overall situation very bad; (*b*) poor but able to survive in some way; (*c*) poor but able to satisfy basic needs; (*d*) middle level (majhari); (*e*) rich (dhoni).

The socio-economic conditions of the boys' families at Tagore varied significantly. The majority (67) were majhari or rich; 39 boys belonged to the third category; 40 were poor; and 17 extremely poor. There were far fewer girls. However, most (14 out of 20) came from majhari households, four from the second category and only two considered themselves very poor. In the girls' college I could only manage to distribute the questionnaire to 83 girls out of about 250 registered in the first and second year. Of them, 62 defined their households as majhari or dhoni, 13 considered themselves poor but able to satisfy basic needs, 7 were poor, and only 1 extremely poor. The results of this small investigation suggest that class is one factor that conditions, and more so in the case of girls. However, it must be underlined that both colleges are partially privately funded, have been set up by voluntary organisations, and, unlike government colleges where only girls receive a stipend, they offer incentives to poorer boys that probably encourages their enrolment and attendance.

New Social Spaces

Primary and high school offers a social space for school children to develop friendships with classmates of the same sex and it also allows limited cross-gender interaction during lessons and at the school premises. However, this social space is highly constrained. High schools are likely to be very close to one's village so that most of the students know each other or mix mainly with those who come from the same village or neighbourhood. Parental control is favoured by the proximity of the school and by the fact that the teachers belong to the same community and are known to parents. In their free time between classes, boys play cricket and football in the courtyard or use the common spaces in the school, while girls tend to go back home. So for girls who do not continue studying beyond high school and get married only a few years after puberty, little has changed. Their short period as unmarried adolescents is intended as a time for learning their future duties and responsibilities as wives. Purdah circumscribes the opportunities for mobility and social interactions. Social control in the village is favoured by the lack of privacy and the continuous interaction that adolescents have not only with their parents but also with their neighbours, relatives and attiyo swajan (one's own people, see discussion in Chapter 3).

Attending college away from the village opens up new spaces. Colleges are usually further away from the homes of most students and thus going to college gives both boys and girls a chance to move away from their usual network of acquaintances. They are allowed, as part of their new acknowledged status as college students, to be away for some time from the environment where they have grown up and legitimately enter spaces where different practices can take place.

The distance of the two colleges from most of the students' homes is at the same time a source of difficulty and of opportunities, and both are strongly gendered. For girls, the distance they have to cover every day is a source of inconvenience and insecurity. They all emphasised, especially during our first meetings, the problems and the risks. While boys can travel by bike or by bus, girls are forbidden to ride bicycles and would feel ashamed if they did. They do not like to use crowded buses where they may be physically and verbally harassed by men. Moreover, some of the villages are not directly connected to the main road and students have to walk a distance. Apart from the physical effort, girls perceive the road as an insecure space and blame boys and men for this. During a discussion with a mixed group of boys and girls, the latter expressed freely their difficulties while the boys seemed to understand their complaints only partially.

Merhuna (girl): *Of course we feel bad because we would like to be more independent but we cannot. Girls cannot get around freely. We cannot rebel against this situation, we will get into trouble because not all the boys are good.*

Prodip (boy): *There are a lot of stupid boys, so even if they (girls) really want it (be more free) they cannot go out.*

Areef (boy): *It often happens that you can see a girl in the street and some stupid boys try to approach her.*

During the same group discussion, Merhuna referred to acid attacks as an example of the violence women are subjected to.

Merhuna: *Boys can do what they want, girls cannot. A lot of boys would force you (to have a sexual relationship), they do a lot by force.*
Areef: *No, nothing happens by force.*
Merhuna: *Just have a look at the newspapers and see. A girl who refuses a boy can be disfigured by acid.*

Girls, in line with dominant public discourses, identify unemployed youth as the main source of danger. Taslima exemplified a common concern saying that the only danger on her way home is represented by some 'bad boys who sit doing nothing at Tala bazar and shout at girls when they pass by'. I was told the same by Shompa who also commented that 'to avoid being disturbed I keep my eyes down and I do not talk to anybody'. All these worries are surely justified. Between 2000 and 2003, three cases of acid violence were recorded in the sub-district. All of them concerned female college students approached by males as they made their way to school and all harassed with propositions of a love affair.

Veiling (wearing burqa) is one of the strategies that many girls use to feel safer, as it allows them to remove themselves from the gaze of others. Veiling allows them to keep going out, be mobile, avoid violence and deflect criticisms from other members of the samaj. Provided they maintain a modest attitude, girls can actually experience the new spaces in positive ways. Travelling offers some opportunities to prolong the time that can be spent out of the village without reprimand. On a few occasions I travelled with some girls to their villages and I noticed how confidently they behaved all the way along and how they answered people's questions about me, introducing me as their English teacher. Tala market, apparently a potentially dangerous place, turned out to be also the place where both male and female students of both colleges went to buy books and cosmetics during their free time. Some of them used to attend computer classes in a small shop where they could talk indiscriminately with male and female friends.

In the mixed college, physical separation between boys and girls coexists with other innovative initiatives. The courtyard informally belongs to the boys who spend their free time there chatting in groups, while the girls have a room of their own for studying and chatting. There, the girls enjoy much more freedom than in the more controlled neighbourhood or in their homes. No male can enter this space without their permission. The girls, however, are free to leave the space. They can also observe boys from their room, comment on them, share their likes and dislikes with the group and eventually go out and hang around on the verandah. Here they can exchange information with the boys about exams, class routines, homework, and so forth.

In the classroom, boys and girls usually sit separately but nobody would reproach them if they did the opposite. During my spoken English classes the girls were initially very shy when I asked them to participate in role playing or group discussion activities with their male classmates. After the lesson their immediate reaction was to request me to split the group into two and have single-sex classes because 'we feel ashamed'. After some discussion, however, they concluded that they would rather face the problem and try to overcome their shame.

Being a student also allows boys and girls more opportunities to meet outside college. As classmates, boys are allowed to visit girls at home to study together and help each other with homework. Boys and girls go together on school trips and participate together at public events in town, like rallies or meetings at religious or political festivals.

Even the students in the girls' college seemed to find places where they could freely express themselves. They were more open with me at college and far more reserved when I visited them at home. During meetings with me, they were extremely curious about the differences between what they called 'western culture' and 'amader (our) culture'. A minority stressed their Islamic belonging through their dress and attitudes. Some claimed that they preferred religious programmes or the news to romantic comedies that they consider non-Islamic. They explained their choice of wearing burqa as a way to obey a religious dictate: 'It is because of our 'dharma' (religion); it is written in the Koran'.

Wearing a burqa does not necessarily go hand in hand with a shy and shameful attitude. On the contrary, most of the girls in both colleges interacted freely with male and female school mates, with the teachers and the administrative staff. In doing so they demonstrated a lot of self-confidence. In Begum Rokeya College, towards the end of the school year, a day long *onusthan* (celebration/ceremony/gathering) was organised that consisted of different games and competitions involving teachers and students. This was followed by a meal. On this occasion, a group of girls staged a short theatrical performance. Those who played male characters dressed in jeans and t-shirts—clothes that girls would never dare to wear either at home or in the village spaces. At college, however, they were not embarrassed wearing them.

In both colleges, the importance of purdah (of which wearing burqa is only one aspect) was stressed by the same students. During group discussions students referred directly to Islamic law and precepts as a source of norms or behaviour. In the village and among adult women there does not seem to be a correspondence between economic condition or social status and a more or less accentuated observance of purdah, expressed by wearing burqa in public spaces. In the Tala area, well-off families such as the ones of Morol para in Tarapur, seem to adhere to a secular mentality and code of conduct. One strategy to achieve this is to refer to 'Bengali culture' rather than to Islam when explaining certain practices. Local NGOs play an important role in reinforcing the idea of a common cultural belonging, secular in nature and not exclusive to any communal group. Both Tagore and Begum Rokeya Colleges intentionally recruit teachers from all three religious communities represented in the area: Muslim, Hindu and Christian. Some of the teachers in both the colleges also work for local NGOs. In this context, many Muslim girls belonging to well-off families feel proud to show a modern, secularist attitude even in the way they dress. The majority of them, as I will discuss later, view education as linked to wider employment opportunities.

Peer Relations and Friendship

Being a student and being more mobile implies significant new opportunities for interaction and relationships between boys and girls. As discussed in Chapter 1, the formation of same-sex or cross-gender groups of boys and girls sharing school-based common experiences and leisure activities is considered by many theorists of adolescence to be an important feature of the process of identity formation. This is so because it widens the adolescents' social world and 'distances' them from the network of relationships that characterise infancy and childhood. In the South Asian context, Osella and Osella (1998) talk of 'cinema culture' in which Malayali young men's socialisation is nurtured through group outings to the cinema. Nisbett (2004) describes and discusses the activities of a group of friends around a cyber café in Bangalore. These authors underline the egalitarian character of these relationships that cross-cut community and class and view young people's friendships as a challenge to prevalent norms of hierarchy. In the Tala area, college students seem to constitute a peer group, but one that is organised by age categories and associated with particular spaces of interaction. In these contexts, the idiom of community and family-based social relations is less forceful.

I came to know a particular group of male friends (bondhu)[4] very well. The core members were: Prodip, Nasser, Sharif, Montu, Kamal, Francis and Joy. All except one were second-year students at Tagore in 2002–3. All of them were Muslim, except for Francis whose family belonged originally to the Rishi group but had converted to Christianity. Prodip, the poorest, played a role as leader of the group in 'love' matters and his reputation was signalled in his nickname of 'romantic hero'. The fact that he was also a good cricket player contributed to his leading role in the group. Francis and Kamal were the best academic students and everyone used to turn to them for advice while preparing for exams. Sharif was teased by the others for spending more time flirting with girls than studying. Montu was considered the most 'responsible' since he spent much of his leisure time helping his father in their shop. Joy was married, a 'love marriage', in 2002.

Prodip and his friends, like most of the male students at Tagore College, were mostly busy studying but they also had to find ways of earning their pocket money by selling vegetables at the marketplace (Sharif), helping their parents with their work (Montu), or playing football for small local teams (Prodip). Although they had clear ideas about young people's fashion and aspired to possess tight jeans, sunglasses and heavy, black leather shoes (which was the only type of shoes that they would refer to with the word '*shu*'), they could not normally afford these items. They relied on their parents giving them such gifts or waited to receive some clothes or other items during religious festivals. Despite this, dress and physical appearance were very important for them and they tried to express both a desire for conformity and a sense of uniqueness in the way they looked. As soon as Montu bought a pair of fashionable trainers, Sharif and Nasser did exactly the same. On the other hand, before Eid, Prodip went to a barber shop with the declared intention of having a haircut different from anyone else's.

For these boys, the bazaar was only a limited space for alternative socialisation: they could not afford to buy drinks or food, or even if they could, their movements would have been controlled by adults. Once Montu was seen eating sweets at a shop and was criticised by some elderly people because he used his left hand while eating. While at college or when playing football, Prodip without any lojja would take a leading role in the group, proposing and then organising new initiatives for his friends. In the village, however, he had to conform to his status as the son of a poor landless labourer. For example he had to avoid wearing items such as sunglasses and had to tolerate the high school principal reproaching him for his long hair.

During the school year, these boys spent most of the day at college attending classes but they also chatted amongst themselves and with other students during their free hours. Since the college was close to Tala town they could also visit the bazaar where, unlike in Tarapur, there was less chance of meeting known fellow villagers. Neither in Tarapur nor in Tala were there spaces for specific youth activities apart from the football grounds. In the afternoon, after a few hours of study, Prodip and his friends used to meet with others and play football or cricket. On holidays or special occasions, they would spend more time together at the bazaar commenting on the girls who passed by and eventually trying to approach them.

This suggests that these boys did not have much time to spend hanging around or doing 'time pass' as described by Nisbett (2004).

Unlike this urban group of middle-class unemployed youth, Prodip and his friends did not have many resources at their disposal, and had very few opportunity to carry out transgressive behaviours. Alcohol in the village was absolutely unavailable and smoking too expensive. Cinemas, which Osella and Osella (1998) identify as important sites for the formation of young people's identity, are considered off-limits in rural Bangladesh for both women and young men. If young people attend them often, their behaviour is disapproved of. So boys would resort to renting a video or a DVD to watch at home. This however meant that older siblings, parents and elders controlled what younger members watched.

Being a student however entailed some privileges. Prodip and his friends were not expected to help their fathers in agricultural labour. Instead, their parents tried to spare them hard work, to put them in the optimal situation to do 'their own job'. At home they were allowed more privacy than any other member of the family. Each of them had a little space of their own in their parents' house where they slept, studied and received friends. They could hide the love letters they received from girls in their drawers and decorate the mud walls of their rooms with calendars and posters portraying their favourite actresses and singers.

In the rural reality of Tarapur, young males as well as females have limited spaces for peer group sociability. Despite this, it is evident that the boys I have described here enjoy a status and a range of possibilities that are distinct from those enjoyed by their neighbours, who at the same age are not in full-time education. Sohag was a primary school classmate of Prodip. He was poor and married at 15. Since then he had been working as a sharecropper with his family. Despite his acquaintance with Prodip, he addressed him in public with the honorific form. Once he came to visit me when the whole group was present and he refused to stay, saying he would rather come again later because he felt embarrassed.

For students, friendship is associated with solidarity and with sharing concerns and experiences. This is well exemplified by the story of Joy's controversial marriage and the involvement of Sharif and Prodip. When Joy married he was about 18 and was attending the second year at college. Hameeda, his bride, was a high school student, but her parents had withdrawn her from school after discovering her involvement with Joy. Sharif and Prodip told me how they used to help Hameeda and Joy to meet secretly in the night, emphasising the risks they faced in the name of friendship. At one point, the couple eloped and went into hiding in a village 20 kilometres from Tala for a few days. Hameeda's father and brothers accused Sharif and Prodip of being Joy's accomplices in the kidnapping of their daughter and filed a case against the two boys at the local police station. After some time, Hameeda's parents accepted the fait accompli and the couple were able to settle down with Joy's parents. Although Sharif and Prodip got into trouble because of the case, in recounting the story to me they were very proud of the role they played in the whole affair. They faced the risk of being beaten by Hameeda's relatives and then of being charged with kidnapping. This however was accepted as part of the price of friendship. Although scared, they helped Joy because otherwise they would not have been 'good friends'. In their accounts, friendship was equated with brotherhood and this entailed equality, solidarity and taking risks and making sacrifices for each other.

In terms of spaces and mobility, girls were more constrained, and college constituted the only alternative to the house or the neighbourhood. What follows is an abstract from a conversation that I had at a college with a group of girls attending first year.

Madam[5]: *Where do you usually meet your friends?*

Fatima: *At college most of the time.*

Madam: *Is there any other place where you can meet your friends?*

Rina: *No nothing like a club or a park for example. The only place apart from home is the bazar at the time of Eid for example (all together).*

Dipali (hindu): *At the time of puja we can go to the temple...otherwise we can't go anywhere... But for boys there are other places.*

Madam: *Would you like to have a place to meet?*

Reka: *Of course. If there was an arrangement like that, in the afternoon we could see our friends.*

Madam: *What do you normally do in the afternoon?*

Rina: *We stay inside the house and the neighbourhood. Some girls play.*
Others: *… some study or play or help parents or sleep. The girls usually*
           play 'ludu' at home. Here girls cannot go out, people would think
           it bad (manshi kharap mone korbe). It is better if they sit at home
           and play.

Unlike boys who play in public places and can freely move in the bazaar and in the village, adolescent girls have fewer opportunities to spend time in groups doing some kind of outdoor activity. They can pass through the bazaar on their way to college or stop to buy books, but this should never occur in the evening, or without a specific purpose. Girls are more likely to spend their leisure time chatting in their rooms at home or sitting together watching TV. If their parents can afford it, they may have their own space at home and like boys they may decorate it with posters of their favourite movie heroes and heroines and pop singers.

Girls talked of friendship (*bondhutto*) mainly in terms of sharing one's intimate thoughts and feelings (moner kota). Having a good friend means having someone with whom you can talk freely and openly, someone who can be trusted. However, there are constraints. Girls do not easily permit newcomers to become intimate and stressed the importance of relationships that dated back from high school saying that long-term friends can be trusted more. Thus, while acknowledging that college opens further opportunities to meet people, girls tend to a have fewer very close long-term friends. It seems that the social control they are subjected to makes them suspicious of other girls whom they do not know, and prevents them from sharing with them their experiences, opinions and thoughts. I realised this when I noticed that in group interviews boys were more eager to speak and less worried about what the others thought of them. Girls tended to be more reserved and less direct unless they knew each other very well. Once, during a group discussion and after the majority of girls had left, the two remaining girls invited me to ask them more intimate questions if I wanted. They explained that they would not have felt comfortable answering such questions in the larger group setting.

On another occasion, when I started asking about friendships with boys, Tonu, a high caste Hindu attending the second year and a self-confident person, claimed she trusted boys more than girls. She believed that boys were more direct and sincere than girls. According to her:

It is possible to be friends with boys. Because if I manage to build a good 'somporkko'[6] (rapport, relationship, friendship) with a boy, it will be possible to talk with him of the same things I can talk with another girl…and many times girls are envious of girls, boys are not envious at all. Boys will try to make their friends happy, will try to give time to them, will look for their advantage. That's what boys want and this is why a 'bondhutto' (friendship) between a boy and a girl is a very good thing.

Tonu underlines an aspect that was also mentioned by others. There is a discourse of rivalry and competition between girls that frustrates the possibility of complete trust except in cases of very close and intimate friends. I was present during a conversation between two girls that seems to confirm Tonu's view. Mamtaj and Taslima were criticising Shompa, a classmate, because she had been seen several times walking in the marketplace with a boy. Mamtaj and Taslima remarked that 'she (Shompa) is old (18) and still in the 11th year because she does not study much, she is too busy flirting with boys'. Girls have to protect themselves from gossip, even from their own classmates and this explains their reserved attitude and the fact that they do not feel as free as boys to speak 'from the heart' (*mon theke*).

Tonu's comment on the desirability of friendship between boys and girls is also interesting because it stresses that cross-gender interactions are not always seen as implying intimate relationships; they can also simply be friendships. Cross-gender interactions take a variety of forms, ranging from friendship to intimate relationships to romance. As love relationships are explored extensively in the next chapter, here I focus on friendships. The hegemonic view about cross-gender interactions is complex. I have extensively discussed in the previous chapter all the constraints on girls' mobility and interactions from puberty onwards, constraints that arise from a belief in the strong force of adolescents' sexuality. Even college students acknowledge that contacts not justified by a specific purpose can be easily misinterpreted: 'People would say that friendship between opposite sexes is bad because it may easily end up in a love affair'. The mixed college directly supervises the interaction between boys and girls. Students are afraid of teachers who may misjudge them and eventually withdraw their support if they engage in 'illegal' relationships: 'We cannot mix too much with boys otherwise the teachers will mind'. Frequent and regular contact between boys and girls is seen as threatening the ability of students to concentrate on their studies.

As it is difficult to establish clear boundaries, common sense and the 'public gaze' prevent boys and girls from becoming friends by very quickly labelling every kind of interaction as having a sexual connotation, and as such being illicit. For example, in reporting how difficult it was to meet a girl he liked in the village, Onup lamented that it would have been easier if they were classmates:

If we could have had a normal somporkko (friendship), if she was, for example, one of my classmates, people would not have minded if I talked to her because they would have thought that we were talking about our studies. But she was not my classmate, she was much younger than me and we were not supposed to have much to say to each other. For example, talking about school would have allowed us to learn from each other. If two people are classmates they get more chances to become friends.

Despite the strong surveillance it is easier to establish cross-gender relations at college because their status as students allows boys and girls to talk to each other about school matters and to spend more time in mixed groups. Moreover, as Onup argues, college boys and girls of the same age are not ideal or viable marriage partners and so their interaction is more tolerated.

In this context, Tonu's comments can be interpreted more as a desire for how things *should be* than reflecting the reality of how they *are* for most young people. Tonu's parents seemed to be quite open-minded. They had relatives abroad, and Tonu and her sisters were allowed more mobility than the majority of their classmates. Tonu was convinced that there should be no difference between same and cross-gender friendships. However, many others expressed a very different, and probably more realistic, view:

Actually we have less contact (somporkko kom) with boys than with other girls. What really happens, the real problem is that if you go around with boys, if people see you around with boys, they will say 'that girl is bad'. It is a problem of our society…where you (pointing to me) live, you can go out with boys, here girls can't.

And again:

You want to know the difference between friendship between boys and girls and one among girls…with other girls you can talk about everything, while with boys… can you talk in the same way? No, you can't. A boy can go out in the evening and at night. Can a girl do that? Where you (pointing to me) live it is possible, here it is not.

From what I observed and heard, I did not find much evidence of friendship between teenage boys and girls. There is rather a strong sense of distance and real difficulty in cross-gender communication. The impossibility of having more regular and closer interaction leads young people to fantasize and dream about relationships. In this process they draw on models of romantic love that will be the focus of the next chapter.

Going to College: What Kind of New World?

As we have seen, college education provides physical and social spaces for young people to socialise and interact in a less structured way than in the village environment. In what follows I discuss the extent to which education brings about other critical changes concerning young people's sense of selfhood, and their expectations and aspirations for the future. I start by exploring how education is valued.

Education is very clearly perceived as being positive and is valued for many reasons by all people, irrespective of age and class. Being uneducated (*oshikkito*) is often associated with poverty and with living in a rural area. Being educated (*shikkito*) is linked to the capacity 'to understand', and is deemed to be a quality that can make a real difference in life. A certain level of education is also associated with a less authoritarian behaviour of parents towards children and youth that allows the latter more autonomy in important life choices. Conversely, violence and antisocial behaviour are often associated with people who are considered oshikkito and not able to 'understand'. Adults and young people alike endorse a view of education as a means to 'enlighten' both the individual and society. Educated people are believed to be better, more open-minded and able to bring about positive changes in society.

However, the perceived advantages of education are different for boys and girls. With regard to daughters' education, those parents who can afford education seem to be more concerned about enhancing the possibility of a good marriage rather than equipping them with skills and knowledge for personal fulfilment. The awareness of limited employment opportunities is another factor that discourages parents from investing in girls' education. Being employed as teachers or NGO workers in programmes run by local NGOs is considered by the adults I talked to as one of the possible available forms of employment for women in the area. However, as I was told, matriculation and sometimes nine years of schooling are enough to be eligible for these kinds of jobs. Although work in garment factories, through the 1990s and 2000s, has become an important source of employment for women, none of the adults or young people I talked to mentioned it as a possible employment opportunity. This might be due to the considerable distance of Tala upazila from Dhaka and the other export processing zone (EPZ), and also to the fact that working in garment factories is perceived as something that would not suit an educated girl. To my knowledge, only one woman from Tarapur had migrated to Dhaka to work in a factory. Amin (1998) and Amin et al. (2006) discuss extensively paid work in garment factories in relation to girls' age at marriage. The latter interestingly point out that 'despite the million strong female workforce in this sector, their propensity to delay marriage in order to work is minimal' (ibid.: 9). Other studies indicate that female garment workers are mainly from poor or impoverished landless households (Naved et al. 2001).

For these and many other reasons considered in the previous chapter, prolonged education for girls is not considered a very viable or worthy option. Basic literacy or a few years of secondary school are deemed sufficient for girls to be able to manage their future children and family. Only a minority of girls proceed to intermediate college and university.

The discursive importance and value attributed to educating girls reflects wider development discourse. Often, NGOs, for example, declare that their ultimate objective is to empower women. In many cases, however, their interventions seem only to reinforce the existing division of labour and responsibilities within the household as a result of projects and policies that are actually strongly welfare-driven, and therefore to strengthen the role of women inside the household as housewives and mothers. In this perspective, a more educated girl will be a more responsible mother and a more supportive wife.

When it comes to college students' perceptions and discourses about the importance of education, there are points of convergence and divergence with the views of parents. For example, students share their parents' 'enlightenment' perspective of education. As Prodip said: 'If a boy and a girl have a relationship and they do not get married, the girl's reputation will be forever damaged ... this happens especially in the rural areas because people are less educated and they lead a "low" (nimno) life'.

Educated people are presumed to be more sensible and reasonable. Education is seen to be bringing about a change of attitude and something that could make the relationships between parents and children easier and less unbalanced. For some, this widens the possibilities for boys and girls to choose their marriage partners.

Prodip (boy):	*Uneducated parents marry off their daughters soon because they do not know about the health risks they might be subjected to because of early pregnancies...*
Zahid (boy):	*Educated sons respect their parents more, and are more likely to be listened to by them and to be able to express an autonomous choice in case of marriage.*
Onup (boy):	*Educated people are more open minded, can discuss and*

be interested in different issues, are less emotional and less prone to violence.

Areef (boy): *I now see a lot of difference from what I used to see in the village when I was little. Now I see a lot of change in people's attitudes, and in religion and people's beliefs.*

Taslima (girl): *Previously parents would not allow girls to study much. Now they do, but only in a few cases. It still happens that if you allow your daughter to study, neighbours will say: 'that girl is growing old and she is still studying'. Many of them say that the girl should be given in marriage.*

Ramesh (boy) while referring to two of his neighbours: *All the time I saw them having trouble and worried. I thought this was not good. If they had studied they could have set up a small business and they would not have got married so early because they would have had a better understanding of what they wanted. For all these reasons I think that studying is useful.*

While discussing her lack of choice in marriage, Najma also added that boys have more opportunities than girls to voice their preferences, and girls would have more power to make their own choices if they belonged to educated families.

For some of the students of the girls college, education is not so much an opportunity for self-enhancement as a way of acquiring general knowledge that will help them to better fulfil their family roles. For example, Lota said: 'If we were educated we could do more in terms of the development of our country and of our family. We would be able to raise our children in the right way and teach them'. This view however was expressed only as a secondary benefit to girls in case they failed to get desirable paid employment. In fact, the immediate answer I received during group discussions about the importance of education was that this could be a means to achieve a settled position ('*protistito howar jonno*') in terms of employment and economic independence. This constitutes the most significant demonstration that adolescent girls at college can imagine for their lives and themselves not only as mothers and wives, whose interests and needs are embedded in those of their families, but also as active participants in wider networks of social relations.

One dimension of *shadhinota*[7] (independence) that girls emphasise is linked to acquiring economic independence through employment. All the girls expressed a desire for independence in terms of 'standing on their own feet' (*'niger pa darano'*). This depended on finding a job after school. When I asked what they were planning to do after college they said: 'We will get a degree and then a masters degree'. When I asked if they were sure that they would pass the final exams they said:

Of course we will, that is why we decided to come to this college. The teachers are good and we are doing our best. Why should we not pass? If we do not, we will sit the exam again. Then we will go to study at Khulna or Jessore or at the least at Kumira Girls College.[8]

They expressed a sense of self-esteem and self-worth in declaring their willingness to 'find a job' after finishing their studies. The assertiveness that they showed in their commitment to study contrasted with their attitude of compliance with respect to marriage. They saw their future employment as the result of their own efforts and expressed self-confidence about their being able to acquire the skills needed to find an occupation. Many of them said that they wanted to become teachers or college professors, others nurses. Thus employment, though not seen as alternative to marriage, seemed to constitute an important terrain for self-expression and self-realisation. Moreover, as education is supposed to make youth's opinions and views more worthy of being listened to, even in the arena of marriage, choice of partner starts becoming an issue, with girls being recognised as deserving more voice in this important moment of their lives.

Girls also claimed that education equips them with the social skills to become full members of the society: *'somaje mixte parbo'* ('we will be able to be part of the society'). I was told by some students, who before college had attended Islamic madrasas, that being able to mix in society means to know and respect its norms and conform to Islamic precepts. In this sense, the ability to integrate is equivalent to the capacity 'to understand', constructed as the capacity to conform.

Other students, however, in attributing value to education emphasised that being able to be part of society means knowing how society works and understanding basic social dynamics. This understanding means people are 'not cheated', and are 'able to take one's own decisions' and 'make one's life better'. Here, the improved capacity to 'understand' is conceived as leading to a more active form of agency. In other words, the capacity to know and manipulate social norms to pursue personal goals and not just in function of adjustment and conformity.

To verify what it means in terms of future life choices and what real opportunities are opened to girls that pass the intermediate exams (at approximately 17–19 years of age), I identified from school records those girls who had completed the final intermediate exams at Tagore College from 1997 to 2002 and gathered information about their current occupation from teachers and other staff at the school (see Table 5.1).

Table 5.1: Present occupation and marital status of girls who sat the final exam between 1997 and 2002, at Tagore College

Exam Status	Marital Status	Employment Status				Total
		Work	Study	Work & study	Housewives	
	Married 14	1	8	1	4	14
Pass 32						
	Unmarried 18	1	10	2	5	18
	Married 18	1	0	0	17	18
Fail 31						
	Unmarried 13	0	0	0	13	13
Total 63		3	18	3	39	63

The most obvious finding is that only 5 of the 32 girls who obtained the HSC were employed and only 1 of the 31 girls failed. Out of 63 girls who sat the final exams, a large number (39) were housewives.

The majority (18 out of 32) of the girls who passed the final exams were enrolled at a degree college not far from Tala. As Mamtaj, a bright second-year student said: 'Girls do not have much choice, boys can go anywhere, to Dhaka or Khulna to study, they can move freely. Our choices are much more limited, we can study at the university only if we have relatives living in town'. Unlike boys, girls are not usually allowed to move to town on their own because it is considered dangerous for their reputation and security. So, unless they can join an uncle, an elder brother or another relative they tend to study in local colleges, many of which do not offer honours degrees and are therefore less valued.

The students' aspirations then may appear, and in some ways are, dreams rather than realistic expectations. The girls are actually aware of the difficulties in finding a job consistent with their level of education. Despite this, I find the meaning behind their words significant for a different reason. What the girls are saying is that they can imagine their lives and themselves not only as mothers and wives, but also as active participants in wider networks of social relations.

The strength of their aspirations and motivation was evident to me not only through what they said but even more through what I observed of their daily lives. In particular, I was struck by the determination with which girls were trying to overcome all kinds of difficulties and obstacles. This was more evident in the cases of poorer girls (and boys). For Taslima, whose father took a second wife and left her and her mother, going to school was like running an obstacle race. To reach the college she had to walk for more then half an hour, cross a river by boat and then take a rickshaw or the bus. At home she helped her mother sew clothes and in other domestic chores. She was not in a position to pay for private tuition and was therefore under the continuous threat of being given in marriage on failing an exam. There was strong pressure from relatives and neighbours to get her married quickly. Taslima, her mother and her grandmother were always under the observation of their neighbours, trying to balance their need for work and mobility with the need to adopt a reserved attitude publicly so that people would not gossip. If it had not been for the foreign family that supports her, Taslima would not have been able to fund her studies even if she was highly determined: 'I have a lot of dreams, I will become a good person, I'll get a job, then my father and mother will give me in marriage'. Poorer girls are also bound to face more difficulties in finding an occupation because of their lack of jogajog or social connections. They are aware of this and of the fact that they could end up with limited choices. Taslima had wanted to study science to become a doctor, but this would have implied too many years of study, as well as studying too far away from home. She successfully completed an honours degree in Islamic history and was in the middle of her masters degree.

Girls from well-off families can afford to think about work, and also the kind of work they wish to pursue. Sonia had argued with her father because she wanted to become a 'manager' while her father had wanted her to study to become a doctor. Kea was more ambitious when she said that she wanted to become a barrister: 'I want to do something important in my life, so that I will be remembered'.

For boys the value of education lies mainly in widening one's chances to get a good job (chakri). This is what Ramesh had to say:

I thought that if I study, I could do something good in the future, I would get a good job. I felt bad because since I was 15 or 16 I could see how difficult it was for the people in the village, for those who worked as peasants. I thought that if I did not study I would have to do the same work, I would not get any other job, it would have been hard. That's why I thought I wanted to study, to get a job or go into business.

Employment perspectives in Tala sub-district are not encouraging. Government posts are considered secure and are very much sought after. However, they are few in number. Competitions for state posts are organised, normally through examinations, at the national level. If successful in the exam, applicants can then be appointed anywhere in Bangladesh. Thus, for example, people living in Tala sub-district could be assigned to a post at the exact opposite end of the country. It is well known that to pass the examinations or to get a job in the private sector good connections, as well as financial resources, are needed. Other opportunities for employment in the area (besides agriculture) are schools and NGOs. Overall, however, in the western part of Bangladesh, where Tala sub-district is located, farming remains an important activity and agriculture is still the largest sector of employment. Compared to the east where services dominate and there has been a consistent growth of the non-farm sector the structure of the labour market in the west in the last 10 years has been relatively static (World Bank 2008a).

Students from Tagore have a very pessimistic perception of their chances of finding a job consistent with their level of education: 'If we do not find anything better we will turn to smuggling' (this illegal activity is actually very highly developed in Satkhira district because of its proximity to the border with India). A group of male students expressed their concerns for the future. Zahir said:

We will continue studying…but the risk is there that after studying so much and spending so much of our parents' money, we will not find a job. To find a job you need to know people, and if you do not know the right people, you need to build connections.

Many young people and adults asked for information about employment opportunities in Italy and the procedures to obtain a visa and an employment contract. Going abroad to study or work is a very attractive prospect compared to what is perceived as complete lack of opportunities at home. Migrating overseas, however, is a much less realistic possibility here than in the eastern parts of Bangladesh. In fact, only 3.9 per cent of households receive remittances from abroad in Khulna district against almost 25 per cent in Chittagong division (World Bank 2008a)

BEING COMPLIANT, DESIRING INDEPENDENCE: BOYS' AND GIRLS' PERSPECTIVES

A recurrent expression that college students (no less than younger adolescents) used during our discussions to emphasise a sense of social constraint is *'mene nite hobe'* ('it has to be accepted') and *'lok kharap bolbe'* ('people will say bad things'). I have already discussed the extent to which the samaj, represented by different institutional figures, the elders, the matobars, the group of attiyo swajan, is an important referent of values and norms of behaviour in the hegemonic discourse. What people (lok) and society (samaj) 'may think' or 'say' is very relevant not only for adults and parents but for children as well. Girls more than boys are aware that their lives can be negatively affected by others' judgements and this makes them very concerned about their social reputation and the risks of being given a durnam (bad name). This sense of constraint was mainly expressed in relation to marriage, an area where a language of acceptance of parents' decisions tends to prevail.

On the one hand, and especially in respect to marriage, girls tended to represent themselves as dependent on and subordinate to adults' decisions, but at the same time they expressed a generic desire for more independence (shadhinota), countering their own situation to mine. I was perceived as *shadhin* (independent) while girls talked of themselves as *poradhin* (dependent or subordinate) and sometimes as *bondhi* (tied). Independence was generically associated with the capacity to manage oneself, to do things according to one's will, and to decide about one's future. I was told: 'You can manage yourself and nobody will tell you what to do. For example, you chose to come to Bangladesh. We have always to ask whenever we want to do something'.

Sometimes girls associated independence with not being subjected to familial pressure and control in terms of mobility and interaction with boys. Most of them complained saying: 'We cannot do what we want, we cannot go where we would like to, especially in the evening. Our parents keep asking us where we go, why we are late and what we are doing. They do not do the same with our brothers'. Girls complained that even when they were allowed to go for a walk in the park with friends, they could not stay for long. Moreover, they could meet only with females. In most of the conversations they stressed the difference between town and rural areas in this respect: 'Here we cannot mix freely with boys, we would get into trouble and our parents would marry us off. In town it is possible to mix, but not here'.

Taslima was a college student from a very poor household whom I visited many times. She always showed great enthusiasm about going to college and had great hopes about her future as an employed woman.

Her attitude to her marriage was much more conformist: 'I will finish studying, I will get a job and then my parents will choose a husband for me'. She said that she could not choose on her own because 'in our "culture" this is not acceptable'. As I described earlier, 'culture' more than 'dharma' was frequently referred to as the ultimate justification for unquestionable and taken-for-granted practices or norms of behaviour. The areas of sexuality and marriage are represented here as beyond discussion and seemed to be the most sacrosanct. This was true for Muslims as well as for Hindus.

Shompa was a wealthy Hindu girl. I observed her behaving in quite a free and self-confident manner at school while she talked with her classmates and teachers, and as she journeyed home with some of her acquaintances. Being Hindu, she would not wear burqa but she used to keep a 'modest' attitude in the street. For example, she always walked looking downwards. Over the period I knew her she voiced contradictory views about her marriage saying on one occasion that she did not want to get married because she wanted to be independent, but on another that she would accept her parents' will, because they had done a lot for her and had borne great hardship.

Girls expressed awareness of the gender disadvantage in society and within their households, and considered themselves bound to be subordinated as females—'amader konno bekti shadhinota ney' ('we do not have any personal independence'). They also felt they were subjected to much control and discrimination with respect to the possibility of talking and expressing an opinion. During a discussion in a mixed group, Merhuna pointed out that girls have to be careful not to express too much of what they feel because they are in a more vulnerable position: 'Even if girls do something good, society will look at them in disapproval (kharap choke dekbe), but boys do thousands of bad things and people will say…"good"'.

However, boys are no less respectful and trustful of their parents. After an English class, I talked to a group of them in the courtyard of the college. As usual, they stopped me out of curiosity and enquired about my 'personal' life and about 'love marriage' in the West. One of the boys said:

I would like to meet my future wife before marriage because liking somebody is not only a question of her being good looking. It is also a question of 'mon' (mind/ heart/thoughts). But in the end we have to accept our parents' decisions 'mene nite hobe'. It would not make sense to marry someone I like if my parents and relatives did not like her. It would be a big problem if they could not get along. They have to like her. It is not possible to have a relationship before marriage and love marriage is not acceptable.

In this boy's statement, loyalty to parents is discursively given prevalence over individual preferences and desires, even if the latter begin to count more than in the past. Sometimes, familial attachment is justified for more practical reasons. At the end of our conversation, the same group of boys agreed that the need to obey parents could be partly attributed to the fact that they were economically dependent on them. At some point this dependence will be reversed and they will have to take care of their parents and provide for their maintenance. Another student said:

Here sons and daughters listen to their parents a lot. They do not argue with them, at least until they are 18–20 years old. Parents have a weapon in their hands. They can always say: 'we are not going to pay for your study any longer'. Boys do not easily leave their parents' house, they do not want to leave.

Shamim, a young NGO officer living in Tarapur with his wife and children and separate from his parental family, explained his loyalty to his parents as a matter of 'culture' (he used the English word). He contrasted this with the western 'individualistic' (he used the English word) society and to what is happening in towns. The village therefore represents a site where traditional good values hold.

We give a lot of importance to the family. Ours is not an 'individualistic' society. If someone wants to get married with someone whom his/her family does not like, it is normally the case that they will end up following the parents' will. There is a lot of affection inside the family in the 'gramer anchole' (at the village level). It is not the same in Dhaka where people are much more 'individualistic'.

He also stressed that other forms of dependence on parents tend to persist even if sons are economically independent, but he associated lifelong dependence on parents' advice and suggestions with a state of not acquiring complete adulthood.

Usually men do not get any job until they are 25–28, but even then they will always discuss every choice with their parents. This will happen even if they are independent and they could live on their own. It is like this as long as the father and mother are alive. Boys and girls never grow up because they always ask their parents before making any decision.

Shamim's words reinforce the discourse of prioritizing family ties, but in criticisng the same values he uses capacity for autonomous decision making as an image of adulthood.

Actually, economic independence and having a separate source of income make young men substantially more autonomous in terms of decision making. This is what the majority of students aspire to. Those that join their father's activities are, on the contrary, much more subject to their parents' authority. So, for example, a young man in his twenties running a shop with his father did not dare to directly oppose his father when he decided to marry him to a young woman he did not like. Instead, he tried to communicate his disapproval through an intermediary, another young man, who was supposed to talk to the father on behalf of the son. He explained to me that this was a matter of man shonman (prestige). The boy ended up getting married according to his father's will.

Another aspect of teenagers' attachment to family emerges clearly from the words of a girl attending the girls' college. I was talking with a group of them about their future and I asked what they felt was their main objective in life. One of them said:

Of course we will get married, marriage is a taken for granted step in our life, so we do not need to think about it too much in this moment of our life. We simply know that at some point in the future we will get married and our parents will arrange everything for us. So now we are busy studying with the hope that we will find a job and be able to help our family. We know that after marriage we will be 'poradhin' (dependent/subordinated), but we have to accept these limitations even if we do not like them. If we rebelled we would be excluded from society 'samaj'. Then

we would not be able to be admitted again (to be part of the samaj) and this means
that we would suffer from the lack of rapport with our parents and 'attyio swajan'
(one's own people).[9] *If we married someone that our parents did not approve of,*
even if we were economically independent, we would suffer a lot because we could
not see our parents. We would be alone.

Here the importance of familial bonds also lies in the sense of security
that comes from belonging. Breaking social and affective bonds with
parents and relatives because of an autonomous marriage decision is
an undesirable choice. It can lead to a sense of social isolation from
the samaj. Some of the girls proudly said that now, more than in the
past, their opinion is asked when a choice about their marriage has
to be made. However, they also said that in most cases this does not
bring them into conflict with their parents because each party will first
attempt to reach a compromise.

   This discourse of compliance does not mean that the students always
expressed complete harmony with their parents. On the contrary, they
were aware of a generational distance from them. During a group
discussion with a mixed group of students, parents were represented
as '*ager lok*' (that is, people of the past). A group of girls admitted that
their parents were not educated because previously (*ager jug,* that is,
in the past) people did not understand the importance of education.
For this reason they said: 'Our parents do not know much about the
country, they do not know about many things. We want to be different
from them'. On another occasion, Tonu admitted to the following:
'There is not much understanding with my father and mother, a lot of
times there is not much understanding'. Taslima Y. reiterated the same
thought saying: 'It is possible that there is no understanding, but at the
end we have to accept what they say ("*mene nite hobe*"). Only a few
times they would accept what we say.'

   I did not come across cases of open conflict but I was told by adults
about a few examples, as evidence, that if children do not accept their
parents' will, a tragic end is likely. There had been in the area at least three
recent cases in which girls or boys unable to get a love affair accepted
by their parents, had tried or had actually killed themselves rather then
accept the partner chosen for them. Adults tend to attribute this to

the bad influence of cinema and TV movies that encourage 'illegal' premarital affairs. Young people also reported cases of elopements and suicides, but I could not establish precise numbers.[10]

I suggest that for both boys and girls, some kind of dependence on their parents is both a source of concern and security. In addition to this, girls on many occasions showed an awareness of their subordinate position in gender relations, and of what this implies in terms of risks and difficulties. However, they seldom expressed a willingness to pursue a radical change in this respect with open or collective actions.

SELFHOOD, AGENCY AND EDUCATION

There is an apparent contradiction between the discourse of constraint with which most of the female students described their present situation and their compliance in marriage choices, and the determination they showed with their behaviour in pursuing education as a means to gain some autonomy. On the one hand, girls, in particular, tended to victimise themselves, emphasising their condition of dependence on parents and society and portraying themselves as dependent and subordinate (poradhin) in gender relations and marriage. On the other hand, they also said proudly that something is changing in comparison with the past, and that they are now in a better position to express their opinion in marriage choices. Even if they complained that their mobility was still more constrained than that of their brothers and male friends, as students they are allowed to travel and this widens their opportunities to be visible in public spaces otherwise reserved for males.

For girls as well as for boys, going to college opens more spaces for social interaction and allows the development of egalitarian forms of relationship. Here the traditional idiom of kinship and hierarchy is challenged by the development of solidarity bonds based on sharing experiences and concerns. Both boys and girls give importance to friendship (bondhutto) where the bond is based on common experiences and activities rather than on familial and kinship ties. Friends are thus chosen on the basis of a mutual choice and affinity of views. The way peer relations are lived and their social visibility are however strongly gendered. Except for the time spent at college and on the journey to and from college, girls cultivate friendships and relationships in the privacy of their or their friends' homes. Boys can more legitimately occupy public areas and their student status allows them time and space for public activities. When a mixed group of students came to my place for a birthday party, two girls, Tonu and Sonia, led the group and took the initiative of stopping a truck to get a lift. However, they were the first to leave because they had to be home before dark.

In the area of Tarapur there is a strong discourse about the value of being educated. Education is associated with development, positive social change and modernity. Educating girls however is, in adult discourse, very much linked to acquiring status and social prestige in function of marriage. In this sense, Jeffery and Jeffery's (1994) arguments about north Indian society are highly relevant. They suggest that when the reason for educating girls is to raise their opportunities of marrying more educated young men, education may result in reinforcing a pattern of dependence and subordination. This argument captures well the motivation of some parents for educating their daughters but it does not give enough weight to the meaning that girls themselves give to reaching higher levels of schooling. Unlike the girls interviewed by Jeffery and Jeffery, the students of Tagore and Begum Rokeya Colleges show a strong personal motivation for studying. It is significant how easily girls considered themselves willing and capable to be economically independent; also notable is the sense of self-confidence and self-worth that allowed one of them to say that she wanted to get an important job so that she would be remembered. Even the capacity to 'understand' is linked to a sense of becoming responsible members of the samaj, capable of negotiation inside both family and society.

Boys and girls would not openly question their parents' authority but they are aware of the changes taking place around them. They view education as a means to secure more control over their own lives. They expressed attachment to their parents and trust in parents' decisions; however, a form of generational distance emerged with education being considered the main difference. In marriage choices in particular, students attributed to themselves a wider capacity to voice their opinions and be listened to, even if they share with their parents a view of marriage as a social institution that involves a much wider network of relationships than the conjugal bond.

Education beyond matriculation, regardless of parents' motivations, has the unintended effect of opening a contested period in which young people of both genders struggle to find a compromise between what the 'samaj' expects from them and their own hopes and uncertainties. This is reflected in the development of a different consciousness and sense of selfhood. Once a girl has experienced college, strong motivation can help her overcome the difficulties she is bound to experience if she comes from a poor family. Her perception of herself changes as she begins to imagine a social identity that is not limited to the performance of familial duties. Even if employment opportunities are objectively limited for women, studying means experiencing a social world that is wider than the village. This is even more true for those who will be able to continue at university in towns. It is very clear from the words of these girls that they identify themselves as having independent ambitions and aspirations. Pursuing an education does not appear to be a decision of the parents. Girls' discourse about education is a discourse centred around the self. A sense of being 'different' from one's parents concerns girls and boys who come from illiterate families. Boys in these cases tend to take a leading role in their family even if their father is still alive.

Students' curiosity and openness about 'cultural differences' and their ambitions for their future indicate that they are aware that they are part of a lucky minority and they want to make the best of that opportunity. Kea dreams of becoming a barrister because: 'I want to do something important in my life, so that I will be remembered'. Isn't this a strong expression of personal motivation and strong self-esteem?

Independence is linked to acquiring more control in one's life in economic terms, enhancing one's capacity to understand and become an active member of the samaj, but never in terms of breaking familial and social bonds. In Chapter 7, where I deal with marriage practices, I explore the modalities with which girls assert themselves in this arena.

NOTES

1. The intermediate college is equivalent in the UK to a 'sixth form college' and the final certificate (HSC) is equivalent to the A level.

2. In other colleges of the area and indeed throughout Bangladesh, violent and factional student groups often cause long-term disruption of school routines.

3. I also collected information on the sources of income; the quantity of land owned, sharecropped (in and out) or mortgaged (in and out); and the level of education of the members of the household. These were used to cross-check the answers to the self-evaluation question.

4. See discussion of the term bondhu in Chapter 4.

5. I was addressed as 'madam' by both male and female students.

6. Somporkko refers to contacts or networks.

7. Shadhinota or independence come froms *shadhin* (independent, or free) which is opposed to *poradhin* (dependent or subordinate). Shadhin is composed of sho (self) and *adhin* (under), while poradhin is composed of *por* (other) and adhin (under).

8. Kumira College is a simple degree college situated in Kumira, not far from Tala. It constitutes the closest alternative for girls who for different reasons cannot afford to go to Satkhira, Khulna or Jessore.

9. See discussion in Chapter 3.

10. The issue of suicide is in itself a very complex one. In the area, and in rural Bangladesh more generally, it concerns also young brides who in most cases kill or try to kill themselves after family rows. Moreover, in some of these cases it is very difficult to establish whether the death is the result of suicide or homicide.

SIX

Living, Writing, Dreaming 'Love'
The Hidden (?) World of 'Lines'

*'The heart (mon) of human beings is like the sky. Inside the human
heart there are as many emotions and sentiments as there are shades
of colour in the sky.'*

Munni's grandfather

INTRODUCTION

As we have seen in the previous chapters, college allows boys and girls the
chance to develop age-based peer relations and same-gender friendships.
Cross-gender friendships and premarital intimate relationships are far
more problematic because of the context of purdah and the strong
hegemonic discourse reflecting and reproducing the idea of a public
separation between males and females. However, young people appear
to be finding ways of challenging these norms, of engaging in more or
less secret contacts and intimacies and creating emotional and affective
links with each other. Younger and older adolescents are involved
in somporkko (relationships) or, as they are colloquially referred to,
lines. The latter term in particular has subtle sexual overtones. In this
chapter I explore the terms of boys and girls' interactions and the
meaning of the forms that these interactions take. This will allow us
to understand how young people interpret the dynamics involved in
the construction of emotional and sexual relationships. I show that
cross-gender relationships preoccupy younger and older adolescents
and that this preoccupation leads boys and girls alike to interrogate

their lives, emotions and behaviour. In some ways adolescents try to reconcile their feelings and behaviour with the values they have been socialised into since childhood, with their parents' wishes and wider social obligations. New models of romantic love, represented in comedies, films and songs, are emerging with the diffusion and availability even in remote areas of TV, video and DVD sets. These are important sources of discourses on love and emotions. In many ways, the modalities in which adolescents in Tarapur experiment with cross-gender contacts and affective relationships and the development of a language to express their emotions is very similar to adolescents in other contexts. However, the significant point is that all this occurs in a context where the separation of sexes is the norm.

This sense of separation was captured by Nasreen Huq, in her statements quoted in the introductory chapter. She argued that acid attacks against adolescent girls may be the consequence of a contradiction between the natural attraction that develops between young men and women and the difficulty of discovering 'healthy' ways of relating to each other.

These are crimes committed by young people against young people…boys and girls can find themselves in situations in which it is very natural to be attracted to each other and in some cases it may happen that this attraction is expressed, may be just with eye contact…This may be enough for a boy to think that the girl has expressed a kind of consent and from that to argue that she already belongs to him. In a society where boys and girls meet each other more freely the tension can be defused, but not here. Where they can mix freely, they can understand a little bit more about each other, but in our society they are totally separated and this is very unhealthy.

Public opinion often blames 'modernity', particular types of movies and women's enhanced public visibility as the causes for acid violence. The solution predictably involves stricter enforcement of the separation of the sexes. Nasreen's comment subverts the terms of the problem and suggests that if boys and girls could meet more freely they could understand more about each other and have a more experiential understanding of the dynamics involved in the construction of affective relationships.

TALKING OF LOVE: FEELINGS, SEX AND RELATIONSHIPS

The quote at the beginning of this chapter was the concluding comment from Munni's grandfather during an informal discussion about the emotional nature of youth. The term 'mon' can be translated as heart, but also as mind, mood and thought. It is often seen as the 'interior domain' of the individual where feelings and emotions mix with thought and reason. Munni's grandfather acknowledges the richness and complexity of human emotions and this seems to clash with the prevalent idea that these same emotions should not be expressed in public. Some boys remarked, for example, in this respect that they were not accustomed to someone like me who would talk freely and openly, 'mon theke' (from the heart). Girls reinforced this with their comment: 'We feel inside much more than we can express'.[1]

However the contradiction is only apparent. Common sense discourses also recognise the emotional nature of Bengalis and make it a cultural trait common to adults and young people. This 'natural' emotionality can be and is legitimately expressed in classical music, traditional comedies (natok) and many other traditional and modern forms of cultural expression. The popularity of these modes, I was told, is due to the fact that they reach people emotionally and create safe situations of emotional expression. In other words, they give voice to sentiments that people cannot normally express in everyday life. After many conversations and observations I came to the conclusion that for the villagers in Tarapur, emotions and sentiments pertain to the human heart but at the same time they constitute a threat to the social order. The individual is not in control of his own passions and cannot subdue them so their management is deputed to society. The convenience of removing from individuals the ownership of their feelings in everyday life is consistent with Appadurai's interpretation of 'praise' in Hindu India as a specific form of verbal interaction. His premise is that in human societies the relationship between language, feeling and the topography of self may differ (Appadurai 1990: 92). In discussing this in the context of India, he argues that in public interactions there is a public play of affect that 'is not a matter of direct communication between the inner emotional states of the parties involved but of a publicly understood code for the negotiation of expectations and obligations' (ibid.: 102), aimed at creating 'sentimental bonds quite independent from the "real" feelings of the person involved'. 'Such bonds are part of the politics of everyday life' (ibid.: 110).

In Tarapur, this is true for adults but even more so for young people. The majority of adults I talked to showed elements of distrust in young people because they are particularly unable to deal with their own feelings. Youth were depicted as easy victims of their own passions for two reasons: (a) their nature as young people and (b) modernity and exposure to the new external stimuli. If emotions, sexual attraction, feelings of attachment, desire and so forth are freely expressed, they may take over and become a disruptive and uncontrollable passion (abeg) that threatens the social order. This is why from puberty onwards boys and girls have to be kept separate. According to many adults even traditional comedies like natoks may have a negative influence on youth. They give the illusion that everything in life can be quickly achieved and so young people do not understand how much struggle and work is needed to reach life objectives and to build up relationships.

Young people were also sometimes depicted as incapable of disinterested love, shotti bhalobasha (real love). Aminur thought that they were only interested and determined to 'possess those whom they like' without considering anything other than the satisfaction of their immediate sexual desires.[2] He cited, as an example of disinterested love, the platonic attachment of a Bengali poet to a woman he could not marry for religious reasons and to whom he remained faithful over a lifetime. Any form of attachment between boys and girls was quickly conflated with sexuality and even the more 'progressive' adults amongst my acquaintances seemed to take for granted that it is inappropriate for adolescents to express interest in and curiosity about sexuality and sexual attraction before marriage. Aleya, a middle-aged, wealthy, unmarried development worker was scandalised to hear that some boys had asked me to explain the functioning of the girls' menstrual cycle. Yet, on another occasion, she expressed the view that it was desirable that boys and girls discuss their problems with adults in order to be guided.

In this context, talking with adolescents about their emotionality and their feelings towards each other may seem an arduous task. Younger female adolescents, attending high school (grades 6 to 10) were sometimes quite reluctant to talk of these issues and were less articulate about them. With boys and older girls, once the barrier of lojja and respect was overcome, it was easier to communicate. They were actually eager to talk openly or 'mon theke' once they understood that I was not going to judge them. They did not seem different from their western counterparts described in the psychological literature on adolescence (Charmet 2000; Coleman and Hendry 1999; Dolto 1990). They were attracted to and curious about the other sex; they had a confused perception of their own emotional and physical needs, desires and fears in 'love' matters. Their moods swung easily, up and down, and they tried to behave as self-confident adults while at the same time showing a need for support and guidance. The pressure and social control of the samaj and the fear of acquiring a durnam (bad reputation) did not prevent boys and girls from acknowledging their emotions and sexuality and from trying to deal with them.

Individual male students, of about 16 years, expressed curiosity about girls and complained about having few opportunities to get to know them. 'Do girls feel towards us the same kind of attraction we feel towards them?' 'Is it normal or not to feel sexual attraction and curiosity toward girls?' They sometimes wanted 'scientific' knowledge, complaining that only science students have the opportunity to learn about the body's anatomy and physiology. The main source of information for young boys and girls on matters related to sexuality are elder brothers and sisters, or friends whose knowledge and convictions are in turn influenced by 'what people say' and by popular beliefs.

In a group discussion at the mixed college, both boys and girls appeared to be lost in, and at the same time aware of, the complexity of affective relations:

Merhuna (girl):   *There are a lot of girls who don't want to get married with somebody they don't know. If their parents don't accept their own choice, they would kill themselves…Girls do it more often because boys have some sort of voice, girls do not.*

Mongiure (boy): *Girls are more emotional.*

Prodip (boy): *Girls are more emotional.*

Merhuna: *No, boys are more emotional but nobody ever blames them. If girls do anything out of the ordinary they are given all the blame.*

Prodip: *Girls feel more sexual attraction.*

Areef (boy): *...You can see among girls and among men...between men and women there is sexual attraction. Sex is human...is normal, natural matter. You have to manage it but a lot of times, a lot of people cannot manage it and behave badly.*

Merhuna: *If a boy loves a girl, he makes an approach to her, if she does not accept... he may throw acid.*

Prodip: *Everyone doesn't love in the same way. Someone has expectations that they may get something* (implying sex). *Love and sex are different things but someone wants to get something...This is not true love.*

Areef: *There is something else to be said, if between a boy and a girl there is true love, sooner or later they will develop a more intimate relation and sex will happen.*

Prodip: *Yes, if there is adjustment between a boy and a girl, there is love...then there could be sex.*

These boys and girls, despite what adults think, are quite aware of and concerned about the different forms that cross–gender relations may take. Here, as elsewhere, they use a repertoire of words to describe different kinds of relationships and each word carries a slightly different meaning. The most common words are bondhutto (friendship), bhalobasha (love), prem (erotic love) and sex (they use the English word). Sometime they see love and sex as incompatible. Bhalobasha is the generic word for love. It can refer to the love between mother and child, between a husband and his wife, and between friends. Prem, from the Sankrit *prema* meaning erotic love, is the word used to mean an affective relation between a male and a female involving some form of physical contact. So for example a *premika* is girlfriend and a *premik* is a boyfriend even though young people usually use the English terms (that is, boyfriend and girlfriend). Sometimes the use of the word prem can be ambiguous. For example, if a couple is described as *'prem kore'* (literally, makes love) it may mean that they have a physical relation, but it can also refer to platonic flirting. In both cases, the reputation of the girl is bound to suffer.

For this reason, girls are more concerned than boys about defining the boundaries of a relationship. They tended to depict as kharap/ *biadop* (bad), those boys who were interested more in 'sex' (English word) and *doihik milon* (sexual intercourse) than in love (bhalobasha). In particular, second-year students at Tagore were proud of portraying themselves as more 'clever' than their younger school mates, stressing that they did not believe such boys and their love offers. They wanted to avoid any physical contact because they understood what boys really wanted.

They want sex and after obtaining it they will leave us. If there is love between a boy and a girl there shouldn't be sexual intercourse. If there is sexual intercourse there is no real love and the boys leave after having what they want. There are also some girls who behave like this, but most of us just need affection (ador).[3]

Girls perceive themselves as vulnerable in sexual relations, and, as we have seen in Chapter 5, they are afraid of being physically and verbally harassed if they make themselves too visible. Moreover, they are aware of episodes of rape and acid violence reported frequently by local and national newspapers[4] and by their own circle of acquaintances. This seems to contribute to their view of boys as potential predators interested only in sex. In this perspective there is a discourse of sex having a negative connotation and being incompatible with love. Girls are afraid of any form of physical contact because they feel that they would not be able to control boys and avoid sexual intercourse. It seems that despite an interest in and curiosity towards sexuality manifested through jokes, songs and allusions, girls do not want to challenge discursively the common view of sexuality as rightly confined to marriage and the importance of premarital virginity.

The concept of 'sex', as implied by the use of the English word, comes in a sense from outside. It is related to the experience of the West and is characteristic of the modern era (adhunik jug). Thus 'sex' is equated with a hedonistic attitude, the search for selfish pleasure and unrestrained freedom and enjoyment. Adults as well as young people imagine the 'West' as a place where 'free sex' occurs regularly. They compare the control and prohibition they experience with respect to sexuality with the image they have of the West as a place of total auto-determination in which individuals decide when and with whom to have sex on the basis of their immediate desires.

College Students and 'Mon'

The frequent references that boys and girls make to 'mon' as the inner site or source of emotions and thought and the importance that they give to it are significant in a number of ways. Mon refers to affection, attachment and emotions and I suggest that it is also a way of referring to the self and to one's individuality.[5] Boys and girls indicate that sharing one's moner kota or intimate thoughts and feelings is characteristic of friendship or bondhutto. They also consider the reciprocal appreciation of one's mon important for a successful marriage. Mon can also refer to character, nature and personality and in this sense boys and girls evaluate their potential partner's mon in the process of deciding whom to marry. They asserted on many occasions that they wanted someone with whom they could have a good 'understanding' and share their moner kota. Marriage therefore, for them, is not just a contract founded on socio-economic considerations but an intimate union based on mon, or what is felt 'inside'.

It is also interesting that during a long conversation with a group of Prodip's friends, mentioned in the previous chapter, they defined as a 'personal' (using the English word) matter the issue of having a 'girlfriend'. I understood this as a way of circumscribing a private sphere, pertaining to the individual. This allows them to name and value a private space removed from social control and from the interference of the samaj. For Prodip and his friends, bhalobasha belongs to this personal domain, and is located 'inside', that is, in the mon. In contrast, 'sex is just for enjoyment'. They also associated bhalobasha with *ador kora* (give affection and care) and the desire that comes from 'inside' of keeping a loved one close to oneself. They all agreed with Montu when he said:

The love (bhalobasha) of lovers, of those who are in love or those that make love (prem kora), is different from a mother's 'bhalobasa'…at the beginning they do not think much about sex, or of having a physical relation…but when they become more intimate, when there is a good 'understanding' (use of the English word) among them…they may then think of sex. Then a relation develops and then they start thinking of getting married.

College students, both boys and girls, value friendship as a relationship based on reciprocal understanding and sharing. This infers that not everyone can be a friend but only those with whom there is some affinity of character and personality, or with whom there is something in common. The same affinity is valued in an intimate relationship and then in a marital union, where they view the partner's personality as an important element to consider in the choice of partner. This draws on an idea that there is a particular person who is meant exclusively for you and who constitutes a perfect match not because of social and economic considerations but because of emotional affinity. Ideally, they would also like to be able to choose their partner on the basis of their feelings. In this sense young people value their emotions and consider them important in motivating serious life decisions such as the choice of a marriage partner.

During my fieldwork I was not able to talk in depth with women who had been married very early about their individual preferences, emotions and feelings in relation to marriage and their husbands. Older women who married 25 to 30 years ago, for example, said that they were too young when they had married, and they had no understanding of 'love' matters. It seems that girls who are married before or soon after puberty tend to comply with the choices made by their parents. Girls and boys unmarried by the age of 18 or 19 pay more attention to their own feelings and have expectations that these will be taken into account especially if they are well-educated. The longer marriage is postponed and adolescence extends in temporal and social terms, the more the emphasis on individuality and attention to what one's heart wants (*mon chacche*), increases. This is a novelty which translates into the notion that individual preferences should be taken into consideration in marriage.

Those boys and girls for whom 'having a girlfriend' is a 'personal' matter, are removing affective relationships from the domain of the samaj. They place them in a private domain where selfhood is defined through relationships of intimacy and sexual relations. However, there is an awareness that ideas about premarital intimate relations cannot be made public because this would not be accepted.

> But all this has to be secret. They cannot show publicly that they are in love... because this is not accepted in our society. So 'prem' does not always mean sex, it may also mean talking, seeing each other, exchanging letters.[6]

The development of an intimate relation over time is problematic. Adolescents are aware that in practice they have very few opportunities to meet regularly, to know each other, to share activities and spend time together. Even those who define themselves as being in a relationship can only meet their partners briefly and clandestinely. Montu, for example, admitted to having a girlfriend whom he had not seen or talked to for a year because her parents did not allow her to go out except for school. This is quite typical of other experiences. There is little communication between the two parties except through intermediaries or letters.

The modalities of adolescent cross-gender encounters vary a lot and I suggest that they can be interpreted as responding to different logics. Even if college students talk of issues related to sexuality and relationships in a more articulate way than their younger counterparts, this does not necessarily mean that they enjoy more mature or committed forms of rapport. Joking and flirting as well as great passion and romantic love are the repertoires from which young people, irrespective of age, draw to sustain what they call lines or somporkko (relationships). In the next section I try to describe what these different repertoires imply for boys and girls.

LIVING 'LOVE': COURTSHIP, 'SOMPORKKO' AND LINES

Flirting occurs among young people and takes different forms depending on the degree of intimacy and emotional involvement. Young people draw from different experiences in their relationships and through their behaviour provide different interpretations of prem and bhalobasha. As we have seen, Montu considered himself in a relationship even though he had not seen his girlfriend for one year. Tonu and Ahis used to communicate by exchanging glances in the courtyard of the college and by talking while sitting on the same van on their way home. They were aware that for the moment their relationships could not be made public: 'We have to be patient until we are established enough to be able to talk with our parents'. On the other hand, Shahin and Tanjila had the chance for more sustained contact. However, when Tanjila became pregnant, the village judgement was that they had to separate from each other. Tanjila's father forced her to have an abortion.

There is an aspect of play and experimentation in 'courtship', flirting and the discovery of sexual attraction and interest towards the other sex. Lines and somporkko are often signalled by small and limited gestures and activities. However, at the same time, people's relationships formed quite a complicated net that linked many of Tarapur's adolescents. Eventually, I was able to draw a map of the adolescents, depicting who loved whom, who had loved whom, and who was aspiring to love whom.[7] This was possible because of the information I received from young people, and also from an analysis of Eid cards, Valentine's day cards and love letters.

Although not very overt, engaging in 'courtship' (pratomik cesta) and flirting is a very dominant aspect of teenagers' daily life. At some point, Raju, a 17-year-old boy, stopped visiting my place to avoid meeting Sultan, another boy of a similar age. They were jealous of each other because both were writing cards and trying to attract Shirin into a line. Mina, a married 15-year-old girl, had not talked to Renu, who was the same age and a high school student, for months because she was convinced that Renu had previously had a somporkko with her husband. Lipy was scared that a photograph I took of Raju and her might end up in the hands of her brother, and this would be taken as proof of their somporkko. She kept coming to my place to make sure that this would not happen. Shirin could not come to my place for some months because her mother was afraid that she would meet Raju there. Sultan was writing to Rina and sending cards to Shirin.

Shirin, a 15-year-old girl, attended grade nine at high school. She was one of the girls most active in platonic lines and somporkko. Unlike other shyer girls, she was willing to tell others (me) of her 'friendships'. She was also uncertain of which of her many suitors to choose. Once, while showing me a flashy card that Sultan had sent her, she asked me what to do. She liked both Raju and Sultan. She then turned towards me and after a deep sigh, said: 'Life…what kind of thing…so much sorrow…because in the end we have to accept what our parents choose and marry whom they want'.

On another occasion she said that 'lines' rarely ended up in marriage. Comparing the situation of the West with her own and that of her friends, she said:

Among us it is almost impossible. Parents do not allow you to marry the person you like because usually there are problems. One of the two is too rich and the other one is too poor. If they are the same it is possible to get married but still there will be problems because boys try to get as much as they can from a girl and then at the end they do not want to marry her. Most boys are bad (biadop, kharap). Girls believe them and girls love more. They give everything and then end up crying. Some even commit suicide.

On another occasion she again expressed her distrust of boys: a boy she met at a wedding party told her, through another girl, that he wanted to have a relationship with her but Shirin did not know what to do because she was afraid that if she said yes the boy would have tried to 'touch' her (*'hat gaye dewa'*). This is also characteristic of how lines develop. Shirin said:

For example, I see someone at the bazaar and I like him and he likes me, so he may tell a friend of mine that he loves me and wants to have a somporkko. Then we may start writing letters. We write 'I love you' and we give flowers to each other.

When we manage to meet, we talk about marriage. There are secret places where it is possible to meet, also in Tala park. In town, of course, there are many more places, but even there it is important to keep everything secret.

This echoes what Govindo, a boy, said:

For example, if I pass by one girl's house every day I look to see if she turns her gaze towards me or not, if she laughs or not when I look at her. There are many signals from which it is possible to understand if a girl likes me or not. But even if two people are sure they like each other, in a village the girls will never say the first word. No girl will say I love you, the boy has to say that first.

In their ethnography of flirting and courtship in rural Kerala, Osella and Osella (1998) underline the importance of eye contact. Describing it as a way of 'direct aggressive confrontation, a challenge', they interpret it with reference to Babb's work (1981) on Indian theories of vision as a 'actual exchange and offer of something' (Osella and Osella 1998: 195). This interpretation is apparent in the comments above, but I would like also to draw on psychoanalytic interpretations of issues such as eye contact. Charmet, while referring to his own clinical experience with adolescents in Italy, reports that glances have an important communicative function in the first instance.

Being able to catch the other's gaze is lived as a manifestation of attention, as the evidence of an immaterial tie. … In adolescence the intensity of the visual approach in affective experience is expression of the narcissistic aspects of the 'falling in love' experience. (Charmet 2000: 277),[8]

Approaching each other through friends is another common feature of courtship, and girls as well as boys use this means of communication. Letters or cards are also used to express one's interest to someone else. Using an intermediary is a device that allows girls especially to keep a modest attitude and to safeguard their respectability. Girls will also pretend to be ashamed if a boy approaches them. Girls and boys will feel ashamed if a more direct approach is adopted. Working through intermediaries allows girls to withdraw easily if something goes wrong. For boys too this is a less aggressive approach. Prodip and his friends act in a similar way when they go out together to watch girls (*meyeder dekkha*). They look around, identify someone they like and then decide on how to start a conversation.

All the relationships (lines) I was told about shared some common features. First, there is an initial brief encounter, usually on the way to school, or at the bazaar, or at a party. This is sufficient to start a somporkko. An exchange of glances can establish a bond and a relationship can be maintained over time through brief encounters or exchange of cards or letters. As relationships of this kind would very likely be opposed by adults, especially by the girl's relatives, the obstacles that have to be overcome to meet or talk to each other constitute a challenge for the clandestine 'lovers'. However, this can serve to strengthen their bond. Sometime a relationship can develop also out of more regular interaction where, for example, the two are neighbours or school mates. Usually, in these cases, there is an age difference between the boy and the girl. As Prodip once said, just before going to look at girls in the bazaar: 'We wouldn't try to approach someone we know already, we would feel ashamed". Girls or boys of the same age are seen as peers who can be friends, someone who can be addressed using tui (you). This term implies intimacy and contrasts with the term (tumi) used during the initial phases of a relationship.[9] After a few secret encounters, people may start to talk of marriage. This is not so surprising if we consider that it is only in the context of marriage that these young people can think of legitimately enjoying intimacy and sex. Marriage is seen by adolescent 'lovers' as the starting point for a discussion of 'being together' and of fulfilling affective and sexual desires.

WRITING 'LOVE': LOVE LETTERS RECONSIDERED

In most cases, lines do not seem to bring what the adolescents hope in terms of reciprocal understanding, sharing and companionship, and even less do they end up in marriage. Communication is difficult, and opportunities for encounters are minimal. These ties however can last for some time, especially if they are kept alive by continuous love declarations. Exchanging cards and letters plays an important role in this.

Letter from Shilpi to Prodip, February 2003

Ser (Sir), *take my love, I think of you all the time, I feel like seeing you. But there is no possibility for me to come, so, you come here! We will talk a lot. I hope to meet you in Godaripur in front of the women's madrasa, next Thursday, So on 6/2/2003 at two in the afternoon.*
 Take care
 Shilpi

A few days later:

Prodip,
 Accept my greetings,
 I hope you are well. Moreover, what have I asked from you? I have asked only for you, you alone. I do not want anything else, just you.
 On Eid day I will go to Godaipur, I'll wait for you. Prodip, I love you, I love you.
 Be happy Prodip, take care. I love you, I do not want anything else but you. Prodip, do not throw me away, my life depends on you, my death depends on you, you are my beginning, you are my end... I love you, only you. Will you give me a photograph? I love you.

During my stay in the village, I collected some love letters that boys and girls had sent to each other. These are significant because they give us a window into the language within which these relationships are expressed. The cards (given above) were written by Shilpi, a girl from a village next to Tarapur, to Prodip after meeting him once on a bus. They had on that occasion only a brief conversation and they exchanged addresses and informed each other of where they were studying. Prodip did not go to the appointment but Shilpi managed to send him a second message through a friend and this was written in blood.

These two notes illustrate well what has been said above about the circumstances that may trigger the beginning of a *somporkko*. Here a brief meeting is followed by a request for a meeting by the girl. After that she writes a melodramatic love declaration where her love for

Prodip is constructed as a matter of life and death and the basis of her existence. An excessively emotional tone is typical of adolescents' love correspondence. As well as cards and brief notes, these girls and boys also write longer letters to each other.

In the same way that the experiences of lines and somporkko are gender differentiated, so too are the languages and imaginaries in which longing and romantic love are expressed. Boys appeared proud of the letters they wrote and received, and they did not hesitate to give them to me. They seemed to be more excited at playing the role of the 'romantic hero' than expressing their attraction and desire for the person addressed in the letter. It was common among boys especially to write a love letter as a sort of exercise, even before actually meeting a possible girlfriend. These letters can even be sent to more than one person. Sultan, whose letters to Rina I discuss below, sent a very similar letter around the same time to Rosina. Sultan and Rina were first-year college students and used to see each other on the college premises. While Sultan was courting Rina, he was also sending cards to Shirin and writing letters to Rosina. The letters from Sultan to Rina were written during the early stages of their relationship. They are interesting because they offer insights into how love is conceptualised.

Letter from Sultan to Rina, February 2003

....I have never been able to think that we will be together, that you will love me. Anyway, I will love you until the end of my life. I will never forget you whether you love me or not.

I do not know if you will believe my words, but I call as witnesses the moon and the mountains created by Allah. For the first time in my life, I spoke of love to you and I have never done this with anyone else.

....I love you. Rina, the day I first saw you, you are the queen of my heart. I do not want to lose you, from my life, Shati, promise me that after reading the letter once you will throw it away....then we will be fine together

...I do not know the day of my death but I hope I will get your love before I die. Shati, I deeply feel for you and I will not survive if you make me suffer. From now on we are partners for life.

Sultan asserts his everlasting and exclusive 'love' but recognises that their relationship is a difficult one. Further, he makes clear that the main obstacle to the relationship is the different socio-economic backgrounds of the two families. Love implies partnership: Sultan addresses Rina as *shati* [10] (partner). His love for her is based on feelings that come 'from the heart' (mon theke), and their strength makes Sultan and Rina partners forever.

> ....*I survive on earth only because of you. Dear you are mine, you cannot be the love of anyone else. For you my home/heart will always be open.*
>
> *R, If I cannot have you in this life I'll pray to be with you in the next. I do not know if one day you will be mine or not. I want you. Dear, I have not told anyone about you, only my mother, my auntie and my brother, believe me dear.*
>
> *I never lie, I love you more than my own life. I have written a lot, have I not Rina?*
>
> *Whether you love me or not I will love you for all my life. I think only of you all the time. Actually this is a mistake because I have never thought that the moon and the sun could get together.*

Love implies belonging to each other exclusively. The last sentence is important: 'The moon and the sun can never come together'. Similarly, the rich and poor cannot hope to marry. So, realistically, Sultan will be able to fulfil his feelings only in the next life. In his words: '...Love does not care about wealth or poverty. Love does not care about kings and servants. Love does not care about prohibitions. Every prohibition is forbidden'.

However, optimism prevails. Love is a powerful agent and as such can overcome any difficulty and prohibitions, and can make everyone equal.

From the letters that I read, Sultan's sentiments for Rina seemed to get stronger the more she was actually absent and de facto unavailable. Her absence as a real interlocutor, the lack of authentic communication between her and Sultan, and the actual insubstantiality of their relationship are in some way compensated for by a language of desperate passion that tries to make the love more concrete.

This is a matter of style, which I noticed was common in all the letters I read. Distance and separation contribute to give dramatic force to the expression of love. I am not sure if Sultan was actually experiencing the emotions he describes. The language of desperate passion and exclusivity has to be contrasted with the fact that he was courting other girls at the same time and that he wrote similar letters to at least one of them. In this sense, a love correspondence like this seems to be more a way of playing or acting than a matter of real emotional involvement. The second point I want to emphasise is that this 'impossible love' is conceived in terms of partnership and exclusivity and something that can affirm itself against social conventions, social differences and against all the social considerations that count in a marriage match. In a conventional conjugal union, husband and wife are not seen as equal partners and the focus of conjugality is not the dual relationship between husband and wife. So the romantic ideal of companionship and exclusive reciprocal belonging are quite alien to the way adults conceptualise conjugality and marriage in my research area.[11]

A second set of letters I want to look at are those that Rosina wrote to Prodip in the context of a more concrete longer relationship. They were neighbours and they had occasions to meet on a daily basis. At the time of their line, Prodip was attending grade 10 at high school and Rosina grade 7 in a local madrasa. They both reported that their prem finished when a jealous friend, Hassan (mentioned in one of the letters), revealed everything to their parents. Consequently, to avoid a scandal, Rosina's parents married her at the age of 14 to the son of the imam of the local mosque. From Rosina's letters, it seems that she was more committed to the relationship than Prodip. She used to take the initiative to meet. She would leave her home late evening with some excuse and knock on the bamboo walls of Prodip's tiny room to attract his attention. Then they would stand under a tree a short distance away from their homes, in the dark and chat. In Rosina's letters to Prodip, melodramatic assertions of love are intertwined with a wide range of emotions. Rosina associates her pain to a kind of gender destiny, portraying herself as highly involved. She then accuses Prodip of being concerned only with his studies. In all her letters Rosina expresses both her hopes and affective investment in the relationship and a sense of disillusionment for what she perceives as Prodip's lack of real commitment. She manifests her anger but at the same time she blames herself for her mistakes. The imbalance that emerges from Rosina's letters reflects a common feature of most of these types of relationship. Boys can flirt without losing much and they are aware that they will not be able to commit to marriage until they are economically settled. Girls, on the other hand, are under pressure to marry from a very early age. The following is the full text of a letter in which Rosina expresses the totality of her love for Prodip and her willingness to give her life for him. Here she calls him '*moner manush*' (partner of the heart or soul mate). In other letters she frequently addresses him as shati (partner).

Letter written from Rosina to Prodip, March 2001

I would give my life for you.

Dear person of my heart (moner manush),

Good wishes with a bunch of roses. I hope you are well. I am well too, thanks to you. Then, what did Hassan tell you? I could hear something, not everything. I do not want to know what he said. Everywhere I go, he follows me. And then he talked to Salima. I also know wherever he goes.

What are you going to do after your SSC exams? Do as you like. I am under a lot of pressure here about marriage. Have mercy on me. Dear, you do not know my sister's news. I'll tell you when the right occasion comes. Prodip, I love you so much. I love you [in English].

I have some more news to tell you, I have to get married soon, I don't understand what my destiny is going to be. And please don't say anything about me to Hassan, absolutely. My writing is bad. Forgive me, dear. I want to win you. Without you I cannot live. Dear I am under a lot of pressure here. How can I survive? Darling I have a request for you. When you go for your exams, inform my mother. And don't talk to me in front of other people. I smile and laugh but there is no joy inside me. I am the only one who knows how I feel. Darling, if you leave me there is nothing I can do. I'll try to be with you for as long as I live, don't forget my words. Some more: I wanted to go somewhere with you but you didn't give me time.

Your sad one (dukkhini).

Answer me and I will believe that we are like husband and wife [in Bengali and in English] *and we will live together, what do you think? I cannot study.*

Prodip was preparing his SSC exams and, talking with me, he said this was the reason he was not available. Rosina was worried because her parents had already started looking for a husband and this, understandably, made her relationship with Prodip a much more urgent matter for her than for him. She was well aware that a marriage with a 16-year-old poor student like Prodip would be unacceptable for both families and she also probably knew that the chances of marrying Prodip were extremely slim. All the letters she wrote have in them expressions of self-effacement combined with assertiveness. She says 'I want to win you' but at the same time she asks for forgiveness, apologising for her writing. Sometime she puts herself in an inferior position begging affection from Prodip and portrays herself as an unhappy person whose life does not make sense without her beloved. She is so emotionally involved that she cannot focus on anything: 'I cannot study'.

Given here are extracts from two letters written respectively on March and April 2001.

...Dear I wrote two letters to you but then I threw them away. Dear, when one's heart breaks, it cannot be repaired. Where do you stay at night? I have no news of you. You do not care about anything else but playing football. Thinking of this I cannot study. If you realize that, have mercy on me. Prodip if I see you with Shirin, I think that you don't love me. Dear, you go around in such a way! I feel that you do not think of me. And you do not want to tell me where you go, that's why I also don't tell you. Keep studying as long as you can. I wouldn't write all this...Prodip don't stay in other people's house

*at night. Use that time to work. Wherever you are, come home in
the evening.*

*...One word: where have you been hanging around? Pray five times
a day. A lot of people are saying bad things about you. You stay for the
night in other people's house. I do not want this.*

In these two extracts Rosina takes a stronger stance and reproaches
Prodip for his behaviour, blaming him for her 'broken heart'. Then
she asks him to pray regularly and reproaches him for staying out too
often.

Extracts from letters written from March to May 2001

*Listen, Hridoy,[12] if you marry me we can make everything right. I
cannot get over what your mother said, I feel uneasy.*
*...If I marry, I won't marry anyone else but you. I will tell my
parents that I will only marry Prodip, otherwise I won't get married
... I have a request for you: make it right at home, ok?*
*...Will you get married after your BA or after you find a job? Will
you marry someone else or will you marry me? Please tell me quickly. I
would have never thought that slowly you became so important to me.*
*P. I love you with my life but because of this love, my life has ended.
I cannot study properly. Dear, someone has seen us talking and has
reported this to my parents. P. if you want us to live together, do what
has to be done.*
... If a boy and a girl love each other, what can their parents do?

These short passages show Rosina's determination to formally engage
Prodip, asking him to take the necessary steps with his parents. She seems
to believe that if he really wants to, he can win over the opposition of
their parents. She is prepared to do whatever is needed. Here is a final
letter, written in June 2001.

*Dear P. How are you? You are probably well. Having left me you
spend your days very well, don't you? I pray that you are well. After*

crying so much for you I have become as hard as a stone. I have waited a lot for you in my life. I cannot wait any longer. You made me suffer a lot, sit and think about it. I had a lot of dreams about you. But you have shattered my dreams. I did not know you were so stubborn. I loved you more than my life, but you did not value my love. The way you made me cry. Don't do this with any other girl. You did well leaving me, I am a spoiled girl, be happy, because your heart is as hard as a stone, you have destroyed our love. You swore with one hand on your heart that you wouldn't marry anyone but me. Do not swear anymore with other girls. I know you have forgotten all our memories. Leaving you I will belong to someone else. I hope that you will be happy all your life.

Are you like before or you have changed a lot?

Perhaps you are worse than before. I will not write to you anymore. I may not be able to write to you again. Please answer this.

…Do not give me any more sorrow. I came on earth to be beaten by my parents and mistreated by you. Why did Allah send me on earth! I do not have any other choice but to die. I cannot bear any longer my parents' beatings. You are a boy, you are bound to happiness, I am a girl, I am bound to sadness. With you, I saw the door of heaven. I won't see it a second time.

Since Prodip seems reluctant to give time to Rosina, her letters turn sour and bitter. The profound sadness expressed in this last excerpt reflects Rosina's actual sentiments about the break-up of her relationship. When I first met her she was already married, was still attending school and led quite a secluded life. We could not talk much because whenever I visited her at home some of her relatives were always present. Once she managed to tell me that she was sorry for having betrayed Prodip by getting married and she asked me if I had a picture of him.

To discuss some aspects of this love correspondence I will draw on Ahearn's (2001a) analysis of the letters exchanged between young Nepali couples, in which she focuses on issues of agency, development and literacy in a changing environment. There is a major difference between her cases and mine because the letters she analyses were exchanged in contexts of long engagements and the love stories she explores were more public and ended up in marriage. However, there are some points of Ahearn's discussion that I find relevant for the analysis of the letters I have read. She asks which conceptions of agency, gender, fate and development underpin the new literary practices that she examines and what are the new structures of feeling that emerge from these practices. Love correspondence constitutes for her an interesting terrain in which to look at local conceptions of agency in terms of how Nepali youth perceive their own possibility to influence the course of events.

The love letters written by Tarapur's adolescents express confidence in the possibility of shaping one's life but this is intertwined with attributing responsibility, or surrendering, to destiny, fate or Allah. On the one hand, therefore, Rosina is determined and reminds Prodip to talk to his parents: if 'a boy and a girl want to be together, there is nothing that their parents can do'. She also states that she wants 'to win him'. However, she then gives up trying to marry him and surrenders to 'her destiny', which she believes is her gender's destiny: 'Girls are bound to suffer, boys are bound to happiness'.

Sultan believes that 'love' is a powerful force that can overcome the social difference between Rina and himself, and he hopes that in the next life he will be able to fulfil his sentiments. Expressions of assertiveness and auto-determination go hand in hand with expressions of hesitation and self-effacement. Boys and girls actively pursue their feelings, but are also very aware of the social constraints surrounding them. For Ahearn (ibid.) the fact that they write 'I love you' in English is a way of overcoming the shame they would feel in using their own language to express such intimate feelings. It may also be a way of putting themselves into a different cultural context where such expressions carry a particular meaning. In arranged marriages, love between husband and wife is something that is supposed to 'happen' to them. This is captured in the phrase *'bhalobasha hobe'* (love will occur). By stating 'I love you' in English or in Bengali, Tarapur's adolescents take ownership and responsibility for their feelings. Girls, as much as boys, take the initiative in writing letters. There is no rule about who has to start, and, in committing their love offers to paper, boys as much as girls probably feel more free from shame. Girls are however much more circumspect about what they do with their letters. This is because letters can be decisive proof of an illicit relationship. They tend therefore to carefully hide their letters from adults' eyes. They trust only very close friends with their love declarations.

From the letters it appears that boys and girls give importance to their feelings, wishes and sentiments. Adolescents value reciprocal attraction and authentic fondness for each other as that which gives sense and meaning to a relationship. Sentiments, what is felt in one's mon, seem to become the only acceptable motivation for choosing a particular person as shati (companion). Individual happiness is a concern for Tarapur lovers and the idea they express is that a union based on partnership, sharing and affinity is what brings happiness and fulfilment in life. As I have indicated, this conception of happiness clashes with the hegemonic view about what makes a marital union successful. The use of the English expression 'I love you' seems a useful mechanism to give this 'love' a modern innovative connotation. Another understanding of the melodramatic tone of the letters is that in the context of the prohibition that I have described, dreams and fantasies are magnified and the difficulty of reaching the object of one's sentiments contributes to emphasising them. Letters are quite a peculiar means of communication. In some way they mark the distance and separation between partners and they cannot but express love in terms of unfulfilled desire, of impossibility and longing. A love object who is impossible to reach is made sense of through language and the imaginary. This is all the more relevant in a context where adolescents know that they have few opportunities to transform their lines into a more mature kind of relationship or into marriage.

WATCHING LOVE: ROMANTIC MOVIES

As Ahearn underlines, love letters are quite a modern instrument of communication. They are linked with the spreading of literacy and secondary education, while their language reflects the idiom of romantic love found in modern comedies and films. Once I asked a middle-aged woman about her relationship with her husband. She looked embarrassed as if she did not know what to say. I was told by Halima, who was accompanying me, that: 'She does not understand what love means because she got married too young and at that time they did not "understand". Now young people know because of TV'. On another occasion Halima also said:

It is true that boys and girls have affairs before marriage. Before people did not understand what love is. They got married at seven or eight but now people understand.

Today, radios are found everywhere in rural areas: these days inexpensive portable radio sets have become affordable even for ordinary villagers. Only the well-off can afford to buy a television, video or DVD player, but these have nonetheless reached even the remotest villages where, paradoxically, electricity has yet to arrive. People and especially students can easily rent a DVD player and DVDs for a day and poor people gather in their richer neighbours' houses to watch TV and movies.

In Tarapur, most families own a radio and only a few a TV. It is common for people belonging to the same para to congregate in the courtyard or on the verandah of the nearest well-off family and watch the chobi (movie) screened by the state channel on Thursday and Friday afternoons. In the towns, rich people may subscribe to satellite TV and watch American and Indian contemporary movies. Cinemas in rural areas are not usually frequented by ordinary villagers; they are absolutely off-limits for women, girls and married couples, while men and young boys are exceptions to this rule. The darkness and dirty condition of the cinema halls means they are associated with illicit behaviour such as smoking, drinking and kissing. The commercial movies screened on TV are mainly Bangladeshi ex-cinema hits or occasionally Indian movies. In Tarapur, watching movies, even those shown on TV, is not an unregulated activity. Young unmarried boys and females are usually permitted to watch them only if the content and the type of movie is not too 'modern'.

We have seen how adults attribute to 'modern' forms of entertainment, like television comedies and films, a substantial role in shaping new structures of feelings among young people and in providing them with models that seem to clash with dominant values. Young people comment on this too although they tend to stress the positive aspects of the diffusion of the media. This is how two students in their late teens view the change.

Ramesh:
A lot of change happens among the youth in Bangladesh because of songs and because of the love movies screened on TV. This is why young people move more in that direction.

And I can say that when I was small, eight- or nine-year-old girls did not know anything about love (prem). Now girls who are 8 or 10, or when they reach puberty, they have a lot of experience in love matters.

…You cannot understand much about those who stay in the village all the time and never watch TV. Perhaps they have got something inside but they do not express it. But those who are grown up and are exposed to TV, those who listen to songs, those who attend cultural programmes, they laugh together and try to do some 'prem'.

Govindo:
This is how love usually happens in the village: village boys and girls understand what love means by going to the cinema, watching films and the way they have affairs in the movies. They write letters, they enjoy being in each other's company so they tell each other I love you.

From these abstracts emerges the role of modern media in proposing a model of love that some young and adult people think is very different from the experiences of the older generation.

It is worth emphasising once again that notions of romantic love and attachment are not alien at all to Bengali and Indian popular culture, even though in everyday life, when marriage matches have to be arranged, sentiments and individual preferences are not given much place in the hegemonic discourse. Even before the advent of TV, adults and young people had access through the radio to the literary production of well-known national writers whose poems, novels and comedies inform popular culture as much as the traditional myths of Hindu and Muslim medieval India.[13] Notions of love and romance are important in the novels and poems of Tagore, Michael Madhusudan Dutt, and Sarat Chandra Chatterjee to name a few of the most popularly known contemporary figures. Beside TV programmes and comedies, where the most famous poems and novels from these authors are taken up in songs and dialogues, young people now access this literature at school. Natoks, the more traditional type of comedy, used to be performed on the radio but now they are screened together with 'modern' movies that take inspiration from Hindi, Bollywood style cinema. The famous novel by S.C. Chatterjee, *Devdas*, narrates the impossible and tragic passion between an aristocrat and a low status woman. Now a famous movie, it was at the time frequently screened in cinemas in Bangladesh and is also available on DVD.

Young people in Tarapur agreed in distinguishing at least two types of contemporary movies: samajik (social) and romantic. The first type is in line with traditional social values, upholding familial and social ties, as well as sentiments of filial and maternal love. The second type is more 'modern' and gives more importance and emphasis to prem or erotic love ('romantic' movies are also called *premer chobi* in Bengali). Romantic movies are usually set in an urban environment; the male characters are dressed in western suits or jeans while adult female characters wear traditional saris, and younger and unmarried women wear western dresses or trousers and skirts. Samajik movies are mostly set in rural environments and the aspect and dresses of male and female characters are completely 'traditional'. Both types of movies contain songs, but in the 'romantic' ones songs are associated with Bollywood style dance. This allows a more explicit display of an erotic nature (Dwyer 2000). 'Romantic' movies are not considered suitable for family viewing because dress lengths are short and because allusive dances simulate kissing and physical contact. Their explicit reference to prem and sexual desire may offend the sensibility of parents and threaten their man shonman. In contrast, samajik movies uphold the traditional values of family and honour, stress the suffering of the powerless good but also their resilience and moral strength. *Srabon meghler din* (A day of monsoon rain), directed by Humayun Ahmed, a famous novelist and script writer, is a good example of a samajik movie. It is set in a rural village and while there are no dances, there are songs interpreted with sentiment by one of the main characters. Feelings of maternal and romantic love and attachment, as well as the pain of unfulfilled sentiment are emphasised in the film. However, romantic love does not triumph, and unable even to name and declare her love, the heroine kills herself when she realises she cannot fulfil her desires. Both types of movies use melodrama as described in contemporary Hindi movies by Dwyer (2000): '…melodrama foregrounds language, as it makes all feelings exterior, through the characters verbalizing, creating discourses on their emotions. In the Hindi film there is an opportunity to do this not just in dialogues or soliloquies but in the song lyric, where visuals and language are simultaneously foregrounded' (p. 109).

Adults and young people in Tarapur are fond of samajik and romantic chobi. The most successful and popular films are those that make people cry a lot. 'Romantic' movies, rarely watched by adults and young people together, are nevertheless criticised by many adults because they offer the wrong models to the youth. Reasons cited for this include the emphasis on the agency of the hero/heroine, their urban setting, and the 'modernity' of the main characters' dress, occupation and everyday consumption. One of the fears that some parents expressed was that their sons and daughters could follow the example of their heroes. Becoming victims of their infatuations they might elope or kill themselves rather than marry someone chosen by their parents. Suicide and elopements are common elements of the plot of 'romantic' films. They are also described by adults as transgressive actions that testify to the extent of contemporary moral degradation and the widening gap between the generations.

Young people in Tarapur have their own taste and favourite actors and movies. They are very attached to romantic movies and two of their favourites are discussed below. 'Romantic' movies like samajik ones follow a defined pattern. They are usually set in an urban middle-class environment with a najok (hero) and a najka (heroine) belonging to families separated either by a long-term rivalry or by socio-economic status. The social distance between the families of the two lovers is a common feature of romantic movies, one of the obstacles that true 'love' has to overcome to succeed. The two protagonists meet casually at some point and an exchange of glances signals that they are attracted to each other. One or both of them may be university students and their encounters take place in modern locations such as restaurants, coffee bars or video shops where young urban people meet. At some point, the heroine's marriage is arranged by her parents to someone she dislikes and the two clandestine lovers have no other choice but to elope. In both *Keamot Theke Keamot* and *Tumi Amar* the lovers take shelter in the forest signalling in this way that they are outside the samaj. Their angry and worried parents search for them, with the help of the police or family friends or mastaans (muscle men). Towards the end of the film, there is an event that cancels the social distance between the two lovers thus making the whole story less transgressive and more in line with the norms of what a proper match should be. Love appears to triumph in the end but normally a final tragic twist is introduced. In *Tumi Amar*, the two lovers manage to be together and to get married but, before that, the hero is severely beaten up by a group of 'bad guys' and the heroine almost raped by their commander. In *Keamot Theke Keamot* the heroine is shot dead and her lover kills himself and dies embracing her body. Thus, love triumphs but only in the afterlife. In the very last scene, the couple is shown walking hand in hand in heaven.

In 'romantic' movies, love has to overcome a lot of obstacles and it usually does so successfully. The lovers declare their sentiments to each other and these motivate all their subsequent choices. In *Tumi Amar*, the heroine asserts her love so strongly, and without any lojja, that her father changes his mind and gives his consent to the marriage (he changes his mind again later, after finding out that his daughter's boyfriend is not as rich as he pretended to be). There is little psychological development of the characters in this genre. Love just happens to them and a few encounters are enough to make them believe that they belong to each other, a conviction that subsequently legitimises all their actions. All this is dressed up with what really gives to 'romantic' movies their flavour: the moments of intimacy between the lovers are shown only as fantasies or dreams during which they dance and sing in gardens and countryside locations. Dwyer proposes an interesting analysis of the symbolism of these scenes, usually shot in gardens full of flowers.

She associates these scenes with fertility. The songs and dances have according to Dwyer another important function, which is similar in most Indian performative traditions. Thus:

...songs fulfil several important functions including advancing the narrative, by setting the scene for future action or enacting crucial turning points in the narrative. They also allow things to be said that cannot be said elsewhere, often to admit love for the beloved, to reveal inner feelings, to make the hero/heroine realize that he/she is in love. (Dwyer 2000: 113)

I think this insight is very relevant to Bangladeshi 'romantic' movies. Dwyer associates the way passion and romance are depicted with the emergence of new notions of the person and of individuality in Indian novels in the 19th century. Notions of erotic love were present in the traditional Hindu and Muslim literature but according to Dwyer were reworked in modern narratives where there is a constant tension between familial and social values and individual sentiments, as well as fantasies and dreams revolving around love, romance and marriage. As in Hindi movies, the strength of individual feelings is opposed to that of hegemonic social norms and the hegemonic form of marriage is more or less successfully challenged by the affirmation of individual preferences and desires.

Romantic movies are very distant from the everyday reality of young people in rural areas. The urban middle-class setting, the opportunities for cross-gender encounters, the levels of consumption and the availability of money, all of these have little to do with what I have described for even the most well-off among Tarapur's adolescents. Moreover, the kind of lines and somporkko I have been discussing rarely survive the censorship and prohibition of parents, and only in extreme cases do they end up in elopement and marriage. However, the movies, the love letters and the fantasy-fuelled way in which young people live intimate relationships have many elements in common. The movies provide boys and girls with a form of language to deal with these emotions and circumstances. Sentiments of love and attachment are imagined as what may give sense and meaning to a relationship. Marriage is seen as a lifelong partnership, an ultimate objective. From this perspective, love relationships become a private matter pertaining to one's mon and linked to self-realisation and self-expression. The language that expresses this in the love letters is the language of romantic love and longing, very similar to the language of the songs and dialogues in romantic movies. Examples here include the constant use of the English expression 'I love you', the melodramatic tone that expresses love as a matter of life and death, the metaphors used, the sense of uniqueness of the beloved and the exclusivity of the relationship, the obstacles that 'love' has to overcome to succeed. In love letters, boys and girls make frequent use of extracts from poems and songs drawing from literature and movies.

Thus, to conclude, we may say that Ramesh's and Govindo's words and Halima's comment at the beginning of this section capture part of the reality. Movies and comedies screened on TV contribute to a more widespread diffusion of certain models of romantic and erotic love than the radio did in the past. Women married in childhood had less opportunity to 'understand what love means' in terms of experiencing premarital courting, flirting and romance. I think, however, that the mere fact that literature, movies and comedies represent 'prem' is not itself an absolute novelty. What is new is that young people, unlike their parents, believe in some way that what happens in romantic movies might also happen to them. They believe that they might marry for 'love', and that what in the past was confined to myth and literature might become part of their daily life. So, I would say, that even if in practice girls and boys still get married according to their parents' wishes, they have time to develop different expectations, fantasies and dreams that in few rare cases materialise into marriage. Hameeda and Joy's marriage is an example of this.

In the previous chapter I briefly mentioned Joy and Hameeda's successful elopement that ended with a secret wedding followed by an official one. Some features of their story resemble those of a romantic movie. Their parents did not want them to see each other, and Hameeda was locked at home for months. Her family belongs to a higher bonghso than Joy's, and this was the main reason for Hameeda's parents' opposition. They had a series of secret encounters with the help of Joy's friends and finally they decided to escape on a bike.

Everyone knows about this episode. During a group conversation, one high school female student commented: 'I want to do as Hameeda did, I want to have a love marriage'. However, I do not know of any other couple in the area that had married in the same way as Hameeda and Joy, although I was told that some married couples had got married on their own (*'nijer biye koreche'*). For most, however, marriage had not been the final step of a long-term relationship. The expression *'nije koreche'* simply underlines the fact that it was not a marriage decided by the two families and that the spouses took the decision on their own. In some respects Prodip and Rosina's love story was similar to that of Joy and Hameeda's. They were all of the same age, all students, and both the girls belonged to higher status families than the boys. But there was one significant difference: Joy belonged to a wealthy family that could afford to support him and his young wife even if he did not finish studying. Prodip on the other hand would have never been able to provide for Rosina had they eloped.

CONCLUSION

Cross-gender interaction in contemporary rural Bangladesh is a complex and contradictory situation. Adolescent boys and girls are undoubtedly attracted to each other and have more space and time than in the past to develop and listen to their own feelings, to try to articulate them, and to fantasise and experience relationships. They view an ideal somporkko as one that is felt inside, one based on a sharing of intimacy and an affinity of mon. Relationships pertain to what they call a 'personal' or private dimension and emotions and feelings ideally constitute the guiding points of reference of behaviour.

Young people deal with their feelings and sexual desires with the instruments they possess: discussing and confiding in friends and older relatives and sharing their anxieties and their enthusiasms inside the peer group. The way they live, 'lines' and somporkko are also an expression of their being in a certain stage of psychological and sexual growth. Flirting, joking and playing are typical of the first adolescent encounters and approaches in many places. The wider context in rural Bangladesh is however one of prohibition and restriction that tends to deny and repress cross-gender premarital attraction and intimacy and also limit the possibilities of experiencing friendly relationships and developing reciprocal knowledge. Thus lines and somporkko rarely progress towards more mature and emotionally involving kinds of relationship or marriage.

While the 'on stage' public behaviour of adolescents conforms to the code of shame and honour, lines do occur in a sort of parallel world, partially hidden to adults. The discourse that gives meaning to flirting and to lines in this parallel world is the code of prem or 'romantic' love, and this is represented in modern terms by comedies and movies. These give adolescents a language to voice and name what happens in their mon. The language of emotions, of bhalobasha and prem, is not new to Bengali literature and artistic expressions. However, in 'romantic' movies it goes hand in hand with the emergence of a new conceptualisation of selfhood and individuality. The beloved is unique; the choice is a private matter based on one's preferences and feelings; the desired relationship is one of companionship that presupposes reciprocal knowledge and understanding. Marital unions are founded on love between two individuals who choose each other on the basis of their sentiments and struggle against social conventions to affirm their inner truth. Even if the reality of rural adolescents is in most respects vastly different from that of their favourite heroes, their imagination and fantasies are nourished by the stories they watch. These provide them with a language for their own encounters.

Despite the attraction they feel for each other, the opportunities to exchange glances, letters and brief encounters in the dark are few and far between. The ideal of partnership, of being each other's life companion, is expressed in letters but it cannot be followed up in everyday life through free interaction and reciprocal knowledge. A model of conjugal union based on reciprocal attraction and partnership does not constitute a realistic, feasible alternative to arranged unions. Boys and girls can flirt and play, but most of them will finally compromise with their parents and negotiate their preferences in the context of an arranged marriage. Hameeda's and Joy's example constitutes an exception; such cases are negatively sanctioned by society.

Does this mean that all the dreams and fantasies have no meaning and remain adolescent experiences to be overcome and forgotten with the move to maturity and adult life? There are of course elements of joking and playing and acting out in lines and somporkko and the degree of emotional involvement may vary. Sultan wrote the same passionate sentences to different girls at almost the same time. Sharif, whom I met recently at the university campus in Khulna, said on that occasion that he does not think anymore about lines because he is grown up and he has no more time for 'playing'. Most of these boys and girls are, like Shirin, aware that this kind of flirting will not end up in marriage. However, I suggest that there is more to love letter writing and flirting than just joking and acting. Rosina may have been aware that her love for Prodip would not end up in a marriage, but her letters are more than a literary exercise. They testify to her commitment and emotional involvement. Some of the interactions described in this chapter are typical of the first experiences of young adolescents in the West. For example, the use of intermediaries to declare love or approach someone they fancy; the difficulties of communication; the sense of experimentation; the shame and curiosity, etc. Often these are indeed overcome with maturity. However, this does not mean that they are less 'real' and that adolescents do not develop expectations and hopes that may clash with their parents' expectations and wishes. The discourse of romantic love that gives sense and meaning to these experiences is also linked to new ways of talking about the self and one's emotions and new structures of feeling (cf. Williams 1977). There is an important contextual element to be considered here. In the West, adolescents are allowed, in fact sometimes encouraged, to experiment, to open up to the social world of peer group friendships and cross-gender intimacies; in rural Bangladesh the opposite is the norm. Adolescent girls' experiences of flirting and relationships are suddenly ended by marriage, and there is no time for them to develop into more mature forms of relationship.

NOTES

1.   This idea of insideness seems to be linked with the notion of shame (lojja) as a social curtain to cover one's feelings. (See chapter 4)

2. This resonates with what Basu (2001) reports about Indian magazines where *prem* as physichal attraction appears to be more valued than bhakti (devotional love), and with the preoccupations expressed by Donner's (2008) informants about the fact that nowadays 'self-less' love have gone amiss' (p. 84)

3. Ador carries the meaning of affection in the sense of taking care of someone and is the word that most married women used to indicate what is expected from a good husband.

4. Ain-o-Shalish Kendro (ASK) reports that in 2002 the newspapers reported 1,442 cases of rape and 262 of acid attacks, of which 250 were against women (ASK 2003).

5. Self is actually translated in Sanskrit as *atman* and in Bengali with the derived word *atta*. This term enters in the construction of words such as atta morjada (self-esteem) and *attabiswas* (self-confidence) but is very rarely used separately. In the Hindu religious tradition atman is the soul, the locus of individuality that is supposed to merge through meditation and at the end of the cycle of reincarnation, with the cosmic conscience, *brahman*.

6. A quote from one of the boys interviewed.

7. I use the word 'love' because most of the time in informing me of their preferences, boys and girls used the English word or the term bhalobasha which was always translated as love.

8. My translation from the Italian.

9. Tumi is a more formal and respectful way of addressing others.

10. Shati is a word used also with the same meaning as swami (husband); married women sometime refer to their husband as '*amar giboner shati*' (my life partner).

11. See Donner (2008) for a discussion about how notions of companionship and common decision making are emerging in the Indian middle class as part of a new conjugal ideal.

12. 'Hridoy' literally means heart.

13. Dwyer (2000) presents some examples of how love has been represented in the Indian literary tradition starting from the myths and stories of the Mahabharata and Ramayana, to the Shastras and the Sankrit erotic traditions of lyric poetry in mediaeval India. Here, a major arena for the depiction of love was religion. The rise in popularity of the cult of Krisna established the Bhakti movement, the tradition in which the popularly known Gita Govinda was written that became 'with its commission of eroticism and mysticism the

classical model of much later Bhakti literature'. In Urdu literature, notions of passionate love, longing and misery were expressed in a major literary genre the *ghazal*. This was taken up by film composers in the 1950s, and in the 1980s was reborn by a new generation of popular singers. According to Dwyer, the influence of this genre on the Hindi film lyric is immense (ibid.: 41). In the 19th century, with the emergence of an indigenous bourgeoisie arose a new literary elite and a new literary genre, the novel, where new ideas of love and romance were expressed. R. Tagore is surely the best literary example of the fusion of mediaeval Hindu literary tradition with the Urdu tradition of the ghazal. One of his novels *Ghore bahire* was made into a film by Satyajit Ray. The film's story is based on the classic love triangle.

SEVEN

Biye Dewa (To Give in Marriage) and Biye Kora (To Marry)

Adolescent Girls' Experiences

'After all...life is birth, marriage and death.'

Saju

INTRODUCTION

Marriage like birth and death is a 'natural' stage in one's life course. Saju's statement, quoted above, forcefully encapsulates the meaning that adults and young people in my study area attribute to marriage as a fundamental phase in the process of growth from childhood and adolescence, a significant life change, and a critical component of women's and men's social identity. As Donner, talking about middle-class families in Calcutta, puts it: '*Biye* (marriage) represents for Hindu and Muslims in Bengal a life cycle ritual that transforms the person into a full human being' (Donner 2008: 65).

Earlier research on marriage in South Asia focused mainly on kinship and caste rules and on formal structures as determinants of the behaviour and choices of the actors involved (Grover 2009). The everyday practices surrounding marriage and marriage negotiations and the individual's motivations were in some ways irrelevant in this approach. Marriage was represented in its structural aspects as an unchanging social institution only partially challenged by 'modern' practices that in some cases could defy the norms of caste endogamy or question the fundamental role of parents in arranging their sons' and daughters' marriages. Arranged 'traditional' marriages were counterposed to 'modern' love marriges as they were two radically opposed forms. The two earlier studies on the transition to adulthood and marriage in Bangladesh (Aziz and Maloney 1985; Kotalova 1993) that I discussed in the introductory chapter focused exclusively on the overall hegemonic discourse and, as a result, identities were described as adhered to passively, especially by women, and there was no real sense of how different subjects experienced and reacted to the social norms. Kotalova (1993) provides an exhaustive description and interpretation of the different phases and rituals of a wedding ceremony, with all its symbolism of passivity and hierarchy, where the bride's behaviour, attitude and gestures express and confirm her adherence to the obligations and responsibilities she has been socialised into since childhood. Aziz and Maloney (1985) likewise described marriage and transition to adulthood using a socialisation approach that focused exclusively on the overall hegemonic discourse and, as a result, girls' sense of personhood was collapsed in their social identity as wives and mothers.

In a similar vein, Veena Das in her study of Punjabi women frames her account in terms of a split between roles and self. She argues that it is precisely in the phase of young adulthood that girls as new brides experience the maximum distance between the two: 'It is in the phase of young adulthood that women experience the maximum role distance and identify their roles as masks which hide their true identities' (Das 1979: 97). This is an interesting formulation because on the one hand girls are seen as having passively interiorized values and norms transmitted by parents and other significant others to take up a predetermined identity as wives and then mothers after marriage. However, beneath this, is a second dimension of their personhood, referred to in terms of a 'true self' that remains hidden and socially irrelevant. The passive performance of external roles has nothing to do with self-perception. Kotalova in the same vein and quoting Davis (1983: 81) subscribes to the view that 'the individual does not enter into thinking in Bengal' (Kotalova 1993:69) and argues that the individual's only aspiration is to fit into the group and carry out one's role.

In these accounts, premarital negotiations, the actual wedding and the initial phases of married life represent a constrained situation where apparently there are limited possibilities to express one's desires, especially for young women.

My interpretation of the stories I present in this chapter resonates better with more recent discussions of marriage and women's status in South Asia. Views of women as passive subscribers to predetermined identities have been extensively challenged in studies that highlight spaces and modalities of women's agency, resistance and autonomy (Ahearn 2001a; Grover 2006, 2009; Kabeer 2000; Raheja and Gold 1994). With regard to marriage, Grover's research on the dynamics of everyday conjugal life in Delhi gives insights on the complexities and nuances of conjugal and wider kin relationships and their changing character (Grover 2006, 2009); while Donner's (2008) study of a middle-class neighbourhood in Calcutta shows how notions of individuality and choice and companionate marriage may coexist with the upholding of the ideal of the joint family and the prevalence of collective interest over individual preferences. Parry's (2004) view of the changes of the meaning of marriage and conjugality in India is even more radical. He argues that public sector employment and the 'modern industrial milieu' play a fundamental role in a process of marriage 'privatization' where the conjugal couple is increasingly the pivot of the household and marriage is increasingly seen as a union between two intimate selves' (p. 312).

As the urban contexts investigated by Grover, Donner and Parry, rural Bangladesh is in flux, invested by processes of change like the new educational opportunities for girls that help open for them different life trajectories. Premarital cross-gender encounters and relationships are nurtured by new discourses about 'love' and intimacy and influence young people's views on marriage and conjugality.

My immediate concern in this chapter is to explore, through case studies of weddings and early married life, the possibilities for girls to voice and to act their aspirations and preferences. In the context of my research, which is broadly concerned with asking questions about how a sense of selfhood is perceived and lived by rural adolescents, marriage represents a critical situation for exploring spaces for choice and self-assertion. The context in which marriage is arranged, the complexities surrounding the decision of when and whom to marry are particularly significant arenas in relation to girls' perception of their desires versus their social obligations towards family and wider kin. The stories of Najma, Saju and Shopna show that, even though marriage is the ultimate and dominant source of economic security and social identity for young women, the reality accommodates different situations where girls explore different capacities to express their feelings and their views vis-à-vis their parents, relatives and the broader society.

Before presenting the case studies, I discuss in the next section the broader context for an understanding of marriage practices in Tarapur area. I discuss how the institution of 'arranged marriage' is sanctioned in the hegemonic discourse as the normative form of marital union and explore the meaning of some of the practices connected with the premarital negotiations and the criteria taken into account in arranging marriages.

MARRIAGE IN TARAPUR: THE NORMATIVE CONTEXT

'Biye Dewa': To Give in Marriage

In rural Bangladesh, the institution of 'arranged' marriage is the dominant culturally sanctioned form of conjugal union. There is no precise Bengali term for the word 'arranged' but the most common verb used in discussions of marriage (biye dewa; literally, to give in marriage) conveys clearly the idea that the two spouses do not take the initiative in deciding when and whom to marry. The alternative verb (*biye korbo*; literally, 'I will marry') is used, but less frequently and normally more by boys than girls. This is consistent with men having more choice than women in choosing their marriage partner and occurs especially in cases involving men with higher educational degrees and those employed in the public or private sector. These men are likely to be economically independent when they get married, and could in some cases be supporting their parents. In this context it is socially accepted that they should explicitly express their preferences. On the other hand, those who are less educated and take on the family business or work on family land are likely to be more dependent on parents' decisions. Education in itself seems to be bringing about some change. Students of both sexes stress that knowledge and skills acquired at school constitute a recognised element of maturity that may bring parents to seek and consider their opinions, especially in the case of boys.

In people's common view, arranged marriage is opposed to what is called 'love marriage' (*premer biye*). A marriage where the parents take the initiative is considered to be a 'proper' one that conforms either to 'Bengali culture' or to dharma, in the sense previously discussed, of norms and code of conduct rather than religion. When a couple decides to get married, without consulting the parents, it is said that they 'marry on their own'—'*nijer biye kora*' or that '*palaye biye koreche*' (they married after eloping).[1] These kind of marriages are uncommon in Tarapur. Adults refer to these marriages as a model imported from the West, and link them to what is perceived as extreme sexual liberty characteristic of western societies.

Almost everyone I met in the Tala area was surprised that I was not married. Once, while chatting to an old man, the question of marriage in Italy and the West in general was raised. He asked me whether marriage is usually arranged by the 'guardians' or whether boys and girls marry on their own initiative (*nijera kore*). He went on to inform me that even in Bangladesh there are 'love' marriages', mostly between college and university students:

Teenagers make mistakes because they dream and dreams and reality cannot match. So after a love marriage a lot of problems come up. They cannot adjust to family life. Some marriages may actually work but most of them will not. There can be problems even in an arranged marriage but in a love marriage this is more likely to happen first of all because the two families are more likely to have problems in adjusting to each other and secondly because love is not enough for a marriage to work, if the material condition is not good and there is nothing to eat.

As we have seen in Chapter 5, male college students tend to express the same preoccupation with unions where the parents are not involved in the choice and yet they are more likely to use biye kora. One of them said that he would have liked to know his future wife before marriage 'because liking somebody is not only a question of her being good looking. It is also a question of mon (mind/heart/thoughts)'. Despite thinking that an 'understanding' between husband and wife is important to make a marriage work, he concluded: 'Finally, we have to accept our parents' decisions ('*mene nite hobe*'). It doesn't make sense to marry someone I like if my parents and relatives don't like her. It will be a big problem if they can't get along'. The same point was stressed by Aleya, a middle-aged unmarried woman from a well-off family. She reiterated a common opinion: 'Love marriage' doesn't work because in most cases the parents are not happy about their son's choice and a difficult relationship with the parents-in-law makes the marriage break down.

It is clear that the focal point of the conjugal union is not the relationship between husband and wife, but that between the bride and her in-laws.[2] This is also apparent in the role that dowry plays in marriages and marriage negotiations.

Dowry in the form of a transfer of money and/or goods from the bride's family to the husband's family is, in the Tarapur area, an important aspect of marriage. It has important practical implications for the success of a marital union in terms of stability and well-being of the parties involved. It is also analytically important as it is an indicator of women's position in gender relations. In the Tarapur area, the word used for the payments in cash or kind that are commonly demanded by the groom's family as part of the marriage transactions, is *joutuk*.[3] The amount of cash to be given either at the moment of marriage or afterwards is higher among the Hindus. My interlocutors informed me that this is because Hindu women do not have inheritance rights on their father's property.[4] A Hindu majhari (middle) household can ask for between Tk 1 and 1.5 lakh,[5] well-off families can ask for 2 lakhs or more; a poor family can demand Tk 30,000 to 40,000. Among Muslims, the amount exchanged in dowry is approximately half. Besides cash, other assets may be requested by the groom's family, such as pieces of furniture, tools for the house and the kitchen, and accessories such as radios, bikes, televisions or motorbikes. The higher the socio-economic status of the groom's family compared to the bride's, the higher the amount of money or the value of the goods that can be demanded from the bride's family. The amount of dowry increases with the bride's age and also if her socio-economic status is lower than that of the husband and if she doesn't conform to the hegemonic ideal of the pure, submissive and innocent girl. Moreover, some physical characteristics of the bride count: for example, the length of her hair, her physique and the colour of her skin. The parents of a dark-skinned[6] girl find it much more difficult to find a husband and will have to pay much more in dowry than the parents of a fair-skinned girl with long black hair and a well proportioned figure.

Adult women in Tarapur suggested that dowry is a relatively recent phenomenon in the area and asserted that their parents did not have to pay dowries for them. Halima, the woman in charge of the guest house where I was living, was 40 years old. She was approximately seven years old when she was given in marriage: 'I was bought by my husband with a doll'. This indicates that in the past a symbolic gift to the bride was sufficient for marriage, especially in cases involving poor families. The issue of changing practices with respect to marriage payments and exchanges in Bangladesh and South Asia as a whole has been discussed in the literature. It is widely acknowledged that in much of the Indian subcontinent, dowry has lost its original meaning among upper caste Hindus[7] and has spread to different castes, as well as to other religious communities (Srinivasan 2005). In India, Subrahmanian (1995) and Srinivasan (2005) argue that whereas in the past dowry could have been seen as having only symbolic value, today it is a coercive transaction. Its commoditisation, especially in rural areas and among the poor, goes hand in hand with a perception of daughters as a source of costs and economic strain. From the time a baby girl is born, the parents' main concern is her marriage and her dowry.

Among Muslims in Bangladesh, there has been a shift from past practices that favoured the bride's family to forms of payment to the bridegroom's family that now de facto represent a kind of obligatory economic compensation for taking the bride off her parents' hands (Lindenbaum, 1981; Rozario 1992, 2009). Demands from the groom's family to the bride's emerged in the 1970s among wealthy Hindu and Muslim families in urban areas. These families had educated sons who had secured well paid jobs. Dowry became a form of compensation for the investment the groom's family had made in their sons' education (Kabeer 2000; Rozario 2009). Where women could not access the same educational and employment opportunities, dowry became the price families would pay for marrying their daughters into a higher status group.[8] Thus dowry acts as a means to display status, both for the receiving and the giving family. Moreover, in rural areas, since the 1970s, economic changes such as the decline in family-based farming, an increase in landlessness, growing poverty levels, and the transition in agriculture from subsistence to marketised production have affected women's position and status in a specific way. The effect has been to increase their economic dependence on men, to devalue their roles and to increase the perception that women are liabilities (Van Schendel 1981:109; Rozario 2009). Thus dowry is connected to negative changes in gender relations in terms of an accentuation of the inferior position of women (Kabeer 2000). Cain et al. (1979) describe this process as one in which the 'patriarchal contract' deteriorates. By this they infer that with the devaluation of women's economic contribution to the family and the rising costs of marrying off a daughter, women are increasingly perceived as economic burdens and the male normative commitment towards them is eroded. Dowry can thus be understood both as a result of changing economic structures, and the cause of a further weakening of girls' and women's position in the household and in the community. Some recent studies (Huda 2006; Naved and Persson 2007; Rozario 2007; Suran et al. 2004) point out how this is happening despite some positive changes in the position of women since the 1990s, brought about by the efforts of NGOs and women advocacy groups in the direction of promoting women's empowerment.

Both in India and in Bangladesh, some of the more evident negative consequences of the practice of dowry include indebtedness of poor families, different types of violence and abuse against young brides such as 'dowry deaths' and an increasing number of cases of divorce and abandonment. These negative consequences have led to major public advocacy campaigns against the practice of dowry. For example, in India dowry has been a prominent issue for the women's movement since the 1970s (Siddiqui 2002; Srinivasan 2005). In Bangladesh, dowry figures are a central matter of concern for NGOs, development agencies and feminist organisations. NGO advocacy against dowry has spread across the countryside, including the Tala area, so that there is a general awareness and a widespread discourse about dowry being an evil that should be uprooted, especially amongst poor people. However, as we will see later in the case studies, this has not stopped people from practising dowry.

Local Interpretations of Dowry and Social Change

In Tarapur, I had a number of interesting and heated discussions, mostly with women, about the meaning of dowry. What follows is an abstract from one of those discussions.

There are bad girls who make love (prem kore) and as they are available anyway, men don't want to get married anymore. In this modern era (adhunik jug) women go out and are visible. Before they were always inside. Men didn't know how they were and they wanted to get married. They couldn't choose and they would marry without looking at physical features... Girls nowadays like men, show too much interest in sex, they like to be touched. So men will harass them and even if girls don't encourage them, men won't stop because men are bad. The only solution would be for girls to stay at home. Society has turned upside down.

Thus, people commonly attribute the spread of the custom of dowry to a sort of law of demand and supply.[9] Women have less value (*dam kom*[10]) than in the past because they are too visible and this decreases their 'value' in terms of prestige. Women blame themselves for this as women are seen to be responsible for attracting men's bad attentions. As a consequence, they are perceived as too easy and less valuable. The suggested implicit solution is for women to withdraw from places like streets, which are male domains. These common views reflect, as Rozario (1992, 2009) underlines, the persistence of dominant values related to honour and women's purity and reveal the extent to which girls and women subscribe to them.

There are however aspects of social change that make the situation more complex and can be linked to the emergence of other competing discourses. The increased visibility of unmarried adolescent girls in Tala area is also undoubtedly due to their increased attendance at high school (grades 6 to 10) and college (grades 11 and 12). Married women's participation in NGO activities, either as beneficiaries or staff, also entails enhanced mobility, as well as increasing the possibilities for them to contribute significantly to the family income. Parents sending their daughters to college and girl students themselves are also proud of their increased mobility compared with the past and with older women. Although older women accuse girls of being shameless, they also regret not having had the opportunities to go to school as girls do today. Thus education and work are perceived as a threat to women and to their families' prestige (man shonman), but also, as has been discussed in the previous chapters, as potential status enhancers. Girls' education and working skills add to their perceived value and mean that a lesser amount of dowry will be asked at the time of marriage. At the same time, as the symbolic asymmetry between husband and wife has to be maintained, the bride's level of education cannot be higher than the husband's. Being too highly educated (and also older) can be an obstacle instead of an advantage in terms of marriage opportunities.

Even the way young men perceive and live some aspects of social change is contradictory. On the one hand, males who are better off may prefer an educated bride, able to contribute with her work and skills to the family income. On the other hand, and especially amongst the poor, education is not really perceived as opening opportunities for employment. So the biggest asset of a woman remains her purity, which, in turn, is better assured if she is younger. A less educated girl would also be more submissive and able to adapt to her in-laws. A group of young men who were studying in Dhaka for masters degrees at the time of my fieldwork, but who were also natives of a village close to Tarapur, had this to say:

We would like to marry with a girl who has studied, but not too much, until matriculation. We would like someone we could talk to, but not a town girl that would be too 'modern'. These modern girls want to go out wearing jeans and they cut their hair. They won't obey their in-laws and their husbands.

Finally, as the case studies I present will show, it should be emphasised that in the Tala area dowry assumes a different practical meaning for poor and rich households. Poorest parents perceive dowry and the subsequent compulsory gifts as an obligation and a price they have to pay to secure their daughters a social identity as married women, a decent level of economic well-being, and good treatment by the husband and the in-laws. The father of Shopna, one of the girls I will talk about later, used to say that he was willing to give as much dowry as was demanded because in this way 'they (the in-laws) would keep her well' ('*je tara take bhalo rakbe*')'.[11] For well-off parents, dowry may well be an occasion to display status and economic power, as demonstrated in Najma's marriage (discussed ahead) and as underlined by some of my informants.[12]

For both poor and well-off households, however, the practice of dowry reflects the inferior status of women and that of their families. A marriage union where the bride belongs to a lower group than that of the husband is possible. However, the opposite is not tolerated, especially if the lineage or the caste of the groom are at the bottom end of the social ladder. Women embody the prestige and status of a household. According to the father of a teenager who was disfigured as a result of an acid attack: 'If the status of a woman goes down, the prestige of the whole group goes down'. Marrying a daughter to a groom of a lower lineage hampers the status of the whole family.

Getting Married and Becoming a Wife: At the Shosur Bari (the in-laws house)

It is clear that parents' main duty is to arrange a match that can secure their children a stable economic condition and married status. Girls' parents have more responsibility because at marriage they will hand over their daughters to members of another household who will assume total responsibility for their well-being. Daughters are 'given' in marriage (biye dewa) more obviously than sons. Residence in Bangladesh is predominantly patrilocal and the wedding ceremony dramatically symbolises the girl's separation from the parental family (see Kotalova 1993). The wedding ceremony is made up of different phases, taking place over several days. The union is formally ratified at the bride's home in the presence of the two parties and after this the couple leave for the husband's village where the bride is accompanied only by one relative, preferably her grandmother. The wedding day is supposed to be a sad one for the bride and her relatives. 'The girl is obviously sad because she has to leave her family and go with strangers but once there, she will adapt to the new family and once she becomes a full member of it, all the problems will be solved'.

People acknowledge the suffering implied in having to abruptly leave one's own family, go with strangers, and the ceremony provides for a ritual expression of it. The new bride is expected to cry and to show sorrow and sadness. Doing otherwise would be taken as a shameless act and an expression of a lack of love and attachment to the natal family.

The phase of *boukal* (literally, 'the time of wifehood'), when a young bride moves to her in-laws and before she has children, is understood as a very troubled time. It is the time when women's mobility is particularly constrained and a time when new brides are literally strangers in someone else's house. They are subjected to a lot of scrutiny from the in-laws and at the same time have to adapt to a completely new environment. It is taken for granted that the relationship between daughter-in-law and mother-in-law is a difficult one and it is the former who has to do most of the adapting. A daughter is taught first by her mother how she is to behave at her in-laws', and this is the substantial part of her training as a future wife. Halima's comments on her marriage were echoed by many other women I met: 'When I got married I did not understand anything'. The instructions she received about how to behave with her husband and his family were: 'Keep your eyes down, obey and make yourself small and invisible as much as you can'. In many cases if the bride was very young, the new couple would not have sexual intercourse before the girl's puberty or the husband would wait at least some time before approaching her.

An affective and sexual relation between the spouses is something that is assumed to develop after marriage and never shown in public. The growing intimacy between husband and wife should not displace the strong attachment between mother and son. Whenever a conflict arises inside a household between the bride and her mother-in-law, the husband is supposed to side with his mother. The wife is usually blamed for her inability to cope ('*mene nite pare na'*). All the young brides I talked to identified the relationships with their in-laws as an important factor for their well-being. However, older mature women voiced more concern about the relationship with their husbands. The youngest brides never mentioned, either in negative or positive terms, sexuality and intimacy with their husbands as an important aspect of their married life. They talked of the advantages and disadvantages of marriages in terms of mobility, and evaluated their married life against their expectations. Rita, whose husband is a middle peasant, is an 18-year-old with two small children and a stable marriage. She underlined that married women are less independent. It is especially in terms of mobility that she sees married women as more constrained.

Happiness in marriage depends on the behaviour of one's husband and parents-in-law. My father-in-law was a nice person but died. My mother-in-law is not so nice. My husband is good because he allows me to go out and visit my natal home frequently. But the dreams I had before getting married have disappeared. My parents were poor so I couldn't continue to study. Before marriage women are more independent, after marriage they can't do what they want (icchar moto). You always have to ask your husband's permission and he can always refuse. I am lucky because my husband allows me to go.

Nazima, aged 20, lived with her husband and a six-year-old child at her in-laws. Her household could be classified as majhari (middle) from a strictly economic point of view. When I asked her about the positive aspects of married life, she said:

They are a lot. After some time you don't feel good anymore at your parental house because people start looking badly at you and you start feeling uneasy. Instead, when you are married you feel that you are on your own, you have your children, your work and then when your husband comes home you are happy. If there is one bad person in the house all the others will try to make it good. Here women cannot think of staying on their own because it is difficult for women to earn money, so it is good to be married and have a husband who supports you. I work a lot because now I live for Minni, I want her to study and marry later than me. I studied until class 8 but then I had to stop. I regret it a bit but now all my concern and hopes are for my daughter.

Neither Rita nor other young brides in Tarapur spoke directly with me of their intimate relationship with their husbands. The most they would say was: *'amar shami bhalo, khub ador kore'* ('My husband is good because he cares for me a lot'). Some of them explained ador in terms of good behaviour and of lack of violence on the part of the husband, while others referred to the fact that their husbands regularly provided oil for the hair, clothes and simple ornaments; in other words, all the items that are considered indispensable for women, even the poorest women. In explaining her negative view of marriage and married life Bina stressed:

Marriage is not good, husbands are bad. They only say: cook, give me water, do this and that. My husband didn't care for me, he used to beat me a lot. I do not want to be married anymore, independence is good, I would be fine if I had some more money.

The stability of a marriage and the well-being of a married daughter are ensured by the tie set up between the two families, which is maintained by further exchanges. Importantly, the obligations of the bride's family towards the groom's family do not end with the wedding. The former is expected to give subsequent gifts to the son-in-law at special events such as religious festivities, or to provide him with cash if the economic situation of the couple is not good. The value of the gifts depends on the economic condition of the two households. For example, Halima, a poor NGO employee, gave a sweater to her eldest daughter's husband during the festival of Eid, while Najma's parents, a well-off household, could afford a motorbike worth Tk 60,000.

However, dowry can also become the cause for a marriage breaking down. Unfulfilled requests for dowry can cause divorce, violence, wife suicides and the murder of young brides, particularly if poor parents are not able to give what was promised at the time of marriage or cannot afford subsequent gifts. In this sense, the commonly held discourse about the stability of marriage and arranged marriages (as opposed to western customs) does not correspond to the reality. Interestingly, amongst all the people I talked to about marriage, only Shopon, a Hindu college teacher, acknowledged that in many cases there is a significant gap between the expectations of marriage as a source of ultimate security for women and the reality. 'Parents want their daughters to marry and settle down as soon as possible but they do not realise that after marriage they will have to bear additional expenses and they may fall into bigger danger'.

People in Tarapur are reluctant to admit and discuss what is considered 'shameful' and morally sanctionable; they tend to cover up cases of abandonment, divorce and remarrying for dowry. However, since the early 1980s, there are well-documented reports of men remarrying frequently as a means to secure new dowry payments (Abdullah and Zeidenstein 1980; Adnan 1988; Alam 1985; Ahmad and Naher 1987; Islam 1979). The same studies offer evidence of increased incidences of divorce, abandonment and domestic violence, so that the rise in dowry seems to be linked to the fragility of marital relations rather than ensuring stability. In Tarapur, too, poor parents live under the constant threat that their daughters may be sent back to them with new requests for payments. If they can't afford to respond, the real risk is that their daughters may be abandoned. I had come across several of these situations while I was working from 1994 to 1996 for a local NGO in Jessore district. In Tarapur, during my fieldwork, I was told about the case of Rokeya who lived in Mollah para, one of the poorest neighbourhoods of the village. Rokeya used to come every morning to my place and ask for money. When I asked about Rokeya I was told that her husband was a daily labourer with no assets, who at some point had obtained a loan of about Tk 10,000 to set up a small business in the wood trade. The business did not work out as expected so he was left in debt and also had to look after his family. He then decided to marry another woman whose parents had promised to pay him Tk 10,000 as dowry. Some months after his second marriage the new in-laws had not paid the dowry and so he sent his second wife back to them. Unable to work because of an illness, he could not support his first wife and their three children. For this reason Rokeya was visiting me everyday asking me for help. The person who told me Rokeya's story, admitted that he felt embarrassed to recount such details to a foreigner because 'you may not understand'. However, he also said: 'Of course you know…you have spent a lot of time among us…you know that poor people sometimes have no alternatives'.

In the cases I am going to discuss ahead, poor parents appear to be no less motivated to secure the well-being of their daughters than richer ones. However, the latter seem to have more choices and room for manoeuvre than the former. Moreover, although parents consider marriage the main way to secure their daughters a stable economic and social position and a basic level of well-being, marriages are not as stable as they are often depicted.

'WHETHER I LIKE MY HUSBAND OR NOT IS NOT AN ISSUE': NAJMA'S WEDDING

Najma, who was approximately 18 years old and a second-year student at Tagore, belonged to a wealthy family in Tarapur and was related to the other borolok households of the Morol para. Her marriage took place during my fieldwork and Najma's behaviour throughout was very striking. I first heard about her marriage when she came to visit me with a group of friends. They explained that she was very quiet because she was not happy with the fact that she was about to be married off. 'It was not her decision, it was her father's decision'. Najma had first seen her husband three or four months before the wedding when he and his relatives had come 'to see her', but she did not have a chance to talk to him. She refused to discuss any detail of the wedding ceremonies, and when I asked her whether she liked her proposed husband, she said: 'This is Bangladesh, not Italy, whether I like him or not is not an issue. We have to accept what our guardians decide'. When I pressed her, asking about her actual feelings (moner kota) about her marriage, she said:

Of course I have my own feelings, in this sense we are the same, but here what I feel doesn't matter. Boys have more opportunities than girls to express their preferences, and girls have more choices in educated families. Another problem is that this is a rural area and people are more religious.

The *gaye holud* ceremony, at which many of the friends, neighbours
and relatives of the bride gather to bathe her and smear her body with
turmeric (this is also done at the groom's home), is usually a very
informal and high-spirited occasion. Children and adults play around
and make many jokes. At Najma's gaye holud she remained serious
throughout, letting the others take care of her and not responding to
their jokes and play.

The actual wedding took place the following day at the bride's
house, with the groom sitting under a canopy in the courtyard and
Najma inside a room in her house surrounded by female friends and
relatives. Both bride and groom have to separately give their 'consent'
to the official registration of the marriage. The officer in charge went
first to the groom who signed the documents and gave his consent
after a brief discussion with the father of the bride about the amount
of *mehr* (a sort of bride price). Then he moved to the room where
Najma was sitting with her school friends and female relatives and
asked her formally whether she agreed to the marriage. The officer
had to repeat the ritual formula three times before she answered. She
sat silently with her head down while some of the women around
incited her to speak: 'Say it, say it, quickly say it'. As she remained
silent, everyone began to look worried and serious until someone
said: 'I have heard it, she said it', and she was given the register to sign.
Najma then had to get dressed in the clothes and jewellery presented
to her by the relatives of the groom as the husband's wedding gifts.
However, in line with her earlier reluctance, she refused to leave the
bed on which she was sitting. She was crying, almost screaming, until
eventually two unmarried middle-aged relatives managed to get her
changed, saying 'this is too much, stop it'. Later in the day, when the
newly married couple were to leave to go to the groom's family house,
a really dramatic scene occurred. Najma refused to go, crying and
shouting 'I won't go'. In the end, she was literally carried to the car
and pushed inside.

The different phases of the wedding ceremony were perfectly
consistent with the way wedding rituals are supposed to be but Najma's
reactions were thought to be extreme. The wedding day has to be a
sad one for the bride and her relatives as it signals her separation from

them. So it was normal for the bride to show that she was unwilling to leave. If the bride had shown happiness at leaving, this would have been interpreted as lack of shame and an inappropriate expression of sexual curiosity and desire. It is taken for granted that young women, like boys, feel strong sexual drives and are eager to get married to satisfy them. I was told: 'Girls giggle and smile when their parents announce to them that they have found a husband for them; they wouldn't show it openly, because of shame, but they are actually happy'.

When Shirin talked to me about Najma's wedding she said that most of her married friends were afraid before getting married because they did not know what to expect. In this she referred particularly to what happens in the *bashor ghor* (nuptial room) on the wedding night.

Najma's behaviour at the preliminary gaye holud ritual was however unusual. Unlike the actual wedding day, this ceremony is supposed to be an occasion of fun for everybody, including future spouses, as it gives them an opportunity to celebrate with their own kin and friends. Mina, a 16-year-old who married four years ago, said: 'We had a nice party when I got married; we did all the preliminary ceremony of gaye holud. I enjoyed it, even if I was very young'. Najma's passive and sad attitude during the gaye holud ceremony was interpreted by one of her close relatives as a sign of the contested nature of the marriage. Everybody knew that Najma, her mother and other close relatives had opposed the marriage particularly because of its timing. Najma wanted to continue studying and her mother did not want to be separated from her so early. However, her father did not want to lose a 'good match' for his daughter. The groom's father had cancer and wanted to see his son married before he died and so had pressed for an earlier marriage.

Najma's case is an example of a typical well-off, landowning rural household marriage arranged by the bride's father even if the other family members were against it. Najma's words and attitude in the days preceding the celebrations were consistent with the sort of compliance with parental decisions that has emerged from some of the other interviews with young and older adolescents. For example, they stressed that they trusted their parents and so were willing to accept the choices made on their behalf. Even if Najma, as she had told me, was clearly aware of her feelings about the groom, loyalty to her parents prevailed. She ruled her feelings out as something irrelevant 'in Bangladesh'. The contradiction between her father's will and her own views became particularly evident when she had formally to express her consent at the wedding ceremony. Even here, however, this did not manifest itself as open conflict. As the bride is expected to show her pain at having to leave her family, it was not surprising that Najma spent the whole wedding day sitting on her bed with a gloomy face while all the relatives and friends were trying to cheer her up. This behaviour could be interpreted as reinforcing prevailing gender norms. However it appeared that she went too far in showing her grief. Rather than 'performing' sorrow, it appeared as if she was in real despair and pain. This was reflected in the faces and the expressions of the people around: the children became very serious, and the adults looked annoyed and worried when Najma refused to pronounce her consent. She was ordered to 'say it'; she was told 'this is too much' when she did not want to get dressed, and at the end of the ceremony she was carried screaming and crying towards the car. All those who attended the wedding probably felt that this 'excessive' manifestation of grief and refusal to leave, expressed 'real' pain and reluctance that had filtered through the barrier of shame (lojja) and effectively was an assertion of dissent from her father's decisions.

In her analysis of narratives of marriage in Nepal, Ahearn describes a similar process during the wedding of Pancha Maya (2001a: 93–97). The Hindu ritual in Nepal entails, according to Ahearn's informants, a ritual defloration of the bride. This is achieved by the application of red powder on her hair part by the husband-to-be, symbolising the consummation of the marriage and loss of her virginity. Pancha Maya tried actively to resist this, fighting to keep her head covered. When she had to move from the right to the left of her husband, symbolising loss of status, she resisted and her husband had to force her with the help of others. According to Ahearn, one plausible interpretation of Pancha Maya's behaviour is that she tried to object to the fact that her father had arranged her marriage without her knowledge or consent. This took place against the background of social, political and economic changes that had been occurring in the village. By the 1990s, elopements had become more common than arranged marriages, with young women increasingly getting married without consulting their parents. Parents were also consulting their sons in arranged marriages. Consent and individual choice therefore were becoming more valued in marriage practices. Ahearn argues that Pancha Maya's protest can be seen as, first of all, a way to 'physically enact and discursively express a culturally constrained but never totally negated agency' (2001: 93). Her behaviour, therefore, embraced elements of accommodation and resistance. Secondly, in the specific historical context, this kind of 'accommodating protest' (McLeod 1992) could actually be linked to the emergence of sentiments and actions that may have the potential to change marriage practices more profoundly.

The physical enactment of what cannot be said is central to Najma's behaviour. Delaying her consent, crying too much, and refusing to leave, all assert her opposition to her marriage. Why did she perform in this way if everyone knew of her disagreement, even if it was never openly declared? Is it possible that she was simply overwhelmed by her grief and emotions? This is possible. However, I believe there is a more plausible interpretation rooted in the fact that from the beginning she knew that she had very little choice. Overt and decisive opposition to her father would have triggered a major familial conflict, and she was always in a weaker position. If she had refused to marry she would have risked losing the support of her family and probably would have had to comply in the end. What she finally chose to do was to manifest her disagreement during the ceremonies through a sort of passive resistance. This is evident in her behaviour during the gaye holud ceremony, her resistance to dressing with the bridal red sari, and her refusal to get in the car that would have taken her away. She chose not to give too much value to her own personal feelings and preferences and not to assume responsibility for them because this would not create any realistic or practical alternative. By complying with her father's decision, even if she disagreed with it, she threw the responsibility of her marriage onto others. As an immediate strategic result, she secured help and support in the event of future problems with her husband or in-laws. If she had chosen to follow her feelings she would have been on her own.

Najma did not 'perform her role' as a bride during her wedding, hiding her 'true self' behind a mask. She knew what was happening to her, and was aware of her own feelings and of the spaces that she could use to manifest them. Before her wedding she stressed to me that she knew very well what she felt, but that in her particular social and cultural context her feelings were of little importance. She also drew attention to the role of some social changes favouring the emergence of different practices. Thus, she pointed out that in educated families children (boys especially) are listened to more; that there is a difference between urban and rural contexts; and between people who are more religious and those that are more conservative. She herself was an educated girl and not so young. This probably enabled her to be so articulate and capable of reflecting on her marriage. It also enabled her to distance herself from the wedding and to reflect on how it was all arranged.

'I DID NOT WANT TO GET MARRIED AGAIN BUT WHAT ELSE COULD I DO'? SAJU'S WEDDING

Saju and Jamirul's wedding occurred a few weeks after Najma's. It was a much more informal ceremony with parts of the ritual being skipped. Saju was a 15-year-old girl who had divorced her husband two years before and was working as a maid for a family in Chadnagar. Instead of the bride's natal home, the wedding took place in Tarapur, in the courtyard of Halima's house. Halima was an affine of Saju, who was the sister of the man who married Halima's eldest daughter. Saju's family asked her to help arrange the marriage. Jamirul was a rickshaw puller in his thirties. He was not related to Halima but lived in the same village as Saju's natal family. A few months before he had been abandoned by his wife, Mamtaj, who had fled to Dhaka with another man to work in a garment factory, leaving behind two daughters. Halima knew the whole story because Mamtaj's natal family was in Tarapur and Mamtaj was one of her nieces. Halima tried, along with other neighbours, to make Mamtaj change her mind. Their efforts failed, and following Mamtaj's departure, they all tried to help Jamirul find 'someone that could look after the family'.

The wedding was organised by Halima and her neighbours in less than 24 hours and there was no gaye holud ceremony. Saju's mother was not present.

Halima played a fundamental role as a matchmaker. Backed by the whole neighbourhood she brought Saju to Tarapur and proposed that she should marry Jamirul. Saju's decision was not straightforward. After refusing the proposal in the first instance, saying that she would rather kill herself, she then spent a night trying to make up her mind. When she finally accepted she was tired and confused: 'I didn't sleep last night, and I didn't eat for a whole day. Now I'd like just to take rest. I feel dizzy and I have a lot of confusion in my head'.

Saju had initially been given in marriage when she was 12 years old. Her father withdrew her from school although she had been a good student and had wanted to continue studying. From her first contact with her in-laws, she understood that her marriage would not be easy: 'The first time my mother-in-law saw me she said "black", and so I thought "this is the end"'. Having dark skin is a physical feature that makes girls much less desirable in the marriage market.[13] Parents of dark-skinned girls have to compensate by paying a higher dowry unless other characteristics, like belonging to a high status rich family, enhance the value of the bride. Saju was poor and not educated. Her mother-in-law's first negative comments were followed by physical violence by both her husband and her mother-in-law. She ended up leaving her husband and divorcing him. After such a bad experience, Saju was initially not willing to get married again: 'I don't like anything, I don't want or expect anything. Having a family means trouble and being alone is better'. She also expressed a low level of self-worth: 'I don't have any value. My father and my brothers don't care about me'. But when she changed her mind, after considerable pressure, she explained her reasons in the following way:

I have decided to get married because I realised I don't have an alternative. I don't have a chance of getting a real job, and nobody wants me. Now I can't change my destiny, let it be, according to Allah's will. If everybody says this marriage is good, it is good for me too. I am not really interested in it. I didn't want to marry again, but what can I do? When my father and mother die I will be alone. Nobody will want me, nobody will take me. Life ends sooner or later, everything is in Allah's hands. Life is birth, marriage and then death—jonmo, biye, mrittu.

Saju knew that her job in the long term would not be enough to ensure her economic well-being, let alone give her an acceptable social identity. In a context where marriage is, like birth and death, inevitable in everyone's life, being unmarried is a most undesirable condition. These considerations were foremost in the minds of those who promoted and attended her wedding. When I commented that Saju seemed so unhappy, one response I got was that marriage was the right thing to do and that Allah punishes those who refuse to get married. 'There are norms that have to be followed and being happy is not the most important thing in life'. The samaj,[14] represented here by Halima's neighbours and a matobar who wanted to help Jamirul, exercised a lot of pressure on Saju. Their assurance that they would look after her and Jamirul held considerable weight in making her change her mind. 'You know all these people here convinced me, because they all think that this marriage will be good, that Jamirul is a good man. They have assured me that they will look after me'.

However, this pressure was also evident during the wedding itself. Saju agreed to the wedding in the morning and it took place the same day. By the time it was dark, nobody knew exactly when the groom would arrive. Some children were playing around waiting enthusiastically for the ceremony, while the adults were busy preparing food and making the last minute arrangements. Saju's father was discussing financial matters with some other elderly people. The two parties had agreed on a dowry of Tk 2,000. While all the others were busy preparing food, Saju was sitting alone in a corner of the verandah of Halima's house. She looked indifferent to what was happening around her and she told me she was feeling lonely because her mother was not there. The wedding eventually took place at 2 a.m., after I had left.

In the days immediately following the wedding, Saju was very distressed and emotional and this caused a lot of concern. Halima's advice was that Saju's brother should take her as soon as possible to her parents' house so that 'she would cool down a bit' (*thanda hobe*) because 'she is too hot' (gorom). Being 'hot' is associated with being too emotional and prone to feel and express strong emotions like anger or grief.

Saju's behaviour before and after the wedding expressed a great deal of ambivalence about her decision. The unexpected proposal found her in a situation of relative well-being in the household where she was working, but she knew that it was not a long-term solution. Once she had accepted Jamirul's proposal she remained unconvinced, and in some senses freed herself from the responsibility of her own destiny saying that everything is in Allah's hands. This is consistent with her attitude from the moment she took the final decision. Her wedding was something that was happening to her, but in which she was not really involved. A fatalistic attitude helped her to reconcile getting married with the impossibility of following her immediate will. The troubled decision she had to take and the dilemma she faced however resulted in her being emotionally overcharged and made the overall situation particularly dramatic. The day after the wedding, she was thought to be excessively emotional, too gorom. So her relatives were concerned about 'cooling her down'. Like Najma, Saju was not supposed to show her inner struggle as the ritual allows only a moderate and restricted display of emotions. In the public domain, her attitude should have been more cool (thanda). Like Najma, she refused to hide her emotions and to perform as she was expected to, however it is difficult to say whether this was part of a more strategic negotiation of the expression of distance, or an immediate reaction to her inner turmoil.

In Saju and Jamirul's wedding, the parents of the two spouses played a marginal role. Only Saju's father was present at all times to negotiate the dowry and to attend the ceremony. The most significant roles were those of Saju's brother and of Halima (his mother-in-law). Ultimately, it was Mamtaj's neighbours who felt responsible for helping her abandoned husband. They seemed to want to compensate for her behaviour, something that Halima informed me, the samaj (neighbours and matobars of the para) strongly disapproved of. The neighbours and the matobars assumed the role of parents and represented Jamirul in the marriage negotiations. Jamirul's status as an abandoned husband, as well as Saju's status as a divorced and working woman, were both socially anomalous situations. Their marriage would have redressed both anomalies. This is how a local matobar explained the wedding situation: 'We, the samaj told the boy (Jamirul) not to worry because we would have given him in marriage again. The boy is good, he doesn't have any fault and he earns a good income. After some discussion we found the right girl'.

It was clear, however, that Saju and Jamirul's union was far from the ideal of the highly valued first marriage, the proper biye where the full ritual is performed and which has a sacramental and not just a contractual nature.[15] As this was the second marriage for both the spouses, there was less concern for the formalities. The wedding took place late at night and only close relatives and neighbours were involved. Saju's parents did not give her in marriage and she was asked for her consent in a more obvious way than Najma.

'I DON'T LIKE MY HUSBAND, I WILL NEVER GO BACK': SHOPNA

I first met Shopna and her family during a short visit to Chadnagar in 1991, and then again in 1994 and 1996. Shopna's family belongs to Chadnagar's Rishi para. Shopna's father, Ranjan, worked as a primary school teacher. The whole family had survived over the years through the help of missionaries working in the same village. During my fieldwork, Shopna, 17 years of age, was still living with her parents after an unsuccessful marriage that had lasted a few months. I was told the story of her first marriage by Father Paggi, one of the priests in charge of the local Catholic mission. In this account it should be borne in mind that the Catholic mission is an actor rather than an observer in this situation. This account is not verbatim but based on notes I took during conversations.

When Shopna became shekna (mature), Ranjan started worrying about her chastity as she was 'too hot' and she used to 'go around too much'. He was also afraid that she could have been raped as these incidents are common in the area and the victims are mainly poor girls. Ranjan was afraid that if Shopna acquired a bad reputation, no one would then marry her. On the other hand he did not have the money to pay for her dowry and did not have reliable connections (jogajog) with good families. So Shopna carried on studying with the help of the mission.

In 2000 a group of people of the Rishi para took over and managed to arrange Shopna's marriage within a family living in a village nearby. For this service they were paid a considerable amount of taka by the family of the groom to be who had an interest in marrying into Shopna's family. The suitor's family in fact had a status even lower than Shopna's and they would have gained a more respectable social position from the union. Ranjan accepted and Shopna had to agree even if she did it unwillingly. Marriage hindered her plans to study until matriculation (she was in grade nine). The wedding took place according to the Hindu ritual and was not legally registered.

After a few months, Shopna left her husband and went back to her parents, who strongly supported her decision. First, from the very beginning, Shopna had wanted to marry the younger brother of the man that had been chosen for her. Her father said that they had actually been cheated and that only on the day of the wedding did Shopna and her parents see who the groom actually was. Second, her father-in-law tried to abuse her. Despite this, Shopna's husband wanted to keep her so he called for *bichar*[16] (an informal village court) to decide the matter. The relatives of the boy, backed by those who had arranged the marriage, argued that the marriage could not be dissolved because it had been celebrated according to a Catholic ritual. But this was denied by the priest in charge of the mission. While the bichar discussion revolved around the issue of the validity of the marriage, Shopna stood up and asked to speak. Without mentioning the violence she had experienced, she said that she did not like the man she was married to and that she had wanted to marry his brother. She said that she did not care whether her husband liked her or not, and that whatever the result of the hearing she would rather die than go back to her in-laws. At this point the chairman of the bichar, who was also the chairman of the village, turned to the husband suggesting that he give Shopna up as she had expressed her will so clearly. He then decided that nobody could force her to return with her husband and allowed her to go back home.[17]

Standing up during a public bichar was a highly visible assertion of Shopna's wishes and required considerable determination and a strong sense of agency. The public statement that she disliked her husband and was not willing to remain his wife was highly unexpected.

During the previoius 20 years nothing likc this had ever happened in Chadnagar Rishi para.[18] Elopements and 'illegal' premarital and adulterous love stories had occurred, but Shopna was the first woman who had dared to express publicly a refusal to be with her husband on the basis of a personal preference. The final judgement constituted a public acknowledgement that women could have such preferences. The presence of the mission in the area played an important role in giving Shopna a sense of being supported when she chose to leave her husband. Everyday practices in rural areas now involve a wide range of social actors, and, in this case, the missionaries represent, as do the NGOs, an element of modernity and a source of support for poor men and women.

Like Saju, Shopna could not object to her first marriage despite wishing to carry on studying. She had some legitimate right to object to the abuse she had suffered and this legitimised her return home and her refusal to stay married. It also gave her the strength to defend and justify her position in a public arena. Unlike Saju, she was supported by her parents and was able to make the samaj, represented in this case by the chairman, rule in her favour. After this episode Shopna spent more than a year challenging her father's attempts to have her marry a second husband. I saw her arguing with her mother saying, 'I don't want to get married again, you don't love me, the only thing you want is to get rid of me. I would rather finish studying.' Secretly, and most of the para knew this, she was also entertaining more or less platonic relationships with other boys of the village. At some point she asked me to cover her planned elopement with a boy of the same age whose parents would have never allowed him to marry a divorced woman. While I was still lost in the dilemma of what to do, she apparently changed her mind and willingly accepted one of the many suitors her father had managed to secure.

Taken together, Saju's and Shopna's cases suggest that girls have more opportunities and space for self-assertion at their second marriage. The first marriage is a highly ritualised and symbolic occasion, a sort of obligatory passage of status. Having already been married once, Saju and Shopna had to bear less pressure from their parents and were in some senses granted more opportunities to make their own life decisions. After a bad marriage, Shopna actively tried to marry someone she liked, while Saju experienced some economic independence for some time. Both of them tried in different ways to shape their lives according to their desires. For neither of them was the second marriage an easy choice, but after being more substantially consulted they finally accepted arrangements made for them. Saju and Shopna represent a great number of girls who were given in marriage very early and had to stop going to school because of various linked economic and social reasons. After few negative experiences, separation from their husbands allowed them, to some extent, to break free from formal obligations. However, it also left them in more isolated and vulnerable situations. Shopna had at some point asked the help of the mission to complete her secondary education, but she was also aware that this would not have guaranteed her a job. Saju knew that in the long term her job as a maid would not have been enough to secure her survival.

CONCLUSIONS

The stories of Najma, Saju and Shopna give some insights into the kind of complexities that lie behind the public façade of marriages, where apparently neither the bride nor the groom have much space for expressing their choices and where, girls especially, are supposed to be passive and compliant with others' decisions. Marriage is considered a natural step in the individual life cycle and a fundamental pillar of social organisation, a social institution that implicates not only two individuals but a much wider network of relations. Neither boys nor girls are supposed to choose when to get married and with whom, and there is a widespread hegemonic discourse cross-cutting class and religious communities that makes individual preferences and feelings almost irrelevant to the process, despite the hidden, parallel world of premarital cross-gender friendships, 'lines' and somporkko.

The sense of social pressure and constraint, which girls expressed during interviews and conversations, corresponds to the reality of the role played by parents and female relatives in Najma's story, and the neighbours and village leaders as representative of the wider samaj in Saju's and Shopna's stories. In all three cases, there was no open conflict between the three young brides and their guardians at the first marriage. In Najma's case, her opposition to her marriage was evident from her attitude and manifested with her friends, but never expressed to her father. Saju's and Shopna's desire to continue studying rather than marrying had not been taken into consideration by their parents.

However, the way Najma behaved during her wedding shows that the lack of open conflict and the acceptance of her father's will cannot be equated with total compliance and resignation on her part, still less with a lack of personal awareness about her views on her prospective husband. She was quite aware of her own feelings and opinions but she was also aware that, realistically, they were not relevant as they did not constitute a serious alternative project. She was formally asked for her consent but as Ahearn (2001a) underlines, this does not necessarily enhance women's choice if there are no alternative options. On the contrary, as Jeffery and Jeffery (1994) also stress, referring to India, most of the time women do not consider rebelling against their parents or relatives' decisions if this implies losing the support of their existing social networks. In short, the choice that Najma had to make when asked if she consented to the marriage was not a real one, as she did not have a viable alternative. By accepting the marriage she acquired a socially valued identity as wife and entered a defined status and set of social relations in her in-laws' house and village. Having married according to her father's wishes she had secured the support of her own family whose economic means and the large dowry paid had strengthened her position at her in-laws. However, the way she behaved during her wedding suggests that taking up a social position as wife is not the same as masking her 'true feelings' as argued by Das (1979). During the wedding ceremonies, Najma expressed her feelings and her reservations, albeit in covert ways. This means that in future negotiations, as the marriage unfolds and as her relations with her in-laws develop, these reservations and the terms on which she agreed to the marriage will be present as an implicit factor.

The failure of their first marriages had in some way opened for Saju and Shopna alternative trajectories that they tried to pursue. After having the courage to stand up in a public judgement and make the chairman rule in her favour, Shopna tried in different ways to fulfil her desire to choose her own marriage partner. This implied openly contesting her father's authority. As a divorced working woman, Saju had been accorded more substantial power to decide the second time. However, in deciding to marry Jamirul her choice was influenced by the pressure of the neighbours and the realistic fears that she had about being independent but poor and isolated.

All these examples show how difficult it is to disentangle coercion and consent, agency and passive compliance, when it comes to girls' marriage choices. This requires us to rethink in a more nuanced way the meaning of social embeddedness, the nature of selfhood and situations of cultural, economic and social constraint. These are women who are relatively powerless, who lack opportunities and are, moreover, subject to relations of gender and age that allow them little space for assertion and little time for consultation. Nonetheless, they are very far from being passive victims. On the contrary, their stories show that girls are able to express distance from the complex net of social relations that surrounds them; that they are well aware of the cultural context in which they live; and are aware of the limited spaces they have to manifest their preferences and their needs. Young girls have expectations and fears of marriage and married life and these are shaped by their particular circumstances, their level of education, the experiences of their relatives and neighbours, and their own perceptions of the changes happening around them. Education is discursively gaining importance as an element of social change. Not only can it delay marriage, but is also an important factor that can increase the possibilities of agency for both girls and boys. Najma stressed how in more educated families girls have more choices; Saju regretted having interrupted her education to get married; and before her second marriage, Shopna had decided to go back to school in order to convince her father to give up his search for a second husband.

These girls cannot be seen as the final passive product of a process of socialisation that makes them pawns to be moved from the parental house to the in-laws. Even their adherence, once married, to their identity as wives and mothers has to be problematised because they enter this new status with expectations and personal needs that are played out in everyday life, and arguably they will negotiate their own ways of being married over their lifetimes.

It is important to state again that the socio-economic position of a household makes a big difference for parents' and children's agency and power to choose in marriage. Poor girls' parents are more constrained in their choices and this is manifested in the economic sphere (for example, dowry) as well as the social sphere (for example, the social pressure to marry their daughters off as soon as possible). This leaves them with less room for manoeuvre in trying to find better husbands for their daughters.

Finally, marriages are not as stable as the hegemonic discourse would depict them. The commoditisation of dowry constitutes an element of instability and one of the most recurrent causes of divorce and abandonment of young brides, especially among the poor. Once women, either voluntarily or not, leave an abusive relationship, the actual opportunities for economic independence are quite limited and cutting familial ties puts them in the highly undesirable situation of being out of the samaj (family, but also village and community) and of the network of social relations fundamental for surviving. They would in effect be akin to being in a condition of *'amar keu ney'* (I don't have anyone).[19] Recently, NGOs and charitable organisations are playing a significant part in offering women an alternative source of security, but economic self-reliance outside a stable marriage and a familial life is not valued by women themselves as an ideal way ahead.

NOTES

1. Donner (2002, 2008) notices the use of the same expressions in Calcutta. Marrying on one's own does not necessarily imply emotional involvement or long-term courtship but rather that the two partners took the initiative in choosing each other.
2. A hegemonic view that love marriages are problematic and bound to break down more easily than arranged ones emerges also from the Indian contexts of the lower middle-class youth in Bangalore (Nisbett 2004), Delhi slums (Grover 2006, 2008), and Bombay (Abraham 2001), and Calcutta's middle-class households (Donner 2002, 2008). From these studies and from Mody (2002) emerges

the conclusion that great value is given to conformity to societal expectations and to securing the support of the wider network of kin and family for marital unions.

3. In other areas of Bangladesh, people can use other terms to refer to dowry. Rozario (1992), in a rural area not far from the capital city, talks of 'dabi,' literally, demand.

4. This explanation is consistent with some early scholarly interpretations of dowry in India that perceive it as an institution for property transfer at marriage. Srinivasan (2005) cites Tambiah and Goody's (1973: 86) reference to dowry as what 'a woman received from her parents and relatives before and at marriage' and as something 'over which a woman exercised dominion independently of her husband'. This interpretation doesn't consider that in the contemporary context women are excluded from any forms of control over the money or other goods given by her parents to the husband or to the husband's family before or at the time of marriage.

5. One pound corresponds to Tk 110.

6. See Rozario (2002) for a discussion of the issue of 'dark skin' for girls and women.

7. Dowry is present in the Hindu textual tradition as an element of the ideal form of marriage, the Brahmanical *kanyadan*, literally 'gift of a virgin'. The objects that traditionally accompanied the bride in upper caste marriages had a purely symbolic value and were accessories to the main gift that was the bride herself (Fruzzetti and Ostor 1982; Madan 1975; Srinivas 1983: 3). Conversely, the Muslim tradition does not prescribe any form of dowry. Rather it is the bridegroom who should give a *mehr* (a sort of bride price) which is stipulated at the marriage contract. The fixed amount of money is due to the bride as compensation in case of divorce. In the Muslim communities in rural Bangladesh it was rather common to confer a sort of bride price to the bride's family called *pon* (Hartmann and Boyce 1983; Rozario 1992).

8. These cases can be understood also in reference to the hypergamic form of marriage common in north India where it traditionally serves the same purpose. As Tambiah and Goody (1973: 72) argue: '[dowry] is a superb pawn to use in the formation of marriage alliance and in pursuing the status game of hypergamy'.

9. Rozario's respondents in 2004 in northern Bangladesh gave the same explanation for the spread of dowry.

10. Note that 'dam' also means price.

11. The fact that for poor parents' marriage is the fundamental means to secure their daughters a decent future is pointed out even by Osella and Osella (2000: 81) for Kerala. In these cases prestige and wealth considerations are secondary and marriage becomes an end in itself.

12. Gardner (1995) stresses this second interpretation of the practice of dowry. She observed an increase in the payments due by the groom's family in terms of gold, saris and *mehr*. She argues that between families and groups there is competition for acquiring status and that dowry as well as the payment by the groom's family are to be understood in this sense.

13. See also Rozario (2002).

14. I have discussed in Chapter 3 the concept of samaj and its implications when mentioned in the wider sense of the moral community, which guarantees the respect of social norms. The samaj, understood as an abstract moral community, is made concrete in individuals who in different contexts become its representatives. In this case, Halima's neighbours were the representatives of the samaj.

15. Blanchet's (1986) and Kotalova's (1993) observations are relevant for the area of Tala. Even among Muslims, the Hindu ideal of a unique, permanent and indissoluble sacramental first marriage (biye) discursively prevails over the Islamic contractual form of *nikat*.

16. A bichar is the same as a shalish (see chapter 3), i.e. an informal village court. In Shopna's case it took place at the village market place and was chaired by the village chairman. The priest in charge of the mission was called as a witness to respond to issues regarding the validity of the marriage. Shopna and her parents stood against her husband and his relatives and supporters.

17. Father L. Paggi, personal communication.

18. Father L. Paggi, personal communication.

19. See Chapter 2 for an extensive discussion of the meaning of this expression.

EIGHT

Conclusions

In this book I have explored the changing nature of 'adolescence' in rural Bangladesh, on the premise that the spreading of secondary education in rural areas among girls and boys is contributing to the postponement of marriage and, consequently, to a prolonged and more visible transition to adulthood in temporal terms. I have problematised the use of the term 'adolescence' itself, asking whether it is possible to talk of adolescence at all in rural Bangladesh and whether this term is adequate to interpret the modalities of this transition, particularly in view of the multiple aspects that this assumes in a social and cultural context, which is itself undergoing transition and change. In the light of my ethnographic material, I argue that 'adolescence' is emerging as a life stage in rural Bangladesh, although it does not correspond to a recognised social position in its own right. I argue that all this is relevant in shaping the experience of being young in different ways and in giving boys and girls the chance for differentiated discourses about selfhood, for a more articulate perception of their social identity and for more agentful practices as members of their samaj.

WHY ADOLESCENCE

'Adolescence' is linked to an idea of transition and development that has been interpreted in different ways in the psychological and anthropological fields. The Latin verb *adolescere* means to grow up and the past particle of the verb is *adultum* which means grown up. Psychological anthropologists have understood adolescence as a developmental universal stage, characterised by the disjuncture between the biological and the social capacity to reproduce (Schlegel and Barry 1991). Following this approach, other American studies have adopted a cross-cultural comparative view looking at the different ways in which adolescents are socialised into adulthood. Adolescents have been treated as 'unfinished human beings' (Bucholtz 2002) and the cross-cultural comparison between different societies is based on the observation and interpretation of rituals, rites of passage and of the modalities of transmission of cultural values from one generation to another. Bucholtz makes a strong plea for abandoning the term adolescence and replacing it with youth. She argues that to overcome perspectives that confine adolescents to the role of passive recipients of values and norms and that conceptualise adults, but not adolescents, as agents of their own development, a terminological shift is necessary. According to her, only talking of youth and youthhood would allow us to look at forms of agency and 'emphasize the here-and-now of young people's experience, the social and cultural practices through which they shape their worlds' (ibid.: 532).

I retained, instead, the term adolescents because it enabled me also to examine to what extent a psychoanalytic perspective could provide useful insights for my analysis. According to a psychoanalytic framework that revolves around issues of individuation and self-definition, the transition of adolescence has been interpreted in relation to intra-psychic dynamics of separation from childhood's love objects, and acquisition of a sense of selfhood as the base for developing the capacity of engaging in a wider social world outside the network of childhood relations. According to a widely accepted perspective developed in the wake of Erikson's (1968) theorisation, the process of identity formation can however be seen as having a relative and contingent character and its modalities are deemed to depend on the particular social and economic context in which the transition is taking place. If on the one hand puberty brings about physiological changes at the individual level, the way these changes are culturally constructed and their social meaning may take different forms and the acquisition of adulthood may occur through different trajectories. Recent psychological approaches to adolescence point out also the relational character of the process and the indication that the development of the 'I' always takes place within a complex network of relationships resonates with an anthropological notion of the self that emphasises relatedness and relationships (Moore 2004).

In this view, talking of young people instead of 'adolescents' does not exclude a developmental perspective. Young people are (as adolescents) an unstable terrain to explore because they too are engaged in a process of growth. This takes place through the whole life of the individual, and adolescence can be seen as a phase where this process assumes a particular intensity. Precisely by focusing on 'adolescents' and on the process of transition, and by referring to the literature that sees them engaged in an active process and search for self-definition, two important sets of questions can be addressed that put adolescents at the centre of the analysis. The first one concerns young people's sense of who they are, their selfhood in terms of self-perception and the terms on which they see themselves as an 'I' separated from their parents and other formative influences and what kind of social person they want to be. The second set of questions concerns their capacity to act, to choose, to control and shape their own life, especially in relation to the important life choices they face through their 'adolescents' journey'.[1]

SOCIAL EMBEDDEDNESS

In order to answer these questions I have explored the physical, social and cultural spaces available to Bangladeshi teenagers to live 'adolescence' as well as the gendered and classed character of it. Before doing this I have defined the terms of the social embeddedness that characterises rural Bangladesh by discussing in the first two chapters the main features of the economic and socio-cultural context in my research area. I have employed a social relations framework to account for both a material and symbolic dimension in doing this, counter to a 'culturalist' perspective dominated by 'a paradigm of collectivity' that has prevailed in South Asian scholarship through the 1960s and 1970s. Talking in terms of social relations instead of 'culture' means to first recognise 'the powerful role which the economic foundations of a social order or the dominant economic relations of a society play in shaping and structuring the whole edifice of social life' (Hall 1996: 417) and it allows space for exploring how history and power relations define the context in which people live. My discussion has been informed by Gramsci's concepts of social relations and hegemony to allow an analysis of the way dynamics of power and inequality work at the economic, ideological and political levels. These concepts provide a framework to explore a link between a socio-economic structure and the complex of values, norms, cultural representations and ideologies that shape people's 'common sense', their self-consciousness and sense of identity.

Economic relations in the rural sub-district of Tala and in the village of Tarapur are characterised by the dominance of patron-client relationships whose essence is well synthesised by a popular saying, frequently quoted by ordinary people: 'Oil the head of those who have a oiled head and break a wood-apple on the head of those who haven't oil'. The proverb, by saying that people give only to those who have something to return, implies a kind of 'do ut des' exchange and a type of unequal interdependence between people of differing rank and economic position. The ownership of land in southern rural Bangladesh constitutes the basis for establishing relations of production that entail a moral as well as an economic dimension, and in the interest of both parties these relationships are instrumental, reciprocal and long term. The clients, those who define themselves as gorib (poor), obtain from the borolok (rich and powerful) employment, credit and protection in exchange for secure and cheap labour and political support. By claiming a gorib status, a client does not ask only for economic support, but intends to secure himself a long-term relationship that will ensure his survival. Economic relations are thus embedded in a net of reciprocal, although unequal, claims and obligations, and these relationships themselves represent intangible resources, the importance of which is well expressed by the poorest when they say: 'I don't have anyone' to convey the sense of their extreme vulnerability.

In Tarapur and in Tala, as in rural Bangladesh in general, class relations are expressed through the idiom of patronage, and unequal relationships are experienced and made sense of through a complex cultural framework in which preoccupation with ranking and status constitute a central feature. People's everyday life and practices are informed by a set of cultural counters, such as man shonman and samaj, that are the reference points of an hegemonic world view that underpins and sustains economic and political relations. Hierarchy, sometimes expressed in the language of caste, pervades and ordinates the social world of Tarapur's villagers at the group and at the individual level. Status considerations determine people's reciprocal attitude and behaviour as well as their choices. Keeping a respectable social position by keeping intact one's man shonman and by avoiding being given a durnam (bad reputation) is a priority for men and for women because it is the condition for being recognised as full members of the samaj (society or moral community). My description of Jafrul's relation with Razzak's family in Chapter 2 exemplifies the importance that poor people give to keeping a respectable social position, even if this means losing control over land and material assets.

Gender relations can be understood according to the same cultural counters at work in patron–client relationships. Women as daughters, wives and sisters embody the honour/prestige of the whole family or group and their social identity is defined by their belonging first to their parental bari and then to their husband's. The proverb quoted in Chapter 3—'It is better to lose one's life than one's honour'—has been explained referring, in the first instance, to the fact that in order to preserve the honour of the whole family it is preferable for its women to starve and die rather than to work outside the home. To preserve their own and their families' man shonman, to be valued members of a bari, of a group of attiyo swajan, of the samaj, and to be able to claim what this membership entitles them to, women and girls, just like poor clients inside a patronage relation, have to keep relationships working and have to conform to the social obligations that these entail. In a context of strong social embeddedness as described, girls' and women's selfhood and social identity are shaped inside a moral economy of intangible relational resources, that as much as the material ones can be mobilised to pursue one's perceived needs. This is in line with what Ewing (1991: 139) argues for Indian women that despite operating 'within a highly "engaged" interpersonal network of family relationships and expectations' that informs their own perceptions of their needs and wishes, they are nonetheless capable of articulating and pursuing them. In my critique of the 1960s and 1970s South Asian literature, I have established that this is a perspective which is far away from socio-centric interpretations that considered the individual self totally subsumed into group identities.

Age hierarchies and intergenerational relations can be read according to the same framework. In the hegemonic view, adulthood is seen as the capacity to take on attributed and gender-differentiated adult positions and responsibilities. Women's adult status is defined mainly in relation to marriage and motherhood, and men's in relation to their being responsible for the economic support of their families. For the boys, however, this does not imply severing everyday links with the natal family, as it does for girls for whom becoming a wife means to become part of an even wider network of hierarchically ordered relations. Hierarchy is not absent from conjugal and intergenerational relationships but in these domains there is also an exchange of support and loyalty. Bhakti kora (express devotion) is the Bengali term that best expresses the kind of respect and hierarchical love due to parents and elders by young people, as well as to the husband by a wife, while in return, elders, parents and husbands are expected to provide guidance and economic support to their inferiors.

My discussion of the emergence of adolescence in rural Bangladesh is located in the context of social embeddedness as described, which has profound implications for how young people experience and confront the process of transition to adulthood. This process can be interpreted as having a significant social dimension because, especially in view of the changes brought about by modernisation, it implies now, more than in the past, the redefinition of one's relational world and the opening up, outside the boundaries of the parental family, to peer and cross-gender interaction. I have looked at young people as actively engaged in efforts to understand the contradictory expectations that the samaj and all its actors express and to negotiate their own way through it.

Emerging Adolescence in Tarapur

In Tarapur, as we have seen in Chapter 4, there is a hegemonic discourse that ideally collapses puberty and marriage for girls. With puberty, a girl is considered 'grown up' and ready for adult responsibilities. The reality, however, is changing: the value attached to education and the actual spreading of secondary education among boys and girls is linked to the emergence of competing views and practices. The age at marriage for girls is de facto increasing as many parents are willing to postpone it at least for a few years until the end of high school and a minority even further. Boys too tend to be married later, after the completion of tertiary education, as this is required in order to acquire the skills and qualification for a highly desirable white collar job. The modalities of this process are visibly class differentiated: only a small percentage of the girls that complete high school proceed to intermediate college, while many others stop studying to get married before sitting the final exam at the end of high school.

For High School Girls

I have argued, thus, that adolescence is emerging in temporal terms although with different modalities for girls and boys. While girls used to be married at puberty or even before, it is now considered preferable to wait until they are at least 16 or 17 years old. As my ethnography has shown, the girls who expect to be married after only 8 to 10 years of schooling seem to attribute a limited value to their school experience and they talk of marriage as the most significant future step in their lives. Girls comply to parental authority by seemingly conforming to the model of the virtuous and submissive girl, ready to be transformed in the near future into a compliant wife. During group discussions, these girls tended to present themselves as compliant to adults' decisions and quite clear about what their future was going to be. This is exemplified by some of them asserting that their future would consist of 'cooking at their in-laws' and that they 'will study until their parents find for them a suitable husband'. In the view of their parents and elders, by making them study for at least eight or nine years a double advantage can be obtained. On the one hand, sending daughters to school constitutes an acceptable reason for postponing their marriage; on the other hand, literacy and some years of schooling would enhance their capacity 'to understand' and would make them more capable of performing the tasks that the samaj expects, without questioning substantially the confines of their responsibilities as wives and mothers. In Schlegel and Barry's framework (1991), this would be a confirmation that adolescence is no more than a stage of preparation for marriage. It may seem that these girls, having internalised hegemonic values and norms, are smoothly accomplishing a natural process of transition. I argue, on the basis of my ethnography, that if adolescence is emerging for these girls, it is doing so in a much more complex way. Obviously there is not much opportunity for them to develop and to articulate notions of non-compliance in public spaces, but the way they live their everyday reality, at school and in their neighbourhoods, suggests a more complex picture.

Even though Bangladeshi high school girls (12–13 to 17–18) are normatively withdrawn from public spaces after puberty and their social interaction outside the family is limited and much more controlled than that of older college students, de facto they have the opportunity of a wider social world opening up. School gives them a chance to spend time outside the boundaries of their neighbourhood, to share thoughts and emotions with their peers and to ask themselves questions about who they are and who they want to be. My fieldwork was intended to give me access only to the social and cultural aspects of these processes of growing up. I cannot comment here in psychological terms on the dynamics of separation from parents, the first love objects, and on the intra-psychic dynamics of the assumed process of self-identity definition, all of which requires psychological and psychodynamic research. I have however been able to read in the behaviour and discourses of high school girls the footprints of inner work in the direction of establishing the coordinates of who they are. I have discussed how these coordinates reflect the changing social world around them and the discursive and practical alternatives they envisage. Despite the image they give of themselves in public, as compliant and submissive high school students, they appear to be engaged in an effort to find their own way through what the samaj expects and prescribes.

A complex picture emerges from their experiences of friendships, lines and writing of love letters, and from the limited number of cases of young couples who marry on their own initiative, sometimes against their parents' will. During a visit to Tarapur, in 2007, I found that Lipy, who had been a student in grade nine in 2001, had eloped and married a boy her age. I could not talk to her but I was told by a neighbour that Lipy and her husband were still living in their respective homes waiting for an agreed settlement of the matter, because no one would accept the fait accompli. In the same visit I found that Shahin and Tanjila, who during my fieldwork had been forcibly separated after she got pregnant, had kept seeing each other secretly and finally got married. Tanjila was 14 when the relationship with Shahin began. When Hameeda started her line with Joy, she was 14 and when they eloped she was 16. All this is not surprising in view of the love correspondence I have discussed in Chapter 6 and the desire that these young adolescents (boys no less than girls) show for pursuing occasions and spaces for cross-gender contacts. More than this they are preoccupied with their emotions and sentiments, and even if they are less articulate than their older friends, the love discourse they commit to letters carries many interesting meanings. By writing and dreaming of love in this way boys and girls express their adolescence. Behind a search for a partner, for a love object who matches their mon and corresponds to their ideal, there is a search for themselves and for an answer to their own needs for recognition. The emphasis that girls and boys place on listening to what their mon chacche (wants) signals an attention to their own self as a private personal source of emotions and preferences. Nevertheless, we have to acknowledge that some of the high school girls who said that they would like to do as Hameeda had done and marry for love are the same girls who on other occasions said that they were waiting for their parents' decisions and who took for granted their future position at the in-laws. Most girls who marry in their early teens do so according to their parents' expectations and apparently there is not much space for them for forms of self-assertion and for decision making inside marriage. In the public hegemonic discourse, individual preferences, feelings and desires are deemed irrelevant to marriage choices and there is little room for manoeuvre for young brides.

YOUNG ADOLESCENT GIRLS' MARRIAGES

More recent debates on women's agency in South Asia argue for the possibility of agentful behaviour, but risk overestimating women's acts of resistance in a context of structurally unequal gender relations. I have tried to relocate this debate by looking at the experiences of adolescents in the process of defining who they are and want to be. By discussing some experiences of marriage and weddings in Chapter 7, I have tried to gain insights into not only the spaces for decision making open to girls, but also the manifestations of their self-perception and sense of selfhood. Najma's words and behaviour before and during her wedding provide a key to gaining a sense of the extent to which Bangladeshi adolescents are engaged in a process of self-definition in respect to important life choices, like marriage, which apparently demands from them a passive adherence to adults' decisions. Through them, I have argued, she articulated quite clearly her position in respect to a marriage that she did not want but she accepted. She showed that she was far from unaware of her feelings and of the realistic possibility she had of translating them into reality. In commenting that in her own social context, in Bangladesh, one's marriage preferences do not count, she was also able to distance herself from her own position and context and to compare it with others. I believe that Najma' s maturity in understanding her own situation and deciding the best way of dealing with it comes, probably in part, from her being almost 19 years old and a college student; she has had the opportunity to elaborate self-awareness about her own social position. Saju and Shopna, who were younger at their first experience of marriage, were only later capable of positioning themselves and deciding which was the best choice for them, although each in different ways. They finally accepted getting married for a second time according to parental and social wishes, but not without having tried their own way: Saju through work and Shopna through her own search for a husband.

Feminist theory has developed important insights using ideas of trade off (Kabeer 1995, 1998; Whitehead 1981; Young et al. 1981) into the meaning of choice in a context of strong social embeddedness and I refer to these to interpret their final decision to comply. Shopna, Saju and Najma were not the only girls to have hopes, expectations and fears in respect to marriage and married life, and these were shaped by their particular circumstances, their level of education, the experiences of their relatives and neighbours, and their own perceptions of the changes happening around them. Their perceptions of where their own well-being lay were shaped inside the moral economy I have described and I would argue that their decision to comply is the result of a mature consideration of the different possibilities they had. For all of them a situation of security, where they could count on the support of their families and neighbours in the case of further problems with their marriages, was preferable to a more unpredictable situation in which they would have been more independent, but alone, as was the case for Saju and Shopna, while Najma could have risked losing the support of her parents. Saju could have been relatively economically independent but surely in a more risky position, as by refusing to comply with her neighbours' plans she would have undermined familial and communitarian support to which she was entitled as a married woman. These cases show very real constraints on choice and action. For these girls any choice was a very constrained one and this is an expression of their relative powerlessness in relation to other social actors. Saju's, Shopna's and Najma's decisions were taken in a context of highly unequal gender relations and the consequences of their choice did not challenge or alter their subordinate position. However, it is also important to underline that this subordination did not make them the passive results of a process of socialisation or simple pawns to be moved from the parental house to the in-laws. They were quite aware of who they were and what they wanted within the possible alternatives open to them.

COLLEGE STUDENTS

In the case of the college students described in Chapter 5, the issues around the search for self-definition and the acquisition of social identity are more visible and overt. While lines and exchanges of love letters belong to a domain that young people try to keep hidden from adults' eyes, this is not the case for their expectations and dreams about their future. Girls' and boys' efforts to acquire skills and qualifications are supported by their parents. Their aspirations are socially legitimate, even if, for girls, this implies a partial breaking of purdah. Parents value boys' education for its wider opportunities of employment and income and girls' as a marker of status. That is one element that increases their daughters' value as brides. The poorest parents are the ones who are forced to be primarily concerned with their children's future employment, either girls or boys. People's perceptions about education are informed by, and in line with, a development discourse that emphasises it as a means of 'enlightenment'. Parents express quite 'modern' views about the importance of their daughters' and sons' education and employment, two domains shaped and influenced by the discourse of development. In this sense, college students enjoy public recognition of their identity and in this context it is not surprising how easily they articulate publicly their hopes and plans for the future. However, in the value and meaning they attribute to education and in the strong motivation with which girls especially try to overcome obstacles and constraints, there is more than the simple awareness that being more educated gives them more choices for marriage partners or for jobs. In expressing their wishes and hopes of becoming economically independent or at least more responsible and active members of their families and their society, boys and girls show a strong sense of selfhood and self-esteem, for example, in the ease with which they imagine themselves as adults capable of 'standing on their own feet'. Whatever meaning their parents attach to education, it opens for boys and girls a contested period where they have more occasions to experiment with a period of 'psychosocial moratorium', to distantiate themselves from their parents and from other childhood formative influences and to struggle to find out who they want to be and to find their own way of becoming adults.

There are however limited spaces for youth practices in a rural environment. Girls give growing importance to peer group interaction and friendships but they have few occasions for socialising in public spaces. Boys have more access to public spaces, but they lack resources and the village does not offer anything other than the playing grounds or the bazaar for them to get together in groups. Being a college student favours the development of same gender friendships that challenge more traditional forms of interaction. Young people make sense of these relationships through ideas of egalitarian and disinterested love and affection such as brotherhood, and in this sense we can see these relationships as less 'instrumental' than in the village. Boys, especially, aspire to proceed on to university in town and are aware that such an environment will give them the possibility to engage in a wider range of collective activities. In my recent visit to Bangladesh I met Sharif on the campus of Khulna University. He said that since he had started living and studying there he was involved in youth politics because this was one of the possible ways to make 'connections'. Prodip, who lives now in Dhaka, considers himself much more 'literate' in music and cinema. He said his tastes had become more refined, and, after watching Indian and English movies, he no longer liked the Bangladeshi comedies he used to watch in the village.

WORK AND MARRIAGE

Girls realistically envisage the constraints that will limit their possibilities of a career. After attending the intermediate college, most of them continue studying at colleges that offer only simple degrees because enrolling at honours courses would require them to move to town. This is unacceptable to most parents unless there are other relatives already living there. Nonetheless, it is clear that they attach a great deal of importance to education in relation to their futures and their identities. While they perceive themselves subordinated in gender relations and less autonomous than boys in their everyday life, education is seen as a means of self-advancement, at least in the direction of economic independence. Marriage, however, retains even for them a fundamental role in shaping their future and they are not attached to autonomous decision making and independence in this domain. They do not contemplate the possibility of marrying without their parents' consent and generally delegate the choice of a future partner to them. The only concession to their own wishes, they claim, is to have their opinion taken into account. There appears to be a contradiction between the clear way in which girls are willing to appropriate their lives with respect to employment and their compliant attitude about marriage. The words of a college student discussed in Chapter 5 are quite significant:

Of course we will get married, marriage is a taken for granted step in our life, so we do not need to think about it too much in this moment of our life, we simply know that at some point we will get married and our parents will arrange everything for us, so now we are busy studying with the hope that we will then find a job and be able to help our family. We know that after marriage we will be 'poradhin' (dependent/subordinated), but we will accept some limitations, even if we do not like them, because if we rebelled we would be excluded from society 'samaj'. Then we would not be able to be admitted again (to be part of the samaj) and this means that we would suffer for the lack of rapport with our parents and 'attyio swajan'.[2] If we married someone that our parents did not approve of, even if we were economically independent, we would suffer a lot because we could not see our parents, we would be alone.

I believe the key to understanding this apparent contradiction lies in the words: 'If we rebelled we would be excluded from the samaj'. This expresses quite clearly that girls are consciously trading ideals of independence and autonomy for the security and social position that a properly arranged marriage can ensure for them. They are aware of the social sanctions that they could incur if they went against their parents' wishes. Here, as in Saju's, Shopna's and Najma's stories, the feminist notion of trade off describes this kind of decision making. Their compliance when it comes to marriage can be understood not as a failure of agency due to a sort of false consciousness, but rather as a conscious decision based on their own perception of what can ensure their long-term well-being given the constraints they face. They are conscious that employment opportunities are scarce and that economic independence is in most cases out of their reach. But this is not the main reason why they attach such importance and meaning to marriage. Marriage, if lived as a bond between two families, guarantees them a social space and a social position. Economic independence would never compensate for social isolation.

'OUR CULTURE'

This hegemonic view of marriage is linked to a hegemonic view of sexuality, of honour and of gender relations. People refer precisely to the values, norms and cultural referents that pertain to these domains when they refer to 'amader (our) culture'. This expression is often used as an ultimate explanation for attitudes, behaviours and choices related to sexuality and marriage. Including some issues into 'amader culture' means that they cannot be the object of discussion and that they have to be taken for granted. An example is significant in this respect, one that touches precisely on young people. Aleya, a mature development worker, acknowledged that issues related to sexuality preoccupy adolescents and that boys and girls need guidance from adults in these matters. I suggested that one way of granting this could be for NGOs to deal with issues of sexuality more openly and extensively rather than limiting their intervention to reproductive health programmes that de facto exclude unmarried adolescents. Aleya replied that since sexuality is a sensitive 'cultural' issue it is better not to evoke it because this would provoke a strong negative social reaction. 'In our culture sexuality is not an issue before marriage and even after marriage talking openly of sexuality would not be accepted'. She then concluded that while NGOs can easily implement training programmes on 'reproductive health', because people view it as a technical, neutral issue, sexuality cannot be the focus of discussion because it impinges on 'cultural' values.

Adult and young people appear to distinguish and separate discursively two arenas. The first is a 'modern' arena of 'development', well represented by the NGOs, that includes education, work and employment. Here there are no objections to girls studying and women working and individual self-advancement and a struggle towards economic well-being are encouraged and legitimate. But this is possible provided that 'amader culture' is safeguarded so that there are issues that cannot be questioned and barriers in the face of which the development discourse and practices have to step back. This is illustrated by the programme Kishori Abhijan, mentioned earlier. This is a programme that targets adolescents living in rural areas. During my fieldwork, the main implementing agencies were BRAC and CMES and one of the core activities of the programme consisted of setting up village libraries that young people could freely access and were supposed to function as centres of aggregation and peer group socialisation. In the first stages of this programme, boys and girls could not mix and girls were actually the main target. The necessity of keeping boys and girls separated was explained to me in relation to the emotional nature of young people, their being prone to passion and the need to protect girls from boys' sexually abusive behaviour. When I asked the two officers why boys and girls were not instead taught to relate to each other, they objected saying: 'this is our culture'.

This separation is however highly constructed and the relations between the domain of 'our culture' and the modern domain of development work and employment are in practice contested and competing. As this book points out, changes brought about by education are de facto challenging young people's perceptions of themselves, their aspirations for the future, and their position in the samaj. They encourage the questioning of parents' decisions. Although only to a limited degree, young people are contesting their powerless position with respect to adults because they envisage more chances to have their opinions and desires taken into account, for example, in marriage choices. This applies to boys as well as girls, since they too are in a subordinate position as far as age hierarchies are concerned. In the arena of cross-gender relationships, premarital 'lines' challenge discursively, if not practically, the hegemonic views about conjugality, marriage and sexuality. Parents are aware of the existence of a hidden adolescent world of more or less platonic 'love stories' built around love letters, passionate glances and furtive encounters made meaningful by the language of romantic love. However, this parallel world is tolerated as long as it remains invisible and does not openly interfere with the sanctioned public behaviour, thus allowing the hegemonic discourse to keep its consistency and coherence. A female university student I met in Dhaka in 2007 was very conscious about the contrasting pressures she had to bear from her parents:

They expect me to be a successful student and obtain good marks because they say that I have to improve my skills and find a good job, but I cannot go out with my friends and have a boyfriend because they say that this is against our culture. I don't understand what I have to do and it is difficult for me.

Girls appear to be well aware that their situation is characterised by forms of dependence and subordination in gender relations. They appeal to their 'culture' to explain why their mobility and contact with boys are limited and controlled, but on the other hand they are able to name the power unbalance that characterises gender relations: 'This is a country where men have the power'. However, they do not consider the possibility of fighting openly and collectively for a transformation, and their answers and solutions are mainly individual. For example, they prefer to compromise with hegemonic notions of purdah by wearing the burqa or the veil to make themselves symbolically invisible, while at the same time occupying public spaces such as colleges and streets. In this way they also deal with the problem of violence and personal security and try to reach their objective of self-advancement through education.

These examples show that the hegemonic discourse is not all-encompassing and that a developmental modernist perspective in practice challenges what is discursively conceived as beyond scrutiny because it belongs to the 'unchangeable' domain of 'culture'.

However, it is very important to add that hegemony is not only challenged from the outside in a questionable dichotomous perspective that would oppose 'tradition' and 'modernity'. As explained in Chapter 1, by drawing on Gramsci's understandings of the hegemonic social order, this is never without internal contradictions since people's common sense is 'contradictory and fragmented'. The Gramscian concept of common sense implies that subordinate groups may develop a 'critical understanding of self through a struggle of political "hegemonies and of opposing directions" in order to arrive at the working out of at a higher level of one's own conception of reality' (Gramsci 1971: 333).

It is thus important to establish what this book has not been able to do, as much as what it has done. Gramsci's ideas of the always contested processes of non-hegemonic discourses imply that the rural social order in Bangladesh would always have contained subordinate hegemonies. The ones most studied in South Asia have been the subaltern view of rank and class and the submerged discourses of women within the male dominated discourse. My research has not sought to analyse these, although these perspectives are apparent in some of my chapters. In Chapter 3, I have discussed a few examples of how subordinate clients perceive their relationships with their patrons, whether they are the NGOs or the borolok, and the extent to which they are aware of the power that rich people have to define the parameters of what is socially and morally acceptable. This awareness, which undoubtedly constitutes a threat to the coherence and boundedness of the hegemonic discourse about rank and patronage, is rarely manifested in open protest and is confined to a submerged domain and to 'off stage' conversations. The same can be said of the social relations of gender. We have seen how difficult it is to disentangle compliance and resistance and how young girls negotiate their spaces inside the modern domains of school and college and the more 'traditional' domain of marriage choices, continuously reshaping gender relations themselves.

It is likely that for young people, as well as for women and peasants as subordinate groups, common sense would always have been contested and fragmented. As discussed in the first chapter, we could say that hegemony, as the 'discursive face of power' (Fraser 1992: 53) is 'never either total or exclusive' (Williams 1977: 113). A different kind of research is needed to establish these ever-present contestational youth discourses in the past. My own research suggests that, particularly as discourses of development and modernity become available and as adolescence is emerging, there are today more spaces for young people to elaborate and draw from such discourses.

These findings enable us to revisit the issue of acid violence. In the summer 1999, at Dhaka Medical Hospital, I met Shoroni, a 14-year-old high school student, who had survived an attack from a rejected suitor who had thrown acid at her and some relatives who were sleeping in the same hut, causing burns to her face and minor injuries to the others. I was with the representative of an NGO that was planning to support acid survivors. Shoroni's father requested our attention and after explaining how the attack occurred, asserted that plastic surgery is only a limited response to the acid violence emergency. He said:

We did our best to raise them (they had another daughter), but now everything is finished. The samaj will not accept our daughter. Everybody will think that she has done something bad. Nobody will ever marry her because of her face. What will she do? You should do something to make people understand. Our 'culture' should change. Plastic surgery is not enough.

Shoroni's father is one of the few adults I met in Bangladesh who openly advocated a change in 'culture', which he considered was responsible for the serious social consequences that the acid violence was likely to have for his daughter and for the whole family. Because women's sexuality is constructed as a powerful force that men cannot resist, women are to blame for provoking them. In many cases of acid violence against adolescents, people suspect the victim of having started an approach which is later withdrawn. Nobody would openly justify acid attacks, and they are considered criminal acts, nonetheless they are partially explained as being due to the uncontrollable *raag* (anger) that a man would feel after being turned down by a woman. Throwing acid is in this sense a way of reasserting one's power and vindicating the offence to one's man shonman—or prestige. By asserting the need to question 'culture', Shoroni's father pointed to the power relations bound up with the code of honour and shame signalled in the implicit class dimension in the many cases of acid violence in which the attackers belong or are attached to powerful and rich families.

The discursive isolation of a domain of 'culture', to be preserved as something beyond scrutiny and discussion (which I described earlier as consistently brought into play to support particular kind of limited spaces for youth and young girls) is having serious and real consequences for some young women. Acid violence attacks are manifestations of highly unequal and constraining gender and class power relations. Disfigurement and sometimes death are the extreme consequences that some girls face for stepping too far out of line. But there are other more subtle constraints. The fear of violence, harassment and bad reputation de facto prevents parents from sending their daughters to study in town and frustrates girls' best hopes and efforts. I remember Mamtaj, a brilliant college student, saying: 'What can I do? Boys can go to study in town, but we are girls, we are not allowed to go far away from home'. In this context individual answers and negotiations appear to be unsatisfactory because they do not substantially challenge the substance of power relations. We should not interpret the very negative consequences of acid violence to create a negative picture of the development of adolescence in these rural areas. As my research has shown, the situation is far from static and many changes are happening in the everyday life of boys and girls and in the way they perceive and experience youthhood. My research has shown that much is going on under the surface in the development of languages and repertoires of behaviour for young people and that they are making some claims for spaces to negotiate with parents and the older generation. At the same time the ways in which poor people, the young, women and girls, the outcastes bear the brunt of the hegemonic social order remain very apparent and continue to give cause for concern.

NOTES

1. Kishori Abhijan (adolescents' journey) is the title of a current development project that targets adolescents, implemented by UNICEF, Bangladesh Rural Advancement Committee (BRAC) and (Centre for Mass education and Science (CMES). I'll refer to it again ahead.
2. One's own people, see discussion in Chapter 3.

Glossary

Abeg probon	Prone to passion
Ador	Care/affection
Adhunik Jug	Modern era
Apon jon	Relatives
Atman	Soul
Atta	Soul
Attiyo swajan	One's own people
Baper bari	Father's house
Bebsha	Business or trade
Bhabi	Sister-in-law (elder brother's wife)
Bhaddhrolok	Gentle person
Bhaghe kora	Splitting in two parts
Bhalobasha	Love
Bhikka gorib	Begging poor
Biadop	Bad
Bibaho	Marriage
Bigha	Measure of land equivalent to 0.33 acre
Biye	Marriage
Bondhi	Tied
Bondhu	Friend
Bongsho	Lineage
Borga kora	A form of sharecropping contract
Boro	Big
Borolok	Rich or powerful people
Bou	Bride
Boukal	Period or time of being a wife
Boyosh	Age

Boyoshko	Aged
Buddhi	Intelligence or knowledge
Bujha	Understanding
Buri	Old
Burka	Veil or covering garment worn by women
Cashcia	Cultivator
Chakri	Job
Chobi	Movie or film
Choto	Small
Daya	Mercy
Dharma	Religion or code for conduct
Dhoni	Rich or wealthy
Doik milon	Sexual intercourse
Dukkhini	Sad
Dukkho	Sadness or grief
Durnam	Bad reputation
Gorib	Poor
Gusti	Lineage
Hridoy	Heart
Ijjat	Honour
Jat	Caste or kinship
Jogajog	Social connections
Jon dewa	Selling one's labour for wages
Kisor/Kisori	Early adolescence
Lojja	Shame
Loobh	Desire
Madhyo	Middle
Mahajon	Literally, a virtuous man. The term is used to refer to moneylenders and large landowners.
Majhari	Middle
Man shonman	Prestige or honour
Matobar	Village leader
Mon	Mind, thought or heart
Mon theke	From the heart
Moner kota	An utterance from the heart (i.e. genuine)
Murobbhi	Elder
Nichu	Low or lower
Notun bou	New bride
Obhostan ache	To stay or reside

Onusthan	Ceremony
Oshubida	A problem
Parivar	Family
Poradhin	Dependent or subordinated
Prem	Erotic love
Purdah	Curtain or female seclusion
Samaj	Society or moral community
Shadhin	Free or independent
Shati	Partner
Shikkito	Educated
Shoshur bari	In-laws house
Somosha	A problem
Somphod	Inheritance
Somporkko	Relationship
Swami	Husband
Uchu	Upper or higher
Zamindar	Owner of an agricultural estate

Bibliography

Abdullah, T. & S. Zeidenstein. 1982. *Village Women of Bangladesh: Prospects for Change*. London: Pergamon Press.

Abraham, L. 2001. 'Redrawing the Lakshma Rekha: Gender Differences and Cultural Constructions in Youth Sexuality in Urban India', *South Asia*, XXIV (Special Issue): 133–56.

——. 2002. 'Bhai-behen, True Love, Time Pass: Friendships and Sexual Partnerships among Youth in an Indian Metropolis', *Culture, Health and Sexuality*, 4(3): 337–53.

Abu-Lughod, L. 1990. 'The Romance of Resistance: Tracing Transformations of Power through Bedouin Women', *American Ethnologist*, 17(1): 41–55.

Adnan, S. 1988. 'Birds in a Cage: Institutional Change and Women's Position in Bangladesh', Paper presented at the conference *Women's Position and Demographic Change in the Course of Development*, Asker, Norway, 15–18 June.

——. 1990 *Annotation of Village Studies in Bangladesh and West Bengal: A Review of Socio-economic Trends over 1942–1988*. Comilla: Bangladesh Academy for Rural Development.

Ahearn L. M. 2001a. *Invitations to Love: Literacy, Love Letters and Social Change in Nepal*. Ann Arbor, Michigan: University of Michigan Press.

——. 2001b. 'Language and Agency', *Annual Review of Anthropology*, 30: 109–37

Ahmad, R. & M. S. Naher. 1987. *Brides and the Demand System in Bangladesh*. Dhaka: Centre for Social Studies.

Ahmed, R. (1981). *The Bengal Muslims, 1871–1906: A Quest for Identity*. Delhi: Oxford University Press.

Ahmed, I. 2004. 'The Construction of Childhood in Monipur', D.Phil. University of Sussex.

Ahmed, S. 1993. 'Purdah: An Analysis of Ideal versus Contextual Reality', *Journal of Social Studies*, 60: 45–58.

Akhter, H. and S. Nahar. 2003. *A Study on Acid Violence in Mymensingh*. Women for Women Report, Dhaka, Bangladesh.

Alam, S. 1985. 'Women and Poverty in Bangladesh', *Women's Studies International Forum* 8(4): 361–71.

Amit-Talai, V & H. Wulff (eds). 1995. *Youth Cultures: A Cross Cultural Perspective*. London: Routledge.

Amin, S. 1996. 'Female Education and Fertility in Bangladesh: The Influence of Marriage and the Family', in R. Jeffery & A. Basu (eds), *Girls' Schooling, Women's Autonomy and Fertility Change in South Asia*. London: Sage

———. 1998. Family Structure and Change in Rural Bangladesh. *Population Studies* 52: 201–13.

Amin, S. et al. 1998. 'Transition to Adulthood of Female Garment-Factory Workers in Bangladesh', *Studies in Family Planning*, 29(22): 185–200.

Amin, S. and L. Huq. 2008. 'Marriage Considerations in Sending Girls to School in Bangladesh: Some Qualitative Evidence', Working Paper 12, Population Council, Dhaka.

Amin, S., N. Selim and N. Kamal Waiz. 2006. *Causes and Consequences of Early Marriage in Bangladesh*. A Background report for workshop on programme and policies to prevent early marriage, Population Council, Dhaka.

Appadurai, A. 1990. 'Topographies of the Self: Praise and Emotion in Hindu India', in L. Abu-Lughod, & C. Lutz (eds), *Language and the Politics of Emotion*. Cambridge: Cambridge University Press.

Arens, J. & J. van Beurden. 1977. *Jhagrapur: Poor Peasants and Women in a Village in Bangladesh*. Amsterdam: Third World Publications.

Arnold, D. & S. Blackburn (eds). 2004. 'Introduction', in *Telling Lives in India: Biography, Autobiography and Life History*. Bloomington: Indiana University.

Ain-o-Shalish Kendro (ASK). 2003. *Human Rights in Bangladesh*. Dhaka: Ain-o-Shalish Kendro.

Aziz, K. M. A. & C. Maloney. 1985. *Life Stages, Gender and Fertility in Bangladesh*. Dhaka: Centre for Diarrhoeal Disease Research Bangladesh.

Babb, L. 1981. 'Glancing: Visual Interaction in Hinduism', *Journal of Anthropological Research*, 37: 387–401.

Bangladesh Bureau of Educational Information and Statistics (BANBEIS). 1998. *Bangladesh Educational Statistics 1997*. Dhaka: BANBEIS.

———.2006. *Bangladesh Educational Statistics 2005*. Dhaka: BANBEIS.

———. 2007. *Educational Statistics*. Available at: http://www.banbeis.gov. bd/db_bb/secondary_ education_2.htm (accessed 14 June 2009).

Bangladesh Bureau of Statistics (BBS). 2003. *Population Census 2001*, Bangladesh Bureau of Statistics, Dhaka.

———.2008a. *Household Income and Expenditure Survey Report*. Dhaka.

———. 2008b. *Agriculture Census 2008*, Dhaka.

———. 2009. 'Updating Poverty Maps of Bangladesh'. Available at: http://www.bbs.gov.bd/dataindex/povertymb.pdf.

Basu, S. 2001. 'The Blunt Cutting Edge: The Construction of Sexuality in the Bengali Feminist Magazine Sananda', *Feminist Media Studies*, 1(2): 179–96.

Bertocci, P. J. 1970. 'Elusive Villages: Social Structure and Community Organization in Rural East Pakistan', Unpublished PhD Thesis, Michigan State University.

———.1972. 'Community Structure and Social Rank in Two Villages in Bangladesh', *Contributions to Indian Sociology*, 6: 28–52.

Bhattacharya, R. K. 1991. *Muslims of Rural Bengal*. Calcutta: Subarnarekha.

Bhumijo. 1996. 'Religio-Ethnic Minority Groups of South West Bangladesh', unpublished report, Khulna.

Blanchet, T. 1984. *Women, Pollution and Marginality: Meanings and Rituals of Birth in Rural Bangladesh*. Dhaka: UPL.

———.1986. 'Marriage and Divorce in Bengali Muslim Society', Unpublished MS, Dhaka.

———. 1996. *Lost Innocence Stolen Childhoods*. Dhaka: UPL.

Blos, P. 1966. *On Adolescence: A Psychoanalytic Interpretation*. New York: Free Press.

———. 1967. 'The Second Individuation Process in Adolescence', *The Psychoanalytic Study of the Child*, 22: 162–86.

———. 1979. *The Adolescent Passage. Developmental Issues*. New York: International Universities Press.

Boissevain, J. 1966. 'Patronage in Sicily', *Man*, 1: 18–34.

Bangladesh Rural Advancement Committee (BRAC). 1980. *The Net: Power Structure in Ten Villages*. Dhaka: BRAC, Research and Evaluation Division.

———. 2006. *Adolescents and Youth in Bangladesh: Some Selected Issues.* BRAC Research Monograph Series No. 31. Dhaka: BRAC.

Bucholtz, M. 2002. 'Youth and Cultural Practice', *Annual Review of Anthropology*, 31(1): 525–52.

Burbank, V. K. 1988. *Aboriginal Adolescence: Maidenhood in an Australian Community.* New Brunswick, NJ: Rutgers University Press.

———. 1995. 'Gender Hierarchy and Sexuality: The Control of Female Reproduction in an Australian Aboriginal Community', *Ethos*, 23(1): 33–46.

Cain, M., S. R. Khanam & S. Nahar. 1979. 'Class, Patriarchy and Women's Work in Bangladesh', *Population and Development Review*, 5(3): 405–38.

Caldwell, J. C. 1998. 'The Construction of Adolescence in a Changing World: Implications for Sexuality, Reproduction and Marriage', *Studies in Family Planning*, 29(2): 137–53.

Campaign for Popular Education (CAMPE). 2000. *Education Watch (2000) – A Question of Quality – State of Primary Education in Bangladesh*, Volume 1. Dhaka: The University Press Ltd.

Charmet Pietropolli, G. 2000. *I Nuovi Adolescenti*. Milano: Cortina.

Chowdhury, E. H. 2005. 'Feminist Negotiations: Contesting Narratives of the Campaign against Acid Violence in Bangladesh', *Meridians: Feminism, Race, Transnationalism*, 6(1): 163–92.

Cohler, B. J. & S. Geyer. 1982. 'Psychological Autonomy and Interdependence within the Family', in F. Walsh (ed.), *Normal Family Processes*. New York: The Guilford Press.

Coleman, J. C. & L. Hendry. 1999. *The Nature of Adolescence*. London: Routledge.

Condon, R. 1987. *Inuit Youth: Growth and Change in the Canadian Arctic.* New Brunswick, NJ: Rutgers University Press.

Condon, R. 1995. 'The Rise of the Leisure Class: Adolescence and Recreational Acculturation in the Canadian Artic', *Ethos*, 23(1): 47–68.

Daily Star. 2006. Vol. 5, No. 719.

Das, V. 1979. 'Reflections on the Social Constructions of Adulthood', in S. Kakar (ed.), *Identity and Adulthood*. Delhi: Oxford University Press.

Davis, M. 1983. *Rank and Rivalry: The Politics of Inequality in Rural West Bengal.* Cambridge: Cambridge University Press.

Davis, S. S. & D. A. Davis. 1989. *Adolescence in a Moroccan Town. Making Social Sense.* New Brunswick, N.J.: Rutgers University Press.

Davis, D.A. 1995. 'Modernizing the Sexes: Changing Gender Relations in a Moroccan Town', *Ethos*, 23(1): 69–78.

Del Franco, N. 1983. 'Fuoricasta in un Villaggio Bengalese', *Il politico*, no.2, Pavia.

———. 1999: 'Changing Gender Relations and New Forms of Violence: Acid Throwing against Women in Bangladesh and the NGO Response', M.A. dissertation, University of Sussex.

De Neve, G. 2004. 'The Workplace and the Neighborhood: Locating Masculinities in the South Indian Textile Industry', in R. Chopra, C. Osella & F. Osella (eds), *South Asian Masculinities. Context of Change, Sites of Continuity*. New Delhi: Women Unlimited.

Devine, J. 1999. 'One Foot in Each Boat: The Macro-politics and Micro-sociology of NGOs in Bangladesh', D.Phil, University of Bath.

Dolto, F. 1990. *Adolescenza*. Milano: Mondadori.

Donner, H. 2002. 'One's Own Marriage: Love Marriages in a Calcutta Neighbourhood', *South Asia Research*, 22(1): 79–94.

———. 2008. *Domestic Goddesses: Maternity, Globalization and Middle-Class Identity in Contemporary India*. Aldershot: Ashgate.

Dumont, L. 1970. *The Caste System and its Implications*. Chicago: University of Chicago Press.

Dwyer, R. 2000. *All You Want is Money, All You Need is Love: Sex and Romance in Modern India*. London: Cassell.

Economist Intelligence Unit (EIU). 2005. *Bangladesh Country Profile*. Available at: http://www.unicef.org/infobycountry/bangladesh_bangladesh_statistics.html

Edgar, I. 1990. 'The Social Process of Adolescence in a Therapeutic Community', in P. Spencer (ed.), *Anthropology and the Riddle of the Sphinx: Paradoxes of Change in the Life-course*. London: Routledge.

Erikson, E. H. 1968 *Identity: Youth and Crisis*. New York: Norton and Company

Ewing, K. 1991. 'Can Psychoanalytic Theory Explain the Pakistani Woman? Intra-psychic Autonomy and Interpersonal Engagement in the Extended Family', *Ethos*, 19(2): 131–61.

Fraser, N. 1992. 'The Uses and Abuses of Discourse Theories for Feminist Politics', *Theory Culture and Society*, 9: 51–61.

Freud A. 1958. 'Adolescence', *The Psychoanalytic Study of the Child*, 13: 255–78.

Fruzzetti, L. & A. Ostor. 1982. 'Bad Blood in Bengal: Category and Affect in the Study of Kinship Caste and Marriage', in A. Ostor, L. Fruzzetti and S. Barnett (eds), *Concepts of the Person: Kinship, Caste and Marriage in India*. London: Harvard University Press.

Fuller, C. J. & H. Narasimhan. 2007. 'Information Technology Professionals and the New-Rich Middle Class in Chennai (Madras)', *Modern Asian Studies*, 41(1): 121–50.

Gardner, K. 1995. *Global Migrants, Local Lives: Travel and Transformation in Rural Bangladesh*. Oxford: Clarendon Press.

Goetz, A. M. and R. Sen Gupta. 1994. Who Takes the Credit? Gender, Power and Control over Loan Use in Rural Credit Programs in Bangladesh', IDS Working Paper no. 8.

———.1996. 'Who Takes the Credit? Gender, Power and Control Over Loan Use in Rural Credit Programs in Bangladesh', *World Development*, 24(4): 45–63.

Gould, H. A. 1969. 'Toward a Jati Model for Indian Politics', *Economic and Political Weekly*, IV: 291–97.

Gramsci, A. 1934. *Quaderni del Carcere*. Edizione Critica dell' Istituto Gramsci (ed.) V. Gerratana, vol. 4 Torino 1975.

———. 1971. *Selection from the Prison Notebooks of Antonio Gramsci*. Hoare & Nowell Smith (eds and trans). London: Lawrence and Wishart.

Greenberg, J. R. & S. R. Mitchell. 1983. *Object Relations in Psychoanalytic Theory*. Cambridge Massachusetts: Harvard University Press.

Greenberger, E. 1984. 'Defining Psychosocial Maturity in Adolescence', in K. P. and J. Steffen (eds), *Adolescent Behaviour Disorders*. Heath Lexington M.A.

Grootevant, H. and Cooper, C. 1986. 'Individuation in Family Relationships', *Human Development*, 29: 82–100.

Grosz, E. I. 1990. *Jacques Lacan: A Feminist Introduction*. London: Routledge.

Grover, S. 2006. 'Poor Women's Experiences of Marriage and Love in the City of New Delhi: Everyday Stories of Sukh aur Dukh', D.Phil, University of Sussex.

———. 2009. 'Lived Experiences: Marriage, Notions of Love and Kinship Support Amongst Poor Women in Delhi', *Contributions to Indian Sociology*, 43(1): 1–33.

Hall, S. 1916. *Adolescence* (Vols 1–2). New York: Appleton.

———. 1996. 'Gramsci Relevance for the Study of Race and Ethnicity', in David Morley and Kuan-Hsing Chen (eds), *Critical Dialogues in Cultural Studies*. London & New York: Routledge.

Hallowell, A. 1955. *Culture and Experience*. Philadelphia: University of Pennsylvania Press.

Haq, E. M. 1975. *A History of Sufism in Bengal*. Dhaka.

Haq, N. and M. Khan (1990): *Menstruation, Beliefs and Practices of Adolescents Girls*. BRAC Research Report, Bangladesh Rural Advancement Committee, Dhaka, Bangladesh.

Hartmann, B. & J. Boyce. 1983. *A Quiet Violence: A View from a Bangladeshi Village*. London: Zed Press.

Haynes, D. & G. Prakash (eds). 1992. *Contesting Power: Resistance and Everyday Social Relations in South Asia*. Berkeley: University of California Press.

Holland, D. 1997. 'Selves as Cultured: As Told by an Anthropologist Who Lacks a Soul', in R. Ashmore and L. Jussim (eds), *Self and Identity: Fundamental Issues*, pp. 193–221. London: Oxford University Press.

Hollos, M. & P. Leis. 1989. *Becoming Nigerian in Ijo Society*. New Brunswick, NJ.: Rutgers University Press.

————.1995. 'Intergenerational Discontinuities in Nigeria', *Ethos*, 23(1): 103–18.

Holub, R. 1992. *Antonio Gramsci: Beyond Marxism and Postmodernism*. London: Routledge.

Hossain, N. T. 2003. 'Elites and Poverty in Bangladesh', D. Phil., University of Sussex.

Hossain, N. T. 2005. *Inheriting Extreme Poverty: Household Aspirations, Community Attitudes and Childhood in Northern Bangladesh*. Dhaka: BRAC and Save the Children UK.

Huda, S. 2006. 'Dowry in Bangladesh: Compromising Women's Rights', *South Asia Research*, 26(3): 249–68.

Huq, M. 2005. 'Pursuing Peace in Both Worlds: The Formation and Contestation of a Female Islamist Subjectivity in Bangladesh', paper presented at the workshop *Islamist Reformist Movements in South Asia*, SOAS, May.

Inden, R. B. 1976. *Marriage and Rank in Bengali Culture. A History of Class and Clan in Middle Period Bengal*. Berkeley: University of California Press.

Inden, R. B. & R. W. Nicholas. 1977. *Kinship in Bengali Culture*. Chicago: University of Chicago Press.

Islam, M. 1979. 'Social Norms and Institution', in Women for Women (eds), *The Situation of Women in Bangladesh*. Dhaka: Women for Women.

Islam, N. & A. Ahmed. 1998. 'Age at First Marriage and its Determinants in Bangladesh', *Asia-Pacific Population Journal*, June, pp. 73–92.

Jahan, R. 1988. 'Hidden Wounds, Visible Scars: Violence against Women in Bangladesh', in B. Agarwal (ed.), *Structures of Patriarchy: State Community and Household in Modernising Asia*. London: Zed Press.

Jahan, R. 1994. *Hidden Danger: Women and Family Violence in Bangladesh*. Dhaka: Women for Women.

Jahangir, B. K. 1978. 'Peasant Mobilisation Process: The Bangladesh Case', *Journal of Social Studies*, 1: 25–42

James, W. 1981. *The Principles of Psychology*. Cambridge: Harvard University Press.

Jansen, E. G. 1986. *Rural Bangladesh: Competition for Scarce Resources*. Oslo: Norwegian University Press.

Jannuzi, F. T. and J. T. Peach. 1980. *The Agrarian Structure of Bangladesh: An Impediment to Development*. Boulder, CO: Westview Press.

Jeffery, P. and R. Jeffery. 1994. 'Killing My Heart's Desire: Education and Female Autonomy in Rural North India', in N. Kumar (ed.), *Women as Subjects: South Asian Histories*. Charlottesville: University of Virginia Press.

———. 1996. *Don't Marry Me to a Plowman!: Women's Everyday Lives in Rural North India*. Boulder, CO: Westview Press.

Kabeer, N. 1995. 'Necessary, Sufficient or Irrelevant? Women, Wages and Intra-household Relationship in Rural Bangladesh', IDS Working Paper no. 25, IDS University of Sussex.

———. 1998. 'Money Can't Buy me Love? Re-evaluating Gender, Credit and Empowerment in Rural Bangladesh', IDS Discussion Paper no. 363, IDS University of Sussex.

———. 2000. *The Power to Choose*. London: Verso.

———. 2001. Conflict over Credit: Re-evaluating the Empowerment Potential of Loans to Women in Rural Bangladesh', *World Development*, 29(1): 63–84.

Kandijoti, D. 1988. 'Bargaining with Patriarchy', *Gender and Society*, 2(3): 274–90.

Kakar, S. 1978. *The Inner World: A Psychoanalytic Study of Childhood and Society in India*. Delhi: Oxford University Press.

——— (ed.). 1979. *Identity and Adulthood*. Delhi: Oxford University Press.

Kaviraj, S. 2004. 'The Invention of Private Life: A Reading of Sibnath Sastri Autobiography', in D. Arnold and S. Blackburn (eds), *Telling Lives in India: Biography Autobiography and Life History*. Bloomington: Indiana University Press.

Khan, M. R. 1997. *Report on Focus Group Discussion on Maternal Health*. Report prepared for UNICEF, Dhaka.

————. 2000. 'Adolescents' Reproductive Health: Issues and Concerns', in K. Salahuddin, R. Jahan and H. H. Khandaker (eds), *Current Status of Health Care System In Bangladesh: Women Perspective*. Dhaka: Women for Women.

Kotalova, J. 1993. *Belonging to Others. Cultural Construction of Womanhood among Muslims in a Village in Bangladesh*. Uppsala: Uppsala Studies in Cultural Anthropology.

Kroger, J. 1989. *Identity in Adolescence. The Balance between Self and Other*. London: Routledge.

La Fontaine, J. S. 1970. 'Two Types of Youth Group in Kinshasa', in P. Mayer (ed.), *Socialization: The Approach from British Anthropology*. London: Tavistock.

Lindenbaum, S. 1981. 'Implications for Women of Changing Marriage Transactions in Bangladesh', *Studies in Family Planning*, 12(11): 394–401.

Lo Piparo, F. 1979. *Lingua Intellettuali Egemonia in Gramsci*. Roma: Laterza.

Madan, T. N. 1975. 'The Structural Implications of Marriage in North India', *Contributions to Indian Sociology*, 9(2): 217–43.

Mahler, M. 1963. 'Thoughts about Development and Individuation', *Psychoanalytic Study of the Child*, 18: 307–24.

Mahler, M. S. F. Pine and A. Bergman. 1975. *The Psychological Birth of the Human Infant*. New York: Basic Books.

Mahmud, S. and S. Amin. 2006. 'Girls' Schooling and Marriage in Rural Bangladesh', in E. Hannum and B. Fuller (eds), *Research on the Sociology of Education*, vol. 15, *Children's Lives and Schooling Across Societies*, 71–99. Boston: JAI Elsevier/Science.

Maloney, C. (1988). *Behaviour and Poverty in Bangladesh*. Dhaka: University Press Limited.

Mani, L. 1990. 'Multiple Mediations: Feminist Scholarship in the Age of Multinational Reception', *Feminist Review*, 35: 24–41.

Mannan, M. 2002. 'Banghsa: Islam, History and the Structure of Bengali Muslim Descent', in Alam Nurul (ed.), *Contemporary Anthropology: Theory and Practice*. Dhaka: UPL.

Marcia, J.E. 1980. 'Identity in Adolescence', in J. Adelson (ed.), *Handbook of Adolescent Psychology*. New York: Wiley.

————. 1993. 'The Relational Roots of Identity', in J. Kroger (ed.), *Discussions on Ego Identity*. LEA Hove and London.

Marriott, M. 1976. 'Hindu Transactions: Diversity without Dualism', in

Bruce Kapferer (ed.), *Transaction and Meaning*. Philadelphia: Institute for the Studies of Human Issues.

——— (eds) 1990. *India through Hindu Categories*. New Delhi: Sage Publications.

Mars, L. 1990. 'Coming of Age among Jews', in P. Spencer (ed.), *Anthropology and the Riddle of the Sphinx: Paradoxes of Change in the Life-course*. London: Routledge.

Marsella, A. 1985. 'Culture Self and Mental Disorder', in A. Marsella et al. (eds), *Culture and Self, Asian and American Perspectives*. New York: Tavistock Publications.

Mayer, P. (ed.). 1970. *Socialization: The Approach from British Anthropology*. London: Tavistock.

Mayer, P. and I. Mayer. 1970. 'Socialization by Peers: The Youth Organizations of the Red Xhosa', in P. Mayer (ed.), *Socialization: The Approach from British Anthropology*. London: Tavistock.

———. 1990. 'A Dangerous Age: From Boy to Young Men in Red Xhosa Youth Organisations', in in P. Spencer (ed.), *Anthropology and the Riddle of the Sphinx: Paradoxes of Change in the Life-course*, pp. 35-44. London: Routledge.

McCarthy, F. and S. Feldman 1984. *Rural Women and Development in Bangladesh. Selected Issues*, NORAD, Ministry of Development Cooperation, Oslo, Norway.

McLeod, A. 1992. 'Hegemonic Relations and Gender Resistance: The New Veiling as Accommodating Protest in Cairo', *Signs: The Journal of Women in Culture and Society*, 17(3): 533–57.

Mead, M. 1928. *Coming of Age in Samoa*. Ann Arbor: Morrow.

Mines, M. 1988. 'Conceptualizing the Person: Hierarchical Society and Individual Autonomy in India', *American Anthropologist*, 90: 568–79

Mody, P. 2002. 'Love and the Law. Love-marriage in Delhi', *Modern Asian Studies*, 36(1): 223–56.

Mohanty, C.T. 1988. 'Under Western Eyes: Feminist Scholarship and Colonial Discourse', *Feminist Review*, 30: 60–86.

Ministry of Health and Family Welfare (MOHFW). 1998. *Population and Development. Post ICPD Achievement and Challenges in Bangladesh*, Ministry of Health and Family Welfare, Bangladesh.

Moore, H. 1994. *A Passion for Difference*. Cambridge: Polity Press.

———. 2004. 'On Being Young', *Anthropological Quarterly*, 77(4): 735–46.

Murray, D. W. 1993. 'What is the Western Concept of the Self? On Forgetting David Hulme', *Ethos*, 21(1): 3–23.

Muuss, R. E. 1996. *Theories of Adolescence*. New York: Mc Graw Hill.

Nabi, R. et al. 1999. *Consultation with the Poor: Participatory Poverty Assessment in Bangladesh*. Dhaka: NGO Working Group of the World Bank.

Naved, R. T. and L. A. Persson. 2007. 'Dowry and Spousal Physical Violence against Women in Bangladesh: Is Payment and/or Patriarchy the Main Issue?' ICDDR,B, Dhaka and Department of Women's and Children's Health, IMCH, Uppsalla University, Sweden. http://www.icddrb. org/pub/publication.jsp?classificationID=1&pubID=7960

Naved, R. T., M. Newby and S. Amin. 2001. 'Female Labor Migration and its Implication for Marriage and Childbearing in Bangladesh', *International Journal of Population Geography*, 7: 91–104.

NIPORT. 2001. *Demographic and Health Survey 1999–2000*. National Institute of Population Research and Training (NIPORT) Dhaka.

———. 2009. *Demographic and Health Survey 2007*. National Institute of Population Research and Training (NIPORT), Dhaka

Nisbett, N. C. 2004. 'Knowledge, Identity, Place and (cyber)Space: Growing up Male and Middle Class in Bangalore', D. Phil. University of Sussex.

Osella, C. & F. Osella. 1998. 'Friendship and Flirting: Micro-politics in Kerala, South India', *Journal of the Royal Anthropological Institute*, 4(2): 189–206.

———. 2002. 'Contextualising Sexuality: Young Men in Kerala, South India', in L. Rice Pranee and L. Manderson (eds), *Coming of Age in South and Southeast Asia: Youth, Courtship and Sexuality*. Richmond, Surrey: Curzon.

———. 2000. *Social Mobility in Kerala: Modernity and Identity in Conflict*. London: Pluto Press.

———. 2004. 'Young Malayali Men and their Movie Heroes', in R. Chopra, C. Osella and F. Osella (eds), *South Asian Masculinities. Context of Change, Sites of Continuity*. New Delhi: Women Unlimited (an associate of Kali for Women).

Osmani, S. R. 1990. 'Structural Change and Poverty in Bangladesh: The Case of a False Turning Point', *Bangladesh Development Studies*, 18(3): 55–74.

Paggi, L. (2002). 'The Dalits of Bangladesh', unpublished paper.

Papanek, H. 1982. 'Purdah: Separate Worlds and Symbolic Shelter', in H. Papanek and G. Minault (eds), *Separate Worlds: Studies of Purdah in South Asia*. Delhi: DUP.

Parish, S. M. 1994. *Moral Knowing in a Hindu Sacred City. An Exploration of Mind Emotion and Self.* New York: Columbia University Press.

Parry, J. 2004. 'The Marital History of a "Thumb Impression Man"', in D. Arnold and S. Blackburn (eds), *Telling Lives: South Asian Life Histories.* New Delhi/Bloomington: Permanent Black/Indiana University Press.

Raheja, G. & A. Gold 1994. *Listen to the Heron's Words: Re-imagining Gender and Kinship in North India.* London, Berkeley: University of California Press.

Roland, A. 1988. *In Search of Self in India and Japan: Toward a Cross-cultural Psychology.* Princeton: Princeton University Press.

Rashid, S. F. and S. Michaud. 2000. 'Female Adolescents and their Sexuality; Notions of Honour, Shame, Purity and Pollution During the Floods', *Disasters,* 24(1): 54–70.

Richards, A. I. 1956. *Chisungu: A Girls' Initiation Ceremony among the Bemba of Northern Rhodesia.* Faber.

———. 1970. 'Socialization and Contemporary British Anthropology', in in P. Mayer (ed.), *Socialization: The Approach from British Anthropology.* London: Tavistock.

Roy, M. 1975. *Bengali Women.* Chicago: University of Chicago Press.

Roy A. 1983. *The Islamic Syncretistic Tradition in Bengal.* Dhaka.

Rozario, S. 1992. *Purity and Communal Boundaries.* Allen and Unwin.

———. 2002. '"Poor and Dark": What is my Future? Identity Construction and Adolescent Women in Bangladesh', in L. Manderson and P. Liamputtong (eds), *Coming of Age in South and South East Asia. Youth Courtship and Sexuality.* Richmond: Curzon Press.

———. 2007. 'The Dark Side of Micro-credit', Available at: http://www.opendemocracy.net/article/5050/16_days/dowry_microcredit

———. 2009. 'Dowry in Rural Bangladesh: An Intractable Problem?' in Tamsin Bradley, Mangala Subramaniam, Emma Tomalin (eds), *Dowry: Bridging the Gap between Theory and Practice,* pp. 29-58. New Delhi: Women Unlimited and London: Zed Books.

Schlegel, A. 1995a. 'Introduction', *Ethos,* 23(1): 3–14.

———. 1995b. 'A Cross-cultural Approach to Adolescence', *Ethos,* 23(1): 15–32.

Schlegel A. and H. Barry. 1991. *Adolescence, An Anthropological Enquiry.* New York: Free Press.

Schuler, S. R. et al. 1996. 'Credit Programs, Patriarchy and Men's Violence against Women in Rural Bangladesh', *Journal of Social Science and Medicine*, 43(12): 1729–42.

Schuler, S. R., L. M. Bates, F. Islam, and M. K. Islam. 2006. 'The Timing of Marriage and Childbearing among Rural Families in Bangladesh: Choosing between Competing Risks', *Social Science and Medicine*, 62: 2826–37.

Scott, James C. (1972). 'Patron-Client Politics and Political Change in Southeast Asia', *American Political Science Review*, 66: 91–113.

———. 1985. *Weapons of the Weak. Everyday Forms of Peasant Resistance.* Yale and London: Yale University Press.

Sen, B. and D. Hulme. 2004. *Tales of Ascent, Descent, Marginality and Persistence*, Available at: http://www.chronicpoverty.org/pdfs/43Sen_Hulme. pdf

Sen, A. K. 1990. 'Gender and Cooperative Conflicts', in I. Tinker (ed.), *Persistent Inequalities.* Oxford: Oxford University Press.

Sharma, M. and H. Zaman. 2009. 'Who Migrates Overseas and is it Worth their While', Policy Research Working Paper no. 5018, World Bank Working Paper Series, World Bank.

Shilpi, F. 2008. 'Migration, Sorting and Regional Inequality: Evidence from Bangladesh', Policy Research Working Paper no. 4616, World Bank Working Paper Series, World Bank.

Shweder, R. and E. Bourne. 1984. 'Does the Concept of the Person Vary Cross Culturally?' in Shweder and Le Vine (eds), *Culture Theory: Essays on Mind, Self and Emotion.* Cambridge: Cambridge University Press.

Siddiqui, K. 2000. *Jagatpur 1977–97. Poverty and Social Change in Rural Bangladesh.* Dhaka: UPL.

Siddiqui, D. M. 2002. 'Dowry, Ancient Custom or Modern Malaise?' *The Daily Star*, 19 February, Dhaka.

Simmons, R. et al. 1992. 'Employment in Family Planning and Women's Status in Bangladesh', *Studies in Family Planning*, 23(2): 97–109.

Spencer, P. 1970. 'The Function of Ritual in the Socialization of the Samburu Moran', in P. Mayer (ed.), *Socialization: The Approach from British Anthropology.* London: Tavistock.

Spencer, P. (ed.). 1990. *Anthropology and the Riddle of the Sphinx: Paradoxes of Change in the Life-course.* London: Routledge.

Spiro, M. E. 1993. 'Is the Western Conception of the Self Peculiar Within the Context of the World Cultures?' *Ethos*, 21(2): 107–53.

Srinivas, M. N. 1952. *Religion and Society Amongst the Coorgs of South India*. Oxford: Clarendon Press.

Srinivas, M. N. 1983. *Some Reflections on Dowry*. Delhi: Oxford University Press.

Srinivasan, S. 2005. 'Daughters or Dowries? The Changing Nature of Dowry Practices in South India', *World Development*, 33(4): 593–615.

Stirrat, R. 1982. 'Caste Conundrums: Views of Caste in a Sinhalese Catholic Fishing Village', in D.B. McGilvray (ed.), *Caste Ideology and Interaction*. Cambridge: Cambridge University Press.

Subrahmanian, R. 1995. 'Combating Violence against Women: Finding Ways Forward', *The Administrator*, XL (July-September): 145–59.

Suran, L., S. Amin, L. Huq and K. Chowdury. 2004. 'Does Dowry Improve Life for Brides? A Theory of Dowry in Rural Bangladesh', *Population Council*, no. 195.

Tambiah, S. J. and J. Goody. 1973. *Bridewealth and Dowry*. Cambridge: Cambridge University Press.

Tariquzzaman S. and N. Hossain. 2009. 'The Boys Left Behind: Where Public Policy Has Failed to Prevent Child Labour in Bangladesh', *IDS Bulletin*, 40(1): 31–37.

Thorp, J. P. 1978. *Power Among the Farmers of Daripalla: A Bangladesh Village Study*. Dhaka: Caritas Bangladesh

Trawick, M. 1992. *Notes on Love in a Tamil Family*. Berkeley: University of California Press.

Uberoi, P. 1998. 'The Diaspora Comes Home: Disciplining Desire in DDLJ', *Contributions to Indian Sociology*, 32(2): 305–36.

United Nations Educational, Scientific and Cultural Organization (UNESCO). 2009. *Global Education Digest*. Paris: UNESCO.

UNICEF. 1999. *Adolescent Girls in Bangladesh*. Dhaka: UNICEF.

Van Schendel, W. 1981. *Peasant Mobility. The Odds of Life in Rural Bangladesh*. Assen: van Gorcum.

Verma, S. and R. Larson. 1999. Are Adolescents More Emotional? A Study of the Daily Emotions of Middle Class Indian Adolescents', *Psychology and Developing Societies*, 11(2): 179–94.

Werbner, P. 1996. 'The Imagining of Muslim Dissent: Hybridized Discourses, Lay Preachers and Radical Rhetoric among British Pakistanis', *American Ethnologist*, 23(1): 102–22.

Wilce, J. 1998. *Eloquence in Trouble: The Poetics and Politics of Complaint in Rural Bangladesh*. Oxford: Oxford University Press.

Wilder, W. 1970. 'Socialization and Social Structure in a Malay Village', in

P. Mayer (ed.), *Socialization: The Approach from British Anthropology*. London: Tavistock.

White, S. 1992. *Arguing with the Crocodile. Gender and Class in Bangladesh*. London: Zed Press.

———. 2002. 'From the Politics of Poverty to the Politics of Identity? Child Rights and Working Children in Bangladesh', *Journal of International Development*, 14: 725–35.

Whiting, B. B. and J. Whiting. 1975. *Children of Six Cultures: A Psycho Cultural Analysis*. Harvard: Harvard University Press.

Whitehead, A. 1981. "'I'm Hungry, Mum": The Politics of Domestic Budgeting', in K. Young, C. Wolkowitz and R. McCullugh (eds), *Of Marriage and the Market: Women's Subordination in International Perspective*. London: CSE Books.

Williams, R. 1977. *Marxism and Literature*. Oxford University Press.

Winnicott, D. W. 1965. *The Family and Individual Development*. London: Tavistock.

Wood, G. D. 1981. 'Rural Class Formation in Bangladesh 1940-1980', *Bullettin of Concerned Asian Scholars*, 13(4): 2–15.

———. 1994. *Bangladesh: Whose Ideas, Whose Interests* Dhaka: UPL, Intermediate Technology.

World Bank 2008a. 'Poverty Assessment for Bangladesh: Creating Opportunities and Bridging the East/West Divide', Paper no. 26, *Bangladesh Development Series*, World Bank, Dhaka.

———. 2008b. 'Whispers to Voices: Gender and Social Transformation in Bangladesh', paper no. 22, *Bangladesh Development Series*, South Asia Sustainable Development Department Dhaka, World Bank.

Wulff, H. 1995. 'Introducing Youth Culture in its Own Right', in V. Amit-Talai and H. Wulff (eds), *Youth Cultures: A Cross Cultural Perspective*. London: Routledge.

Yates, P. 1990. 'Interpreting Life Texts and Negotiating Life Courses', in P. Mayer (ed.), *Socialization: The Approach from British Anthropology*. London: Tavistock.

Young, K., Carol Wolkowitz and Roslyn McCullagh (eds). 1981. *Of Marriage and the Market: Women's Subordination in International Perspective*. London: CSE Books.

Youniss, J and J. Smollar. 1985. *Adolescent Relations with Mothers, Fathers and Friends.* Chicago: University of Chicago Press.

Zannini, F. 1991. 'Muslim Christian Dialogue in Bangladesh', *Islamochristiana* Rome, 17: 131-67.

About the Author

Nicoletta Del Franco is a researcher with a long-term engagement in Bangladesh where she has worked with NGOs since 1994. A D.Phil in Development Studies from the University of Sussex, she has also taught at Sussex and the University of Parma, Italy.